DORIS FLEESON

DORIS FLEESON

*Incomparably
the
First Political Journalist of Her Time*

CAROLYN SAYLER

SANTA FE

Sunstone books may be purchased for educational, business, or sales
promotional use. For information please write: Special Markets Department,
Sunstone Press, P.O. Box 2321, Santa Fe, New Mexico 87504–2321.

Book and Cover design ‣ Vicki Ahl
Body typeface ‣ Goudy OlSt BT
Printed on acid free paper

Library of Congress Cataloging-in-Publication Data

Sayler, Carolyn, 1934-
 Doris Fleeson : incomparably the first political journalist of her time /
by Carolyn Sayler.
    p. cm.
 Includes bibliographical references.
 ISBN 978-0-86534-759-5 (ssoftcover : alk. paper)
 1. Fleeson, Doris, 1901-1970. 2. Women journalists--United States--Biography.
I. Title.
 PN4874.F5S39 2010
 070.92--dc22
 [B]
                                            2010007910

Published in

WWW.SUNSTONEPRESS.COM
SUNSTONE PRESS / POST OFFICE BOX 2321 / SANTA FE, NM 87504-2321 /USA
(505) 988-4418 / ORDERS ONLY (800) 243-5644 / FAX (505) 988-1025

IN MEMORIAM

Helen K. Fleeson

CONTENTS

ACKNOWLEDGMENTS

I am grateful to members of the Fleeson family—Dick, Bob, Helen and Harry—for their informative and entertaining reminiscences of their aunt. I would like to acknowledge their help and that of Doris O'Donnell; of Robert Parks, archivist at the Franklin D. Roosevelt Presidential Library; Sara Halderman of the Lyndon B. Johnson Presidential Library; Ruth and Dale Evans and their friend, C. Warren Ohrvall, archivist at the Harry S. Truman Presidential Library.

Retired editor Max Moxley provided interesting details and observations, along with his own photos. I also appreciate the contributions of Thelma Pence Tichenor, U.S. District Judge Martin C. Pence, Bernadine Steierl, Helen Jacobs Crooks, Betty Calderwood, Judy Jones, John, David and Catherine Sayler, Dr. Barbara L. Watkins, Doris E. Saunders, Liz Carpenter, Helen Thomas and Mary McGrory.

INTRODUCTION

On June 9, 1954, the Senate-Army hearings produced a dramatic confrontation as Army counsel Joseph Welch blurted to Senator Joseph McCarthy: "Have you no sense of decency, sir? At long last, have you left no sense of decency?"

Doris Fleeson had been following the rise of McCarthyism for three years. Her voice had been among the most prominent in defining manifestations of the brief period in history now known as an era.

Her column had contained vivid denunciations, beginning in June 1951 following the attack on General George Marshall. "For one thing is perfectly certain," she wrote. "If Joe McCarthy can undermine the reputation of Gen. George Marshall, Joe McCarthy can become the dictator of the United States of America."

Rhetorically, Fleeson had prodded Eisenhower to denounce the Senator. Now, following the explosive session in the summer of 1954, she wrote: "That flower of evil which is McCarthyism bloomed in the Senate caucus room late Wednesday, rank and noxious, a fitting funeral blossom for the death of a republic."

Fleeson was in the most productive time of her career, syndicated in seventy newspapers and cited by *Time* magazine as the "top news hen" in Washington. Although she was a well known liberal, her following bridged political lines. Typical was a letter in response to the June 10th column:

> Dear Doris,
>   I invariably read your articles with eager appreciation for you are the most lucid, brief, crystal clear writer in my

humble opinion I know of. Today you surpassed even yourself. What you said was like a diamond writing on glass. I thank you for being so supremely articulate in so few words and for expressing what so many of us feel regarding this creature McCarthy's latest and most revolting action.

The letter was signed Peggy Talbott, with a postscript: "Dont please answer this, just keep on writing!"

Helen Thomas, looking back over fifty years, focused on this essence of Fleeson's writing. Thomas had come to Washington in the middle of World War II, and was "a gofer, or copy boy" on the old *Washington Daily News*. It was at about this time that Doris began her column. "She was very careful when she wrote," Thomas observed. "What struck me was that in conversations she was on her soapbox and could be very vehement. Her columns were straight, balanced, unbiased . . . they were so intelligent and they uplifted you. She was trying to find some sort of logic in things, which I think was wonderful."

Liz Carpenter remembers Fleeson and her long-running campaign against discrimination of women journalists. "She was the top reporter in town when I went there," Carpenter said. "She was short, attractive, thin and full of bustle. She had been president of the Women's National Press Club and, you know, she was well established and you admired this woman who had carved her way into being significant at the President's press conferences and had significant bylines."

The late Mary McGrory, in a letter dated March 29, 1996, on her *Washington Post* letterhead, wrote, "She was my idol. . . ." McGrory, in her "appreciation" following Doris' death in 1970, referred to her as "incomparably the first political journalist of her time." Ben Bradlee, in *A Good Life*, remembers Fleeson as "one of the toughest and smartest political columnists ever."

She was, in fact, the first woman in the United States to become a nationally syndicated political columnist. She began with the Bell Syndicate in 1945, and became affiliated with United Features Syndicate in 1954. By 1958 her column was distributed to one hundred twenty newspapers reaching about eight million families.

She was said to differ from colleagues in that she was first a reporter, and certainly not a thumb-sucker. Readers looked to her for amazing behind-the-scenes contacts. To Eric Sevareid in 1958 she was "the finest woman reporter of the time."

Born in 1901 in Sterling, Kansas, she was a graduate of the University of Kansas, and eager to leave Kansas for the East. She credited early police beat reporting on *The New York Daily News*, where she began in 1927. In 1933 the *News* sent Doris and her husband, John O'Donnell, to open a bureau in Washington at the beginning of the Roosevelt administration. They were young and liberal; Liz Carpenter said she can imagine the O'Donnells being welcome in "that fabulous era."

When the O'Donnells divorced in 1942, the *News* recalled Doris to New York. She left the *News* a year later to become a war correspondent in Europe for *Woman's Home Companion* magazine.

Her column, launched after the war, quickly gathered momentum. She had a talent, *Time* observed, for criticizing public figures without losing them as friends—or sources. *Newsweek* in 1957 suggested that there was almost no Washington figure, Republican or Democrat, "who has not felt the sharp edge of her typewriter."

Although Fleeson publicly characterized the pampering by the press of politicians as a crime so heinous it should be forbidden by law, she cultivated celebrities. Those who became personal friends were Eleanor Roosevelt, Bernard Baruch, Harry and Bess Truman, Jack and Jacqueline Kennedy, Lyndon and Lady Bird Johnson, and Adlai Stevenson.

Jacqueline Kennedy wrote in 1960, when Doris defended her from critics during the presidential campaign:

> I cannot tell you how touched and grateful I am that you should write such a thing—you are so many altitudes above "women's page" subjects—so for you to write about it means more than you can imagine.

Arthur M. Schlesinger, Jr., a special aide in the Kennedy administration, also knew Doris at that time. The historian, considering what Doris was really like, spoke of "her wit, her capacity for affection, her joy in the absurdities of life."

Today, her name is forgotten. That fact must puzzle historians. It would not have pleased Calder Pickett, who was professor of journalism at the University of Kansas.

Pickett in 1978 wrote an article for the alumni magazine relating "a distressing experience" in his history of journalism class. In the final exam he included the name of Doris Fleeson. The students bombed. Some had her confused with Dorothy Thompson, and the rest, he said, "might as well have had her confused with Horace Greeley." Pickett wrote:

> So I went back and looked at my notes, and convinced myself that I had given some attention to the great Doris, and concluded that I must have bombed. Because if there is any 20th Century journalist whose identity I want in the possession of my students it is Doris Fleeson.
>
> For Doris Fleeson was—and is—my journalistic passion. Doris Fleeson was part of a great journalistic tradition. Her column ranked with any of them—not as ivory tower as that of Lippmann, maybe, but oh, how she could write, and how she could dig.

1

STUNT GIRL

She was a lovely gal, "but unhappily intelligent," said Henry Mencken.

William Allen White called her his pet panther, although he addressed her in letters as "Doris, dear child."

Doris' contradictions were striking, even to childhood friends. Thelma Pence Tichenor, looking back over eighty years, observed: "Nobody ever knew she was competing, but she was every minute."

Her small stature was disarming. At twenty-six, as she began employment on *The New York Daily News*, she was impressively attractive—dark hair, hazel eyes, and a strong, straightforward gaze. The latter was a suggestion of the driving ambition and self-confidence that had brought her from Sterling, Kansas, to the University of Kansas, Chicago, and New York.

In 1927, those enigmatic qualities were about to be exploited for the benefit of readers of the nation's first tabloid newspaper. The assignment had elements of deception and drama that would be anathema today, and a label that would trivialize her career. But, historically, Doris was in good company. Margaret Mitchell and others had begun their climb to success in the role of a newspaper's stunt girl.

Considering what had gone before, and the touch of vaudeville in the city's journalism, the pursuit of a story under false pretenses was not the ethical crisis it might be today. On January 14, 1928, Warden Lewis E. Lawes of Sing Sing was on his way to Palm Beach for ten days' rest. His nerves were shattered by the executions of Ruth Snyder and Henry Judd Gray, and he was vacationing on the advice of a physician, The Associated Press reported. The warden, long opposed to capital punishment, was distressed because someone had secretly photographed Mrs. Snyder in the electric chair as the switch was thrown. Moreover, the photograph was prominently displayed in a pictorial newspaper.[1]

Enlarged to fill the front page, the riveting picture was printed in an "Extra" edition of the *Daily News* under a two-inch headline: "DEAD!"[2] The exclusive capped months of coverage and pleas for clemency, with lawyers portraying the lovers as moved to bludgeon Albert Snyder[3] "by an all-impelling psychosis due to sexual excitement."

The feat of taking the sensational photo had been masterminded by new city editor Harvey Deuell.[4] Twenty newspapermen had been allowed to witness the execution, but cameras were banned, and so the *Daily News* imported an out-of-town photographer whom Deuell instructed in the use of a miniature camera. The photographer had hidden the camera and squeezed a bulb in his pocket to snap the shutter.[5] The paper cropped the photo for the front page, but also carried the original in its various editions, including its "Pink" and "Final," showing the feet of a matron in the foreground. The photo that would become notorious in the annals of journalism carried a caption which later would not seem an exaggeration: "This is perhaps the most remarkable exclusive picture in the history of criminology."

The *Daily News*, introduced in 1919 by the *Chicago Tribune*'s McCormick-Patterson dynasty, had by 1928 captured the highest newspaper circulation in the nation.[6] Its sensational style was said to be as inevitable as jazz, as expressive as skyscrapers or the movies. But critics proliferated, even including an organization of New York State newspaper publishers. A study in 1926 showed that the paper gave as much space to crime and divorce as it did to general, foreign and local news. "If this appetite is not curbed, a tabloid a day will soon be a national drug habit," said one of the brethren.[7]

Daily News reporter Frank Dolan had just concluded months of covering the Snyder-Gray murder case when the revelation of a story

⬳

in the making at one of the nation's most exclusive women's colleges provided the next assignment. The headline, "Society Girl Student Lost in Mystery," gave an indication of the unfolding sensation which Smith College had futilely tried to contain during the weekend.

The missing girl was eighteen-year-old Frances St. John Smith, daughter of Mr. and Mrs. St. John Smith of New York, listed in the *Social Register*. She had vanished on Friday the 13th. The *Daily News* was not above exploiting the readership potential, advising in bold face at the bottom of the story: "Follow the search for Miss Smith, who disappeared so mysteriously, in tomorrow's Pink and other editions of THE NEWS."[8]

Dolan was assigned the story, but editors confronted the challenge of penetrating the policy of silence which had "gagged the 2,000 students of Smith."[9] Doris was one of the newest reporters, having been on the paper only two months. With a strategy rivaling that of the hidden camera, the editors decided that she should rent a raccoon coat, travel to Northampton, Massachusetts, and pose as a student.

According to the college, Frances Smith was seen at breakfast on Friday. Her absence was unnoticed until the next afternoon when a classmate went to her room and found an unopened note.

School authorities "first thought that Miss Smith had gone to spend the week-end with her parents in their summer home at Amherst, seven miles distant," it was reported. With its dearth of information, the paper could merely quote her parents and college authorities as saying they were unable to find a motive for her absence, "as she was known to have led a quiet life in school and to have had no trouble with her studies."

The *Daily News* had no photo of Frances Smith, but it ran a file photo of Alice M. Corbett, a Smith girl still sought after her "oddly coincident" disappearance on a Friday the 13th in 1925.

For a day, as it dispatched its top crime reporter and new woman journalist, the *Daily News* was confined to reports of the search by Boy Scouts and students of Amherst, the draining of Paradise Pond and the dragging of the Connecticut River. The scene had now become "proud Smith college, strangely haunted by missing girl mysteries."

But by Tuesday, Dolan and Fleeson had found sources for details and deeper aspects of the case. Smith President William Allen Nielsen continued to temporize: "The girl had no love affairs, she was fairly good in her studies, and I can find no conceivable reason for her voluntary disappearance." From their sources in town, on the campus and at Milton Academy, the reporters found different information. Frances had been inseparable with a friend, Joy Kimball, while attending Milton Academy. She had asked to room with her when they registered at Smith, but was assigned to Dewey House, reserved for upper class women and honor students. Far from being delighted, she was desolate. "It was learned that conditions existed in the life of Frances Smith which might have sunk her into a fit of mental depression," the *News* reported. Overtones of a lesbian relationship were present, but the account mentioned only that Frances Smith was "of an artistic temperament that sometimes threw her into melancholia."[10]

Anne Morrow, a senior at Smith, had just spent Christmas with her parents, the Dwight Morrows, at the Ambassador's residence in Mexico. There she had met Charles Lindbergh, who had flown the Spirit of St. Louis nonstop from Washington, D.C., and was the family's houseguest.[11]

Anne wrote her mother on January 15 of the "frightful torture" of the disappearance. The Smiths and the Morrows were friends, and Anne related that she had tried to help the "terribly depressed" freshman during the first semester. She was convinced that Frances had committed suicide.

The letter, published in the book *Bring Me A Unicorn*, included observations that poignantly foreshadowed her own tragedy four years later.[12]

By the sixth day the parents of Frances Smith were reported to have "practically given up hope that their daughter's fate will be revealed." Joseph V. Daly, state detective, said: "In my mind the case has settled down into a matter of a girl having a nervous breakdown and getting into the river."[13]

While the message in the note was never revealed, the *Daily*

News played the story for ten days, with reports of false sightings, a ransom note attributed to a crank, and the near drowning of two state troopers whose motorboat sprang a leak as they were patrolling the river.[14]

Finally the *News* alleged a whitewash, reporting that the search had covered practically every yard of country within a twenty-mile radius, with the exception of the college buildings and grounds. Information, it declared, had been withheld at the college, and a woman had been imported "especially to deal with newspapermen and to see that they found out nothing." A notice warned the students not to speak of the case even among themselves. Further, two upperclass women were appointed "to play policeman on Joy Kimball, Miss Smith's best friend, lest by chance remark she might shed some light on the mystery."[15]

In a rented raccoon coat she played the role of "stunt girl" for *The New York Daily News*. She disguised herself as a student to investigate the case of a missing girl at Smith College. (University Archives, Spencer Research Library, University of Kansas Libraries)

Headlines revealed the style with which the *Daily News* provoked critics as it drew the masses: "Society Girl Student Lost in Mystery," "Father, In Collapse, Directs Girl-Hunt," "Missing Girl Hunters Hold Maniac Theory," "We'll Find Her Dead Or Alive Pledge Troops in Smith Hunt."

Months later, the body of the tragic Frances was found in the Connecticut River.[16] Doris saved a photo of herself on which she had written: "The job achieved Miss Fleeson rented a raccoon coat to disguise herself as a college student to investigate the case of a missing student at Smith."

The "stunt girl" was a role in which women journalists from the time of Elizabeth Cochrane Seaman (pen name "Nellie Bly") had ascended from the society page to more interesting assignments. "Bly" created her own sensational story after persuading *The New York World* to send her on an assignment appropriate to the newspaper's name— that of traveling around the globe in an attempt to beat the fictional record of Jules Verne's *Around the World in 80 Days*. The eager reporter also had posed as a patient in a mental hospital, worked in a sweatshop, gone to jail, and played a chorus girl.[17]

On the *Atlanta Journal* in 1922, before she wrote *Gone with the Wind*, Margaret Mitchell began with fashion news, advanced to general assignment, and was more than once a stunt girl. One of the first experiences was a hazardous demonstration of the rig sculptor Gutzon Borglum planned to use in carving the Confederate Memorial on Stone Mountain. Mitchell, wearing overalls, was placed in a chair to swing from the cornice of a sixteen-story office building—an imitation mountain. During the demonstration the seat of the chair slipped out from under her, but when men at the top saw that the strap had held, they lowered and dangled her some more before pulling her back up to a window. She was a "society girl," and had attended Smith College, but her nerve in the stunt assignments impressed her hardened colleagues.[18]

Margaret, born in 1900, and Doris, born in 1901, were both remarkably small, or so it seemed to those observing their boldness. Another woman working in the stunt girl tradition was the *San Francisco*

Examiner's Winifred Black, writing as Annie Laurie. She posed as a derelict to enter a San Francisco hospital, and as a boy to report on the Galveston tidal wave.

It seemed especially enterprising, and quite a feat of accomplishment, when Eleanor "Cissy" Patterson disguised herself as an out-of-work maid to investigate unemployment in Washington in 1931. The former countess and heiress of the Medill-McCormick-Patterson newspaper dynasty was editor of Hearst's *Washington Herald*.[19]

In looking back, Kay Mills wrote in her book, *A Place in the News*:

> However one defined it, news received a different slant from some women from their earliest professional days. In part, that was because women could get into places where men would have been suspect. They could get victims to talk more readily. So they had different information and wrote different stories. Those who succeeded also dared to be different because they had little to lose, and they weren't going to get the job or be able to do it if they didn't have a gimmick such as going around the world or exploring the seamy side of life.[20]

Doris in a raccoon coat, submerging her driving ambition as she posed as a daughter of privilege, helped Frank Dolan write his sensational bylined stories from Smith College. It launched her career. She was not apologetic about her experience in a city room beat.

In 1956, national news commentator Eric Sevareid called Doris "the finest woman reporter of the time." Admirers singled out her ability to dig as much as her ability to write.[21] She was considered different from the "thumbsuckers." H.L. Mencken pronounced: "Your pieces are excellent stuff—simple, clear, succinct and effective. You get as much into 400 or 500 words as the comrades get into columns, and it is better told."[22]

"It is the kind of reporting all us old-timers cut our teeth on," wrote another.[23] Speaking to the Boston Press club in 1958, Doris proposed that "reporters today are eggheads. They come out of the university instead of off the street or out of the hellbox."[24]

Looking back at her early years on the *Daily News*, she observed that the front pages were "ripe as a camembert and their (the Pattersons') story was that if the good Lord let human folly happen, they were not too proud to publish it."[25] "I belonged," she said, "to the 'who the hell reads the second paragraph' school of journalism."[26]

2

MAIN STREET

In 1901, the year that Queen Victoria died and Doris Fleeson was born, a "vessel of wrath" was exploding in Kansas. Matronly, dressed in black alpaca, Carry Nation was a prairie Victorian with a mission against drink, tobacco, and more.

She had been the dominant partner in two marriages—the first to an alcoholic physician, and the second to an ineffectual minister whose sermons she monitored from a front pew in the church. "That will be all for today, David," she might declare.

From her town of Medicine Lodge she began a crusade which at the turn of the century made her a much discussed woman. In the waning months of the nineteenth century—on a Saturday afternoon in the summer of 1899—Mrs. Nation with another minister's wife made the first foray on a saloon in Medicine Lodge. Then, advancing alone, she visited the rough border town of Kiowa near Indian Territory, inflicting damage with rocks and bricks.

On December 28, 1900, she wielded her cane with a heavy iron ring attached to wreck the luxurious Hotel Carey bar in Wichita, slashing its life-sized painting of "Cleopatra at the Bath."

As an active member of the Woman's Christian Temperance Union she had served as "jail evangelist" in Medicine Lodge, but now she was herself an inmate, in the Sedgwick County Jail.

Released on January 12, she rallied W.C.T.U. stalwarts to a new attack on Wichita bars, in which for the first time she carried a hatchet.

The Wichita tempest sparked newspaper articles throughout Kansas, and the story soon spread to the Eastern press. On January 22, *The New York Times* carried nearly a column on page one about Mrs. Nation. The only larger headline was that given to the dying Queen Victoria on her deathbed on the Isle of Wight.[1]

As Carry Nation stirred the instincts of prairie reformers, she could have found no more fertile field that Sterling, Kansas. It was seventy miles northwest of Wichita and about thirty years removed from the frontier. Sterling, or at least a segment of its citizenry, aspired to a life of high-Victorian propriety. If nominally the Victorian age ended with the death of the old Empress, it was just dawning in Sterling. Ornate houses represented a peak of optimism and prosperity in the little town of about two thousand people. Their parlors were grand.[2]

While saloons were illegal in Kansas, the enforcement was token, and a temperance league was active in Sterling.[3] Within two weeks of her release from the Wichita jail, Carry Nation appeared in town at the United Presbyterian Church. "Mrs. Nation, who gained considerable notoriety by smashing a saloon in Wichita, lectured to a large audience at the U.P. Church Saturday evening," reported the *Sterling Bulletin*. "As to her personal appearance we may say she is a matronly looking woman about 55 years old, stout in build. She isn't a woman that the casual observer would take for a masher, especially of the saloon kind."[4]

The Victorian ideal was in full flower in Sterling as the young Sinclair Lewis and H.L. Mencken germinated their invective against Main Street and the small-town puritanical mentality.

Doris was born on Main Street in Sterling on May 20, 1901, to William and Helen Tebbe Fleeson.[5] William, fifty-seven years old, had been in Sterling since 1885, the year he arrived from St. Louis[6] to begin business as a bootmaker.[7]

He was born on October 13, 1843, to James and Mary Fleeson in Westmeath County, Ireland, where the family reportedly had come from Flanders to escape persecution by the French.

Helen Hermine Tebbe was born in St. Louis in 1855 to a family in the Forest Park section of the city. Information transcribed from a church record indicated that Helen's grandfather came from Vielefeld, Germany. Helen Hermine, a widow, came to Sterling in 1882 with a son and three daughters, including twenty-seven-year-old Helen. Soon after arriving she opened a boarding house.[8]

William, forty-five, and Helen, thirty-three, were married on January 13, 1889, in her mother's home.[9] In the next twelve years their six children—William Jr., Elizabeth, Ray, Howard, Richard and Doris—were born.

The Fleeson store was a center for political discussion, as factions clashed and William Allen White wrote "What's the Matter With Kansas." But as Populism collapsed and agriculture prices doubled, coinciding with good crop years, Sterling prospered. There were new brick sidewalks, a $10,000 Masonic temple, the Fair mansion, a crowning example of Victorian architecture, and a large, handsome residence built by the Jewish merchant A.L. Mincer. Beyond the Mincer family, speculation suggests the presence of a small Jewish element, as was the case in other towns where Jewish entrepreneurs had followed the railroads westward. According to Helen K. Fleeson, granddaughter of William and Helen, it was believed that several who had discarded Judaism were members of the Presbyterian and Congregational churches, and that the Fleesons were among them.[10]

On Main Street, Sterling's leading residential avenue, were the new showplace houses, with trees fed by the Arkansas River underflow, an advantage not shared by other Kansas towns. In contrast to the neighbors' homes, there was no ostentation in the Fleeson residence. Thelma Pence Tichenor, Doris' childhood friend, said that it was "very, very modest . . . a cottage . . . meager." The house gave the impression of being close to the ground, "only one stone up." In addition, the lawn was indifferently kept, and there was no curbing. It was just one more indication of a feeling by some that "the Fleesons lived a little differently."[11] A competitiveness and a driving ambition seemed to affect all of the family in some way. This was attributed to the "terrible temper" and competitive nature of William Fleeson, who had to win always—at business, at cards (if he didn't win at cards, he would pick them up and throw them in the stove, said Helen)[12]

To other children, the Fleeson parents seemed foreign and terribly old; their home "was never anyplace that children wanted to go," Tichenor said. She described William as dark, with a grizzled beard, a hook nose, and speaking with an accent ("He could have passed for an Arabian.") Helen was small, quiet, and spoke with "a heavy accent." Increasingly deaf, she and a sister conversed with each other with ear trumpets.[13]

William drove the boys to excel in the classroom and on the athletic field, and when the boys brought home report cards, they were expected to have A's. This seemed inevitable for the studious Elizabeth (Elsie), who was ten years old when Doris was born.

There was a strong attachment between the sisters. Doris, a beautiful dark-haired child, bright and talkative, idolized Elizabeth, her mentor. And others could not help noticing their exceptional abilities. Writing forty years later, in an article for *The Kansas Teacher*, Doris related:

> It was a former teacher in the Sterling, Kansas, grade schools, W.B. Dunmire, who was able to persuade my somewhat Victorian father that his eldest daughter, Elizabeth, could profit from any quantity of higher education as well as his sons could. Her two degrees from the University of Kansas and a Doctor of Philosophy from the Yale Graduate School proved Mr. Dunmire a prophet and her achievements opened the door for me.[14]

At the end of first grade Doris might have passed on to third, so impressed was her teacher. It was only to prevent demoralizing her brother, Richard, that her mother rejected the proposal (Doris did skip third grade.) Advanced and strong minded, she did not seem to attract many friends, Tichenor related. "She was never really taken in." She was close only to the Pence children—Georgia, Thelma and Cornelius. She played with them in their yard and in their attic,[15] but the children never went to the Fleeson home.

When members of the family in later years spoke of Elizabeth as the patriarch or powerhouse, it was a serious reference. Her departure for the University of Kansas was critical not only in the careers of two extraordinary women, but had implications for Fleesons of two generations. As Elizabeth approached high school graduation, Mr. Dunmire wrote a letter to the chancellor at the university, commending a deserving student. It was a fateful act. Soon afterward, Dunmire left teaching and spent thirty-five years as Sterling's assistant postmaster.[16]

William Fleeson died of uremic poisoning at the age of 73 in 1917. Elizabeth now was assistant superintendent of the student hospital at The University of Kansas. Howard also was at the university.[17]

Doris was not quite seventeen when she graduated as valedictorian of the Sterling High School class in 1918. Students in boxes at the Morris opera house showered her with flowers.

At sixteen, valedictorian of the Sterling (Kansas) High School Class of 1918.

She entered Cooper College in Sterling that fall, a time of national absorption with the war.[18] Word came in October of Howard Fleeson's heroism in the American Army Air Service on September 12, when he, as observer, and a pilot carried out a difficult mission on the first day of the offensive at Saint Mihiel. After being driven back twice by a patrol of enemy planes, they made a third attempt and found American lines. They were shot down but fell in Allied territory. For "extraordinary heroism in action," Howard received the cross of the Distinguished Service Order. The battle had been under the command of General William Mitchell, who had massed nearly 1,500 planes in an unprecedented show of air power.[19]

The end of the war on November 11 was subdued by new confirmations of deaths of young men from the community, and by the flu pandemic, the Spanish influenza, which closed Cooper for four weeks.

Although Doris did not mention the college in later years in her writing and public speaking, nor did the college recognize her, the year spent as a student undoubtedly was influential. Her precise writing, so colorful, yet with unexpected quotation of the classics, might have reflected a little of the freshman English teacher who taught "cultured speech," crusading against slang and use of the "inelegant and unrefined" word.[20]

Doris at seventeen was the star of the Cooper College debate team. More than seventy years later classmate Helen Jacobs Crooks remembered her on the platform, flippant and swirling around. Was she a show-off? "Very." Was she competitive? "Always." "Miss Fleeson has such a forceful manner in delivery that even her opponents were compelled to comment upon it," said the *Cooper Courier*.[21]

The party that Helen Fleeson gave for Doris on her eighteenth birthday was a "huge success," Doris wrote Elizabeth. She also thanked Elizabeth for a telegram and gift:

> Elizabeth dear,
> The telegram! You darling. I just choked up at receiving it and almost sent you a return wire at once to tell you that

I <u>will</u> make you proud of me, just see if I don't! And the ring is beautiful, Elsie, I am desperately proud of it and shall be always. Dick wrote me a long letter which is "Dick all over" and consequently I love every word of it. He ordered me a "K" pin set with pearls but it hasn't come yet . . I know I shall like it as I have wanted one for a long time and of course I should for no other reason than my baby brother got it for me.[22]

Doris finished the year at Cooper with thirty-five hours of A and two of B (solid geometry). With the "K" pin she turned toward Lawrence and the University of Kansas.

3

IDEAL UNIVERSITY

Doris began her studies on Mount Oread in Lawrence at about the time of the coming of the Ise age. The latter was a reference to the arrival of the singular professor John Ise, who began in 1916 a "self-imposed mission" to shock students and the public, almost lusting after controversy.[1] As the KU Alumni Magazine described it, "The Mighty Ise age came grinding down upon Kansas, ponderous, irresistible, moving all before it, changing the intellectual landscape."[2] Ise was thirty-one years old, with a doctorate in economics earned two years earlier at Harvard. His doctoral dissertation on the U.S. forestry policy was the forerunner of his 1926 book, The United States Oil Policy, now considered a socio-economic classic.

After she became the nation's first woman political columnist, it was sometimes reported that Doris had graduated in journalism at the University of Kansas. According to her nephew, Dick Fleeson, she received her bachelor of arts degree in economics rather than journalism, which she had considered but rejected as not meaty enough.[3] Doris at first intended to follow Elizabeth's lead, majoring in biology, but her grades in science were merely passing, not acceptable by her perfectionist standard. On the other hand she could quickly grasp the humanities and social sciences and receive high marks. "Medieval Hist. under Patterson (Professor David L. Patterson) is hard work but wonderfully interesting," she wrote Elizabeth, now at Yale. "The man himself has personality I think. I like to hear him talk and express his views. I don't begrudge him his 3 hours a week of my time in class (the third hour is a quiz section—oh how I force my opinions on them!)"[4]

For a bold and questioning student arriving on campus on the brink of the Roaring Twenties, the provocative classes of John Ise must have had a magnetic attraction. And Doris had heard something of the nonconformist professor. Speaking of her early radicalism in an interview in 1937 she remembered that "it created quite a sensation in our Republican household when my brother Dick came home from an economics lecture of John Ise's at K.U. and announced that John Ise scoffed at the then widely held notion that Calvin Coolidge was a perfect President. I welcomed this support and hastened to enroll in John Ise's courses."[5]

Although he riled Kansans, sometimes to the point of a threat of withdrawal of alumni support, Ise was himself a native "as crusty as the Kansas sod."[6] He was born in 1885 on a free claim near Downs to Rosie and Henry Ise, whose pioneer life he portrayed in the classic *Sod and Stubble: The Story of a Kansas Homestead*. The Ise family story was one of virtually every hardship known to the prairie land. John, one of twelve children, was stricken with polio as a child. It crippled him for life, resulting eventually in the amputation of his right leg. As seemed to have been an element in the Fleeson family, his parents had a "Germanic faith in education;" after Henry's death Rosie sent nine children through college, and some on to Harvard, Yale, Columbia, Stanford and the University of Chicago. Ise was so talented and complex, such a study in contradictions as a prolific scholar and an intellectual gadfly that others did not know what to make of him.

He had impressive academic credentials before he was thirty: from KU, a degree in music in 1908, a bachelor's degree in economics in 1910, and a bachelor of law degree in 1911; from Harvard, an M.A. degree in economics in 1912 and a Ph.D. degree in economics in 1914.[7] He had spoken of an increase in public ownership in his study of forestry policy, and his book on oil policy in 1926 outraged many Kansas oilmen with its condemnation of the results of private ownership and exploitation. As if it wasn't enough to mention the inflammatory "severance tax,"

Ise observed that "it ought to be clear to any mind above that of an orang-outang (sic) that the people of the present generation are only life tenants . . . and that "vast amounts of our irreplaceable reserves of oil are being used—we may well say wasted—by fat-bellied bankers. . . ."[8]

Ise was described as a teacher who used the Socratic method of prodding students to drop their self-righteous shields and to think.[9] His exciting classes were filled with wit against the pretense of popular culture. His respect for the student was high: "The longer I teach the more I love students . . . by and large they are about the finest people in the world, kind, generous, honest . . . and most punctilious in avoiding any effort to ingratiate themselves with the professor," Ise said in later years.[10]

For Doris, not only did the study of Iseian economics provide an unmatchable entrée as a journalist into New Deal politics,[11] but the encounter remained vivid for years. The student and professor share pages of his book *The American Way*, published by the economics department at the time of his retirement in 1955. In a forward, Doris wrote: "When John Ise retires from teaching at the University of Kansas, as very sadly he is soon to do, it will seem as if some unkind person had tunneled away Mount Oread itself and left the University on a dull plain." Doris told of attending a dinner at Bowdoin and finding herself seated next to a professor of economics. She introduced herself and asked what texts he was using. "'We think, and many colleagues agree with us, that we have the best economics text,' he replied. . . . 'Oddly enough it comes from Kansas. . . .'

"Throwing Emily Post to the winds, I interrupted. I was right, of course, John Ise wrote that text.

"I pass over that phrase 'oddly enough.' When I went east to work I became accustomed to the question: 'What was your college?' Meaning of course, did I go to Vassar, Mount Holyoke, Bryn Mawr or Smith. I always answered haughtily, 'College? I went to a University'. . . . Then I moved away before they could ask me how long it had been since Oxford admitted women.

"The fact is that I went to that kind of ideal university which was in President Garfield's mind when he said that the ideal university was a log with a boy at one end and Mark Hopkins at the other.

"Fortunately for me, KU is co-educational, and fortunately also, John Ise was at the other end of my log."[12]

At the time Doris arrived at KU it was a custom in some still Victorian parts of Kansas for mothers to accompany daughters to college, to "make a home" for them. When Helen and the remaining members of the Fleeson family all went to Lawrence in the fall of 1919, the circumstances were a little different. Howard, back from the Air Service, was ready for his final year, and Richard was continuing studies, now released from the Student Army Training Corps.

In 1919, on the turning point between the war and the twenties, the nation was on a threshold of everything revolutionary—the jazz age, Sinclair Lewis' *Main Street*, the lost generation, and the Age of Mencken. Doris joined Chi Omega, Elizabeth's sorority, but she became less and less certain about a field of study.

The school year of 1919–1920 ended with the four Fleesons taking divergent paths—Helen returning to Sterling, Dick remaining at KU, Howard entering Yale law school, and Doris taking a teaching job in Pondcreek, Oklahoma. At home for Christmas in 1920, she wrote Elizabeth of attending a dinner-bridge party. "I was bored to extinction but concealed it nobly," she confided. "Hate to waste my vacation thusly. Brentano's sent Dick 2 books from you—'Main Street' by Sinclair Lewis and 'If I Were Twentyone' by William Maxwell. I hate to start even glancing around for a means of returning to the Creek."[13] The stint was brief, but she was remembered years later by one of her pupils, an Oklahoma oilman working in her home county and chatting with her nephew, Harry Fleeson, bus boy at a hotel. With the year in Pondcreek refinancing her education, she was back at the university in the fall of 1921.

Staff members of *The University Daily Kansan* in 1921–23 changed positions as in musical chairs, trying a new job each month. With the addition of Doris in 1922, the masthead read like a future Who's Who, including Deane Malott, future chancellor of the university, Fred

Ellsworth, future alumni secretary, and Ben Hibbs who would become editor of the *Saturday Evening Post*.

From the Kansas labor unrest of 1922 came William Allen White's Pulitzer Prize-winning editorial "To an Anxious Friend." The Emporia editor wrote his classic defense of free speech in the face of Governor Henry Allen's Court of Industrial Relations, created by the Legislature with a vague authority to suppress public discussion of cases until they had been heard. It was in this atmosphere that Doris first worked on a newspaper, reporting for the *Pittsburg Headlight* in the coal-mining region of southeast Kansas during the summer between her junior and senior years.[14]

In 1923 when Doris left Kansas, Lewis' *Main Street* had gone through more than thirty printings.[15] Lewis ushered the decade of contempt for mid-American conformity, but it was Mencken's and George Jean Nathan's *American Mercury* that fixed the image of Kansas. The *Mercury* was the status magazine for those of "liberated intelligence;" its bright green copies flourished on the KU campus, and its contributors were relentless against Kansas as the symbol of repression and hypocrisy. Charles Driscoll, a former *Wichita Eagle* editor recruited by Mencken, analyzed the "Kansas Complex," and said that it was a medical condition, "a pathological desire to do good." This echoed Mencken's views on the middle ground, the far places which he called "the Methodist prairies of the Middle West." He defined the puritanism of inhabitants as "the haunting fear that someone, somewhere, may be happy."[16]

When Doris renounced Kansas, it seemed more than a response to a fashionable idea, and the judgment showed no sign of abating through the years. She frequently joined chroniclers of Kansas provincialism, sharing examples from the *Sterling Bulletin* with her friend Mencken.[17] There was no expression of nostalgia in her great volume of commentary on the national scene. In fact, she spoke or wrote so derisively that Kansas publishers virtually banished her column. At the time it was nationally syndicated in one hundred twenty newspapers, it was seen in relatively few in Kansas.

In 1923 Doris was sure she wanted to be a reporter. She left with

Elizabeth, who was enrolling in the Yale graduate school for a Ph.D. in public health. But during two years in New Haven she could not find a newspaper job and was employed as assistant production manager of the Acme Wire Company.

As Elizabeth left to teach bacteriology at Vassar, Doris remained unsettled in her plans. During a visit home, she went to Lawrence where she encountered her friend, Esther Clark Hill, author of "The Call of Kansas." At the urging of this "loyal supporter," Doris went to see Marco Morrow at the *Topeka Capital*. She apparently did not convey a sense of enthusiasm for a job in Kansas, for Morrow, after listening patiently, wearily told her that she had better "go East young woman. You'll never be satisfied unless you do."

Doris thereupon left for Chicago. She later gave this account of the experience:

> I arrived on the Chicago doorstep of Maureen McKernan, K.U. '15, on a Sunday morning to find her recuperating from a scoop she had pulled off for the Chicago Herald and Examiner—the identification of a suicide. I was sure then I had to be a reporter and emulate this glamorous friend of my sister and brother. But while I invaded editors' sanctums with monotonous regularity, I was not appreciated in Chicago and made my living as a clerk for Byllesby & Co. Mary Capper, Senator Arthur Capper's sister, was a great help to me. She used to invite me to lunch at Marshall Field's on Saturdays when I'd be free and then tactfully order herself an enormous luncheon so I'd feel free to stoke up for the weekend.
>
> Finally a Chi Omega sorority sister on the Evanston News Index got me a job as society editor.

Evanston was headquarters of the Woman's Christian Temperance Union, and little could surpass the seven-year-old Volstead Act, and the controversy it created, as newsworthy copy. Escaping the confines of the society desk, Doris soon scored a front-page bylined account of a

Prohibition conference at the Chicago Women's Club. With a prosaic headline, "Dry Leaders Spread Note of Optimism," and an unwieldy lead of eleven lines, the story almost toppled of its own weight. Yet it exhibited Doris' gift for seizing reader attention: "One dissenting voice was raised by Mrs. D.V. Gallery who was asked to speak that the conference might have the opinion of a leading Catholic laywoman. She said that she did not wish to bring back the saloon but that she expected to vote wet, because she thought 'the wets are dryer than the drys.'"[18]

Doris left Evanston after eight months when James Lyne, a friend from college who had first suggested journalism, helped find a job on the Great Neck, Long Island, *News*. She began work there December 14, 1926, collecting and writing news, editing and making up the paper. And, as she later recalled, on her days off she "began to get intimately acquainted with the ante-rooms of the New York newspapers." She achieved her goal in November, 1927, when after a fifteen-minute interview she was offered a job on *The New York Daily News*.[19]

4

GOLDEN ERA

Two events in November 1927 brought members of the Fleeson family into the establishment of newspaper journalism as it was practiced in two of its most dissimilar forms. For Doris it was an entry into the world of the New York City tabloids. For her brother Howard it was a union with a family dynasty in the period known as the "golden era of Kansas journalism." The wedding of Howard Tebbe Fleeson and Katherine Allen Murdock was an event of November 21, 1927, in the elegantly decorated Wichita home of Katherine's parents, Mr. and Mrs. Victor Murdock.[1] Victor was the son of Marshall M. Murdock, founder of *The Wichita Eagle*, and had returned three years earlier after a political career in the House of Representatives from 1903 until 1915[2] and on the Federal Trade Commission. He had been considered an insurgent congressman "battling against the forces of entrenched conservatism," and also "a true newspaperman all the way." The latter, pronounced by journalists, was usually their finest compliment. Victor was back at the Eagle, where colleagues noted that the flair he had developed as a young reporter had not deserted him.[3] The prominent young Independence oilman and rising political star, Alfred Mossman Landon, was a friend.[4]

Doris said that the colorful Kansas editors influenced her choice of journalism. Once at the University of Kansas she had put on her "best pink middie blouse," and had led William Allen White around the campus by the hand.[5] In this period Kansas reigned as a newspaper state, with the passionate editors who had been attracted to "Bleeding Kansas" little more than a generation earlier, and others who had become stars on the national stage. Edgar W. Howe, from his small *Atchison Globe* attracted a national following and wrote a dozen books, among them his classic *The Story of a Country Town*. White, with his famous editorial "What's the Matter with Kansas," in 1896 and his Pulitzer Prize for editorial writing ("To an Anxious Friend") in 1923, was at the pinnacle, although described as "a Kansan to the core and never departing from his home land as a base."[6] The famous stimulated their colleagues, and the repartee on Kansas editorial pages was awaited daily as editors battered one another with insult and opinion. While Doris looked toward the East, her classmate Ben Hibbs was beginning his career on the Goodland (Kansas) *News-Republic*, en route to editorship of the *Saturday Evening Post*. Hibbs was a native of Pretty Prairie, Kansas, and also a 1923 graduate of the University of Kansas. His writing characterized the provincial style that at times entertained the rest of the nation:

> E.E. Kelley of the Topeka Capital speaks of the perpetrator of this column as 'the new editor of the Goodland News-Republic.' It is true that the 'new' editor has lived in Goodland less than four months, but even at that he has been here long enough to be called a Democrat by the Republicans and a Republican by the Democrats, a Catholic by the Klansmen and a Klansman by the Catholics; to be accused of helping bankrupt the county by campaigning for a new courthouse . . . long enough to be favored by a special visit from 'God's Last Prophet,' self-styled, and to be told by that venerable personage that the News-Republic building will soon be swallowed up by the earth. . . . It doesn't take long for the 'new' to wear off of a 'new editor' of a Western Kansas town of 3,600.[7]

Charles Driscoll, a former editor of *The Wichita Eagle*, became a pariah when he began contributing essays on Kansas to Mencken's *Mercury* in the 1920s. He found a following among exiles such as Doris, in this period when the Eastern press was said to be "exuding anti-Kansanisms from every pore." He wrote of a "resplendent jewel" in the center of a Bible Belt from Canada to the Gulf of Mexico. "This jewel," wrote Driscoll, "is Holy Kansas."[8]

The Fleeson-Murdock nuptials took place at eight o'clock on a Monday evening with the Reverend Otis E. Gray of St. James Episcopal Church officiating. As a violinist and pianist played the bridal chorus from Lohengrin, the bride and her father descended the stairway to enter a living room "lighted solely by candle glow and quantities of greenery and numerous baskets of yellow and bronze chrysanthemums." The auburn-haired Katherine wore "a severely simple creation of silvercloth," with a court train of ivory satin and a veil of white tulle "arranged into a becoming nun-like head dress."

A buffet supper was served in the dining room.[9] Reported the Eagle's Society column: "Mrs. William Allen White was her usual gracious and charming self. She was attired gorgeously in a white beaded gown." It was mentioned that Mrs. William Fleeson of Sterling, mother of the bridegroom, had assisted throughout the evening.

As the newlyweds left, Katherine tossed her bouquet to her friend, Louise Wilson of Lees Summit, Missouri. As a going-away "costume" she wore a dress of green satin, a coat of green velvet, a "tight fitting" hat of green French felt and a double red fox piece. The bride's gift to her matron of honor, Mrs. Oliver C. Mosman, was a black suede cigarette lighter trimmed with diamonds.[10]

Howard, partner in a prestigious law firm (now renamed Brooks, Brooks & Fleeson) which he had joined upon receiving his degree at Yale,[11] gave his bride a diamond bracelet. The couple left for a month's tour of the South.

"It was all perfectly wonderful—and all Social Wichita is restlessly waiting the marriage of another captivating debutante. . . ." wrote the Eagle's columnist. In Wichita, as in New York City, the golden bubble of the twenties had not yet burst.

5

A TABLOID A DAY

Enough of the tabloid media!
Enough of tabloid television!
—Elizabeth Taylor, "The Jackson
Family Honors," Las Vegas, 1994

Tabloid. The word was a trademark for a tablet ("condensed medicine") and it was true that a newspaper acquiring the name in the early twentieth century was a bitter pill for its critics. Elizabeth Taylor's protest came seventy-five years after the appearance of the nation's first and foremost, *The New York Daily News*, a tabloid because of its small size, half that of the "blanket-size" newspapers of the day. One factor of its instant appeal was its convenience for readers on the subway.[1] Appropriate to the origin of the name, it was seen as offering the "literate but uneducated workers an escape, an entertainment, a thrill, an opiate."[2]

It was light years from J.E. Junkin's *Sterling Bulletin*, and the Cooper (College) *Courier* which had printed Doris' first articles. But Doris, dissatisfied with Kansas, restless in Chicago and merely marking time on Long Island, wanted a position on a New York City newspaper. She told Washington correspondent Duke Shoop of *The Kansas City Star* in 1937:

> I did everything on the Great Neck News, collected the news, wrote it, edited it, and then made up the paper.

And on my days off I began to get intimately acquainted with the ante-rooms of New York newspapers. On one dark November night I walked into the New York Daily News and demanded that I see the editor. I got him and for the next fifteen minutes I did myself no injustice whatsoever. He had a vacancy, wonderful to relate, and I was a full-fledged New York reporter at last. The News was new and vigorous. We had that in common. When it turned out to be liberal as well, I liked it even better. And that it gave an equal chance to men and women reporters instead of shunting women off on the 'woman's angle' was another stroke of luck.[3]

Joseph Medill Patterson, erratic founder of the *Daily News*, became Doris' champion and, finally, almost an agent of destruction. Although he provided her break in 1927, he forced her resignation in 1943 after abruptly pulling her off politics and proclaiming that she had no gift for political reporting.[4] Patterson had been born into great wealth, the grandson of Joseph Medill Patterson and son of Robert W. Patterson of the *Chicago Tribune*. Medill began the family newspaper dynasty when he arrived in Chicago (population 85,000) in 1885 and with a partner purchased a share of the eight-year-old *Tribune*. Medill built the *Tribune* in the epitome of personal journalism,[5] and his son-in-law, Robert Patterson, became managing editor and later editor-in-chief.[6] Eventually the family empire would include interlocking ownerships of three powerful newspapers—the *Tribune*, the *Daily News*, and the *Washington Times-Herald*.

Joseph, reared on Chicago's fashionable North side, was sent to private schools in Chicago and France, to Groton and Yale. In contrast to his studies, a stint between his junior and senior years as an aide to a reporter covering the Boxer Rebellion in China for Hearst's *New York American* was a taste of real excitement.

Leaving Yale, he went to work for the *Tribune*, but thought it dull in comparison with the Hearst papers. In 1903 he turned to politics, joining a municipal reform movement in Chicago. He seemed to have experienced his first real satisfaction in life when he was elected to the Illinois Legislature, and soon started a riot during debates over Chicago's "traction" problems. It was a blow, therefore, when his father asserted that his victory was the result of a bargain between the *Tribune* and Republican party leaders.

Patterson, nevertheless, remained in politics, and two years later a new mayor of Chicago named him commissioner of public works. In that office he launched a campaign against sweatshops in the bargain basements of the leading department stores, and in 1906 announced his conversion to socialism. Soon he was planning to become a farmer, to take a course in agriculture at the University of Wisconsin, to work on an Illinois farm, and to write a book on socialism.

Purchasing a farm near Libertyville, Illinois, he wrote two novels, and three plays which were produced on Broadway—one, the successful "The Fourth Estate". By the time of his father's death in 1911, he had abandoned socialism; he thereupon returned to the *Tribune*.[7]

Patterson and Robert Rutherford McCormick, "the royal cousins," began their ascendancy on the *Tribune* at the beginning of World War I. Although isolationist, as would be their position even more notably in a future war, they advocated invasion of Mexico in 1916 and entered military service themselves. McCormick, heir to both the Medill empire and that of his grandfather, Cyrus McCormick, inventor of the reaper, joined the conflict as a cavalry major. Patterson, in keeping with his more proletarian image, declined a commission and enlisted as a private in the National Guard. He was a second lieutenant when the war began, six months after the *Tribune* had made a complete swing from its isolationist stance to one of superpatriotism.

Shipped overseas, he was gassed and wounded on the battlefields of France and was made a captain. McCormick, who went to Paris as a member of General John Pershing's staff, and later to the front, gave commendable service and attained the rank of colonel. The two would be known by their military titles throughout their lives as they commanded their journalistic realm.

Was the *Daily News* conceived on a manure pile? Future critics liked to emphasize the assertion as they deplored the tabloid style and its astonishing readership. Seemingly they were correct about the meeting in France in 1918 at which the cousins first discussed the idea. McCormick was en route home, assigned by Pershing to return and recruit a million more men. Patterson, meanwhile, had been thinking of a rival for Hearst's *American* and had used a furlough to visit Lord Northcliffe of the *Daily Mirror* in London. He had heard of the *Mirror's* success and Northcliffe's opinion that New York was ripe for such a venture. The meeting of McCormick and Patterson took place in a farmhouse used as a field headquarters, but when the noise inside made it difficult to converse, the two climbed out a window to sit on a manure pile in the backyard. They drank scotch, watched artillery barrages flashing in the night, and planned for the future.[8]

The opportunity came more quickly than they had expected, when the war ended within the year. Slightly more than seven months after the Armistice, Patterson rushed the *Daily News* into production in rented quarters in the New York *Evening Mail* Building at 25 City Hall Place. Summer Blossom, formerly of *The Kansas City Star*, was city editor, and the paper was printed on the *Mail's* presses. The venture was financed by the *Tribune* which had just distributed a three-million-dollar bonus to employees, in an outburst of unprecedented generosity. As author Silas Bent, grandson of the oceanographer and a former journalist and professor, summed up the situation in his 1927 book *Ballyhoo*: "The sensational, boastful and vulgar *Chicago Tribune* had made so much money (thanks to the volume of advertising wherewith Big Business sought to decrease payment of swollen post-war taxes to Uncle Sam) that the owners of the paper were hard put to it to find an outlet for their own surplus."

Adopting its London predecessor's format, the *Daily News* displayed a banner featuring the illustration of a camera and proclaiming it to be "New York's picture newspaper." The focus was "the drama of life," with emphasis on sin and sex, and especially the domestic follies of those in the *Social Register*. In the beginning the newspaper was a joke,[9] with journalists working on it only as a last resort. But extraordinary public response was quickly apparent. The *News* and the tabloid rivals it spawned began to seriously worry the established media. Their aggressive competition with ever larger contests and prizes finally resulted in a federal postal ban against advertising of lotteries in newspapers. But the stunts and gimmicks elevated readership, and by 1921 the *Daily News* acquired a five-story building at 23-24 Park Place. By 1925 it had passed the million mark in circulation, and in 1927 Patterson obtained an Associated Press franchise by paying the Ridder brothers $500,000 for the financial *Commercial Bulletin*.[10]

Their gains had not really been at the expense of their big brothers, Bent maintained. The eight-column papers had been in a "blue funk" for years, he said, "even after it became apparent that . . . the newcomers had but dipped down into subcirculation strata," capturing "a semi-literate audience."[11] The tabloids were considered a natural response to the appetites and restless energy of the twenties. "What then," asked Bent, "are the tabloids, which supply to a multitude of morons the kind of pictures they like to see, and the kind of stuff they like to read? Satisfying instinctive appetites and emotions, and fitting neatly into the scheme of an industrialized democracy, they are a natural flowering of modern journalism. They are the daily printed folk-lore of the factory age."[12]

Except for his privileged childhood, Joseph Patterson might have been the prototype for Gail Wynand in Ayn Rand's *The Fountainhead*. (The fictional Wynand was publisher of "the New York Banner the most vulgar newspaper in the country.")[13] Six feet tall, with gray bristling hair, a square face and deep-set eyes, Patterson presided at his thirty-six-story building at 220 East 42nd Street. Built in 1930 at a cost of $10,700,000, it featured a giant compass on its lobby floor, and above it a twelve-foot revolving globe tilting with the earth's inclination, and illuminated from below. At the entrance was the odd motto Patterson had chosen: "The Lord must have loved the common people, He made so many of them." Inside, too, the publisher's influence was pervasive.

Patterson was described in unflattering adjectives: impulsive, erratic, impatient, unpredictable. He cared nothing for appearance; was dressed in a way that would shame his reporters, it was said. Beyond this, he liked to dress even more shabbily for incognito mingling with the masses, often taking the subway out to Coney Island.[14]

He engaged Raymond Hood, the *Chicago Tribune*'s architect, to build a home in Ossining on a seventy-acre wooded estate overlooking the Hudson, but ordered it painted gray so that it would not be a showplace.[15] Historian Tebbel found an "appreciation" written by former employee Burton Rascoe to be the best single estimate of Patterson: "A man who acts and works on hunches. He is devoid of all except the most elementary reasoning powers, and his mistakes have been made through the initial errors of assuming that he was thinking when he was merely feeling, and of attempting to apply a logical process to matters of pure instinct and emotion."[16]

6

THE NEWSPAPER GAME

Inspired by a classic play, the 1994 movie "The Paper" recreated the cynicism and exhilaration of newsroom life. For this new version of big-city daily tabloid journalism,[1] director Ron Howard and screenwriters spent time at the *New York Post* and the *Daily News*, with the script of Ben Hecht and Charles MacArthur's 1928 hit, "The Front Page." Compared with its fabulous rise in the twenties, the *Daily News* was close to collapse following the death at sea of its most recent rescuer, British publisher Robert Maxwell. When magazine publisher and real estate developer Mortimer Zuckerman finally acquired the paper in January 1993, it had been under bankruptcy protection for thirteen months and was fighting to hold its circulation of just under eighty thousand. Zuckerman began a bloodletting in the newsroom, cutting one hundred seventy employees in what he termed an effort to save fifteen hundred other jobs. In the past decade the paper had lost more than $100 million.[2]

Although the modern filmmakers still found enough tension and absurdity in the newsroom, the aura of the great "newspaper game" portrayed by Hecht and MacArthur was gone. On metropolitan dailies which had struggled for existence against the competition of television and the suburbs, the atmosphere was one of fear and head-hunting. It was more melancholy, still, when contrasted with the Runyonesque world of New York journalism in the twenties. Players were Damon Runyon, Ring Lardner and Rube Goldberg—and such others as Hype Igoe, Heywood Broun, Bob Ripley, Arthur Brisbane and Irvin S. Cobb, and the young sportswriters Ed Sullivan and Gene Fowler.[3]

Although Doris began in a subordinate role to the stars of the *Daily News*, she soon earned her own assignments.

Forrest Davis, who became an author and a *Saturday Evening Post* editor, wrote as he left for greener pastures: "Dear Doris: It is reassuring to know, as I enter on my new career, that you will not permit our separation to impair your feeling for me. In the hope that our acquaintance may ripen into lust, may I subscribe myself. Yours devotedly, Forrest."[4] But it was the lust for the story that mattered most. To Terrence Rafferty in *The New Yorker*, that style of tabloid muckraking seemed "the sexiest, most exciting work you could do without getting arrested."[5] The comic example was the 1940 Howard Hawks movie remake of "The Front Page". When Hildegard Johnson (Rosalind Russell), who has been "six weeks in Reno," turns up in the newsroom, ex husband and editor Walter (Cary Grant) deals mercilessly with new fiancé Bruce (Ralph Bellamy). "You're getting a great newspaperman," he congratulates him. When "Hildy" announces that she and Bruce are "taking the sleeper to Albany," Walter knows he must rescue her from a lifetime of boredom. He knows she can't resist the big story, "the greatest yarn in journalism," about to break. "You know I can't do that kind of thing," he pleads, "it takes a woman's touch."

As the Great Bull Market of 1928 and '29 rushed on, few heeded the market drop in prices in June 1929. Newspapers devoted their columns to other concerns, with Prohibition often a theme, as in a *Daily News* story headlined "Feather King's Son Nabbed In Hard Stuff Raid." The son of a millionaire feather goods dealer had been arrested "with an expensive store of choice liquor" when police "turned their attention on the ultra-ritzy oases in the Forties and Fifties." Readers followed the didoes of Edward W. "Daddy" Browning, in the habit of adopting teen-age girls. The filing for separation by the wife of an eminent professor began a story that sizzled through August. "The efforts of handsome Prof Walter Edwin Peck of Hunter college to translate into personal experience the sex vagabondia of his three literary heroes—Shelley, Byron and Keats—was revealed last night in astounding charges of immorality filed against one of America's greatest authorities on the romantic poets," wrote John O'Donnell. Scarcely had that story subsided when the *Daily News* was covering a new sensation headlined "City Unmasks Rector as Head of Fake Sex Clinic." Implicated was the Episcopal minister who was national secretary of the church temperance society, and now accused of "grave sex abuses against young women and the practice of medical quackery."[6]

Jack Alexander wrote in *The New Yorker*: "By turns sobby, dirty, bloody, and glamorous, the News covered each in the manner that would most effectively appeal to the more elementary emotions of a truck-driver, and to the truck-driver in everyone."[7] John Tebbel said that probably more than any other New York newspaper the *Daily News* developed its sources with police, lawyers and even judges.

It was a prevalent suggestion that money, pleasure, and bizarre fads were the chief preoccupation of most of the population. On the sweltering streets that August "the pajama idea" brought forth a new attire even more liberating for men than shorts skirts and bobbed hair were for women. Five pioneers from the *Daily News* wearing cool, sensible pajamas, took the subway to Roxy's theater where ushers outfitted in heavy, buttoned suits cast envious looks. Others showed up in pajamas to drive trucks, stroll the streets, or relax on Coney Island.[8]

New York Mayor Jimmy Walker defined the twenties as beginning with the celebration of the False Armistice of 1918, and ending with the election of Roosevelt, a period in which he saw Americans dancing to a pied piper that plays after every war.[9] It was also the lifespan of the Volstead Act. Few thought that the festival or carnival could end, except possibly the austere, incongruous leader Calvin Coolidge. When Doris arrived on the *Daily News*, Lindbergh had just returned from his solo flight across the Atlantic. Three years earlier George Gershwin had introduced symphonic jazz with "Rhapsody in Blue", and two years before that, the classic literary works defining the age had been published: Sinclair Lewis' *Arrowsmith*, Theodore Dreiser's *An American Tragedy* and F. Scott Fitzgerald's *The Great Gatsby*. Did Coolidge have some foreboding when in the spring of 1928 he announced that he would not run again for the presidency?

"There was a volcano boiling under him," wrote Mencken, "but he did not know it and was not singed."[10]

The race of the skyscrapers in New York City in 1929 seemed proof, if anything, of soaring prosperity. A surge of buying and building was under way. Overtaking the 792-foot Woolworth Building were two new towers in progress, Chrysler's Art Deco design near Grand Central Station and "40 Wall Street," a sober limestone and brick edifice a half block from the Stock Exchange.

The candidate for Mayor of New York City in 1929 was five feet, two inches tall, an Irish American who was a Republican and an Episcopalian, and had grown up in Fort Whipple, Arizona. He had come from Congress to challenge the high-living Tammany incumbent, Walker, who was presiding over a city of revelry. Some have thought Fiorello "The Little Flower" LaGuardia the greatest politician of all time, and his campaign, which was Doris' first major news coverage of politics, marked a turning point for her. She did not forget LaGuardia, for whom she developed great admiration and personal friendship. That, too, although it might be out of favor in journalism today, became a defining style. She overtly cultivated celebrities with letters and gifts, and many found in her something that made them eager to respond.

After Alfred E. Smith lost the presidential election he reportedly was sensitive to signs of disloyalty, a feeling exacerbated when Mayor Walker's police commissioner retired several of Smith's aging friends. As Walker was considering options in private life rather than a second term, Smith determined to test his power as still head of Democratic politics in New York State. He asked Walker not to run for re-election, which assured his candidacy. With his great personal charm and brilliance as a speaker, Walker easily deflected his critics and entertained the electorate with a style that seemed fashioned for the heady times.

LaGuardia had served in the U.S. House of Representatives from 1917 until 1921, and again since 1923, when the allegations of malfeasance and misfeasance against Mayor Walker propelled him into the race as the "Fusion" candidate. Born in New York to immigrant parents, he had moved with his family when his father took a job as bandmaster for the U.S. Army's Eleventh Infantry, and was nine years old when the family arrived in Fort Whipple, Arizona. In 1898, Achille LaGuardia was sent to the Spanish American war, even though he was more musician than soldier. Ill from food poisoning, he received a medical discharge and an eight-dollar-a-month pension. He then took his family to New York and later to Trieste, where he died in the native city of his wife Irene. Fiorello, now supporting his mother, sister and younger brother, found passage back to the United States as a translator on a British ship, carrying among its passengers eighteen hundred immigrants. Stirred by the immigrants' plight and skilled in languages which he had studied in Trieste, he found work on Ellis Island to support night classes at New York University Law School.

After law school he opened an office in an impoverished neighborhood, representing clients in an often pro bono capacity, and joining the Republican party as a protest against Tammany. His chance to run for Congress came in 1914 when Republicans of the 25th Assembly District, a district in which no Republican had won, were casting about for a name to place on the ballot. LaGuardia lost the election, but returned in 1916 to score a stunning upset which sent him to Washington. But the nation's entry into World War I intervened. LaGuardia had learned to fly in a school on Long Island, and in 1917 he left Washington to join an American fighter squadron in Foggia, Italy. He returned as a major in the Air Force, decorated with an Italian medal. Although he had only a week left in which to campaign for his seat in Congress, his New York constituency elected him to a second term.[11]

With his strong populist idealism, he was drawn back to New York into the race against Mayor Walker in 1929. Backed by reform groups, he went through neighborhoods, speaking Italian, German, Yiddish and even two kinds of English, according to Walker. The leasing of The Casino in Central Park, which recently had been rebuilt into a lavish restaurant, was a key issue in allegations of graft. And accompanying the charges were petitions sent to Governor Roosevelt demanding that the administration be investigated.[12]

The campaign was entering its last days when disaster brought the "great hush" on Wall Street. The election was a resounding defeat for LaGuardia as dazed New Yorkers clung to an illusion and re-elected their debonair mayor to bring back the good times. It would be four years before LaGuardia would begin his legendary tenure as mayor.

Doris considered LaGuardia the ideal public servant. Upon his death in 1947 she wrote:

> American politics has lost its best interpreter and persuader of the common man of its cities and industrial regions. . . . There is not now anyone to strike his note of peculiar concrete aggression against the ills that beset people coming up from behind in the American social and economic system.
>
> With his own tremendous capacity for enjoyment— of contest, power, food, music, fires, family life—Mr. LaGuardia understood that most people want a bird in the hand. Compared to Mr. LaGuardia, Henry Wallace is palely academic, a prey to visions and systems. Comparatively, Messrs. Taft, Truman, Dewey, have a faintly patronizing flavor of Papa-Knows-Best.[13]

ENVIABLE COUPLE

Doris easily attracted men. They were not necessarily put off by her abilities. "She was a striking-looking, young, petite woman," said her niece, Helen Fleeson. "She had many gentlemen friends. She was wooed, and she went after them." Forrest Davis, the newsroom suitor, typed hopefully on March 22, 1928: "Dear Doris I have been faithful to you all day and hope you have been the same. Lovingly, Forrest."[1]

Faithful though he was, Davis remained a footnote in Doris' career, his notes saved in her files. The rival with whom he could not compete was a rising star on the *Daily News* staff, described as "dashing, tall, dark, brilliant and unpredictable."[2] (Actually, John Parsons O'Donnell was five-feet-nine-inches tall, according to his daughter, Doris O'Donnell). In background he seemed as ill suited for the world of tabloid journalism as did Doris, although their lives had been quite different in every sense except their shared Irish ancestry. O'Donnell, born July 23, 1896, in Somerville, Massachusetts, was the son of Dr. Louis P. O'Donnell, a radiologist at Johns Hopkins Hospital. John attended St. Joseph's Academy in Wellesley, Massachusetts, and graduated in 1920 from Tufts College in Boston. He served as an Army lieutenant in World War I. Before going into full-time newspaper work, he took graduate studies in literature at Harvard.[3] Articulate and socially adept, he easily charmed persons in all walks of life, even *Daily News* publisher Patterson who was known to have "a strange contempt for writers." O'Donnell fortified Patterson's isolationism as World War II approached, and he and Patterson traveled together to the wartime Pacific in the last years of Patterson's life.

After joining the *Daily News* in May, 1927,[4] seven months before Doris' arrival, O'Donnell rapidly proved his versatility. He could write as compellingly of disasters at sea, as of crime, politics, or the sex scandals of rectors and professors. In December 1927 he was sent aboard a Navy vessel into a fierce winter storm off Cape Cod in the effort to rescue fifteen men trapped in the submarine S-4, which had been rammed by a Coast Guard destroyer. O'Donnell filed stories as divers attempted to save the victims, and then recover bodies, in a futile attempt lasting through Christmas.

With their talent and drive, Fleeson and O'Donnell earned choice assignments. In May 1929 he accompanied a pilot over New Jersey and phoned in a dispatch, in a test of a Western Electric air telephone, a "revolutionary device" by which pilots and passengers could keep in constant touch with the ground.[5]

O'Donnell had an enduring, if turbulent, career as *Daily News* Washington bureau chief for more than twenty years. Colleagues liked him and admired his writing skill; columnist Helen Escary called him "that journalistic Rock of Gibraltar."[6] However, one bizarre incident involving President Franklin D. Roosevelt places him in the annals of American journalism. The O'Donnell Iron Cross matter was a lapse difficult to explain, since FDR was a president whose press relations were among the most successful and who considered himself "one of the boys."[7]

The *Daily News* and O'Donnell, after supporting the Roosevelt administration for eight years, had become bitter critics as war approached, attacking any kind of aid to the Allies and advocating appeasement of Japan. Patterson, after a trip to Europe in 1939 in which he unsuccessfully sought to interview Hitler, dismissed him as a mystic. In October 1941 the paper editorially branded the conflict "Roosevelt's War." The transformation, or betrayal, should have surprised no one, contended author John Tebbel, for the *Daily News* could be equally venomous to all. Wrote Tebbel: "For example, John O'Donnell, News political columnist, in 1940 subjected Wendell Willkie to the kind of attack for which Mr. O'Donnell is justly celebrated, if one may so use the word, and only a year later he was writing in exactly the same vein about Roosevelt."[8]

After the bombing of Pearl Harbor, O'Donnell and others somehow were able to report the exact losses in Hawaii. Author Betty Houchin Winfield writes that Roosevelt secretly ordered the FBI to investigate news leaks, and threatened O'Donnell with withdrawal of "all privileges that go with the relationship between the press and government and direct appeals to their subscribers."

By 1942 O'Donnell had further irritated FDR with satirical war coverage from the Pacific. Two colleagues, he said, were turning to "flutes and piccolos just to keep their fingers nimble for a time when censorship lets them beat the keys of their portable typewriters and turn out a tell-all story." Roosevelt was reported to have been livid.[9]

At this point, journalist Larry Lesueur, who had just returned from Russia and the Middle East, was taken to a White House press conference by his friend Eric Sevareid. The two remained afterward for a private talk with FDR. Later, Lesueur was not quite sure how it happened, but as they were about to leave he pulled out of his pocket a German Iron Cross on a ribbon. He knew that the President liked souvenirs and said he would like to give it to him. Roosevelt asked if it came from a body. Assured by Lesueur that it was one which the German High Command planned to award to victorious troops after the fall of Moscow, Roosevelt placed it on his desk. According to Sevareid, Lesueur suddenly laughed as they left the White House and said: "Damn it, I really wanted to keep that medal. I don't know why I gave it to him."[10]

With pressures mounting and the war going badly, Roosevelt shocked correspondents at his next press conference (December 18, 1942) when he handed the Iron Cross to broadcaster Earl Godwin with instructions to award it to O'Donnell (who had been at the press conference but had departed). Roosevelt called the "flutes and piccolos" column the most unfair story of the war. O'Donnell replied that the comments were so "obviously facetious" and "fantastically exaggerated" that he was "amazed and bewildered" at the lengths to which the misunderstanding had gone. Except for the gleeful H.L. Mencken who himself had been accused of sympathy for the enemy,[11] journalists were astonished at the personal attack. A Berlin radio broadcast featured the *Daily News* and other McCormick-Patterson papers as examples of what the American press faced: "These newspapers, being true American papers and representing the majority of the American people, are being persecuted by the Roosevelt Administration, even to being accused as saboteurs of the war effort."[12]

In 1930 Doris' assignments were turning to politics and investigation. "I was never a sob sister," she said. "I was always too practical for that."[13] Her story headlined "Radium Death Leaves Tot in Peril," told of deaths of sixteen former employees of the United States Radium Corporation. A twenty-seven-year-old woman who had painted watch dials for the company for five years before her marriage was the latest to die. Now the chief medical examiner of Essex County advised tests for her three-year-old daughter because children of other victims had become ill. Doris wrote of lawsuits by two women, incorporating the possible peril to their small children. "While the question of legal responsibility for poisoning a child through its mother is new in jurisprudence," she reported, "the fact that radium may be transferred from mother to child has been attested before." She noted the death of the five-year-old son of a radiation victim.

The Fleeson-O'Donnell romance began in the revelry of the twenties; it culminated in marriage in the sobering first year of the Depression. They, as top reporters, were enviable survivors of the catastrophe, since New Yorkers, if they could buy little else, would not be without newspapers. But Doris and John were sensitive to developments as financiers took the desperate plunge, and heads of families sold apples on the street. News of the farm crisis was inescapable. Doris sent a refrigerator, her own electric model, to her brother Dick, his wife and baby, caught in the Depression in Kansas.[14]

For their wedding, Doris chose an engraved announcement conforming to the best etiquette of the day:

Mr. and Mrs. William Fleeson
announce the marriage
of their sister
Miss Doris Fleeson
to
John Parsons O'Donnell
Sunday, the twenty-eighth of September
One thousand, nine hundred and thirty
New Haven, Connecticut[15]

John, a Catholic, had been divorced the previous year after a two-year marriage to Kathryn Mullin.[16] The wedding took place on Sunday morning in the home of Doris' sister Elizabeth and her husband, Robert Jordan, an administrator at Grace New Haven Hospital[17] whom she had married in 1926. The *Sterling Bulletin* carried a story, reviewing Doris' life from childhood, relating that "for the past few years (she) has been on the editorial staff of the New York Daily News. She has a splendid position and is making good there. Her own personality and perseverance have won for her an enviable position on the editorial staff of the News." The article concluded: "The groom is not known here, and we have no information concerning him other than that he is a reporter for the New York News. Miss Fleeson is almost a stranger here, as she has been away for so long, but she still has a great many friends in Sterling who will be pleased to hear of her wedding, and who will wish for the happy couple the best that life holds."[18]

The enclosure card informed friends that Mr. and Mrs. John Parsons O'Donnell would be at home after the first of November at 304 East 42nd Street, New York.

8

POLITICAL BAPTISM

Malfeasance, misfeasance and nonfeasance.[1] Eventually all were included in the charges against Jimmy Walker, the "little gentleman" mayor of New York City from 1926 until 1932. Irving Berlin sang his song, with such Berlin tunes as "We'll Walk in with Walker"[2] and "Gimme Jimmy for Mine". The Society of Tammany at 331 Madison Avenue, which had wielded its powers as a political machine since the time of Boss Tweed, had supported him during sixteen years in the Legislature. He was "the jaunty Senator from Greenwich Village" when he won election in 1925 with the backing of Broadway friends S. Jay Kaufman and George Jessel,[3] and a letter of praise from Mrs. Franklin D. Roosevelt.[4] As biographer Gene Fowler observed: "A war-tired city's discovery of the gay, well-dressed phrase-maker, and its adulation of him, made Walker a hero, and finally a victim of the age. He became irrevocably bound to the times, and would rise and fall with the era which created him."[5]

Walker had a topcoat lined with sable, a gift from wealthy publisher Paul Block. He allegedly made lavish trips to Europe with mysterious letters of credit. He had at his disposal a "Chanel Number Five dungeon" arranged by Tammany supporters for his time with his mistress.

During his first term he could do no wrong; he was "the life of the party," said Fowler. In 1928 Roosevelt nominated Governor Alfred E. Smith at the national Democratic convention. Walker nominated Roosevelt for Governor at the state convention. They were a triumvirate in New York State Democratic politics, and the ascending Smith and Roosevelt certainly had not wanted a City Hall scandal.[6]

Soon after her coverage of the LaGuardia campaign Doris became immersed in a three-year saga which, as it brought down others, brought recognition of her talents. Opposed to the Walker administration, she in 1929 took the alternative of registering as a Socialist and voting the Republican ticket.[7] Doris remained on the story when, at the beginning of Walker's second term, his foes moved in to allege misconduct in the municipal courts and other departments.[8] Roosevelt, in 1929 in his first year as Governor, refused to consider charges, and in January 1930 he stayed Republican State Senator Samuel Hofstadter's effort to launch an investigation of the Magistrates' Courts. In June he rejected the Socialist Party's plea for an investigation.[9]

With the outcry increasing, the New York Court of Appeals ordered an "extraordinary grand jury" naming retired State Supreme Court Justice Samuel Seabury as referee. Public hearings began in September 1930, just before the O'Donnells' marriage in New Haven. On September 29 Roosevelt entered the inquiry, denouncing the refusal of high-salaried city officials to waive immunity and testify before the grand jury. He ordered the mayor to demand compliance in the investigation of a job-buying scandal.[10] Then came a recess of seven weeks, and Roosevelt's landslide re-election victory. When the public hearings resumed in November, bombshells began to explode. It was testified that plain-clothes members of the police vice squad had employed stool pigeons to frame women for prostitution. It was alleged that hundreds, many of them innocent, had been sent to jail.[11] Several magistrates resigned and others were removed from the bench.

At this point Doris had a role in the investigation. Ishbel Ross wrote of Doris in her 1936 book *Ladies of the Press*: "During the first Seabury investigation she did some unofficial sleuthing for Chief Magistrate Corrigan, decking herself out as Daisy Smith of Broadway, a gaudy girl."[12] In any event, ten years later that involvement was warmly remembered by the "glacial" Samuel Seabury when he wrote: "Many thanks to you for your kind letter and birthday congratulations. I was delighted to have a line from you. I know what a great help you were during the trying years when, from a newspaper standpoint, you covered so many of my activities."[13]

A sensational development which Doris covered and which was heavily played by the *Daily News* was the murder of Vivian Gordon, an important Seabury witness who was found strangled in Van Cortlandt Park in the Bronx. Mrs. Gordon had testified concerning her arrest by the vice squad, and Seabury was expecting further, more damaging information.[14]

The death set up a new tide of public sentiment. By 1931, with Republicans in control of the Legislature, a resolution to investigate city government was passed and Roosevelt withheld his veto. The vocal critic, Senator Samuel Hofstadter, was chosen to chair the legislative committee, and Seabury was engaged as investigator.[15]

The protagonists were in place, presenting vivid contrasts. Walker and Seabury, native New Yorkers, exemplified the city's diversity.

It was said of Walker as a youngster: "It was Jim's desire always to please everyone." He played the piano and longed to write songs. But prodded by his father, a minor city official in the Tammany hierarchy, he enrolled in New York Law School off Union Square. Walker received a law degree, but was strongly attracted to music and the theater. The theatrical world welcomed him when in 1908 he wrote the hit song "Will You Love Me in December as You Do in May?" He was elected to the Legislature from Greenwich Village.[16]

The studious Seabury became a young magistrate, and served on the New York Court of Appeals and the Supreme Court. He had run for Governor in 1916, feeling betrayed when the support he expected from Theodore Roosevelt did not materialize. Gene Fowler wrote: "In his chambers he overawed even the newspaper reporters, addressing them in glacial stage whispers. It was said that members of his own family spoke of him in the third person even when he was present. Perhaps he was more admired as a jurist than beloved as a man, for outwardly he was as aloof as the ice-cap of Mount Everest."[17]

Doris, inheriting almost all the stories of the city investigation, was now pregnant. For some quality she had, she found favor with the ominous prosecutor.[18] Disclosures of widespread abuse in the issuance of dumping permits in the Bronx sparked the hearings on March 16,[19] with the imposing Seabury at center-stage and harboring, some said, thoughts of presidential nomination.

At this point Doris was the beneficiary of an action not likely to have been repeated in American jurisprudence. The birth of her first child was early—the baby was entangled in the umbilical cord, and a Caesarean was performed by Dr. Mary Halton on March 24. The naming of "Little Doris" has been attributed to John O'Donnell's fear that Doris would not survive. She was seriously ill and her hospital stay was lengthy. Duke Shoop, Washington correspondent for *The Kansas City Star*, wrote in a profile of Doris: "Judge Samuel Seabury of New York, who conducted the investigation of the colorful Mayor 'Jimmie' Walker, recessed his hearings so Doris Fleeson, the Sterling, Kas., girl, might have her baby and not miss the climax of the biggest political story New York knew before Mr. Roosevelt entered the White House." Noted Ishbel Ross: "Her daughter, Doris, was born in March, 1932, while she was doing the Seabury hearings, but she worked almost to the last day, and was back in time for Mayor Walker's dramatic day in court."[20]

A third reference, disputed, appears in Barbara Belford's 1987 *Brilliant Bylines*: "She asked Judge Samuel Seabury to delay Mayor Walker's testimony, the highlight of the inquiry, while she had her first and only child. Two days after the birth of her daughter, Doris Fleeson was back in chambers to hear Mayor Walker testify."[21]

The story exploded on March 27 when Seabury announced the conclusion of his investigation of the magistrates' courts, castigating the mayor for assurances of cooperation "as insincere as they were loud." The prosecutor reeled off cases to emphasize allegations of fixing, bribery, extortion, oppression and political intervention in the courts. Seabury charged that in almost every case of framing exposed during the inquiry the bribery and fixing had occurred in a police station.[22]

The *Sterling Bulletin* carried a birth announcement on March 31:

A Girl in the Fleeson Family

> Mr. and Mrs. John O'Donnell, of New York, have a little daughter born Thursday, March 24. The little girl weighed 5 1/2 pounds. Relatives here have not yet learned her name. Mrs. O'Donnell was formerly Miss Doris Fleeson.

On May 25 a crowd began to gather at seven o'clock at the County Courthouse of Foley Square. Mayor Walker's day in court had arrived. It was a warm May morning, and the square was a circus. When an attendant mistakenly opened the doors of the hearing room, more than seven hundred spectators tried to fight their way inside. Police were called to clear the area and admit only those with passes from the Hofstadter Committee. By that time the throng had grown to several thousand in the corridors and rotunda, and outside the building, and members of the press and the selected spectators had difficulty getting through.[23]

Doris had just turned 31 on May 20; her baby was two months old the previous day. Now after twenty months of covering the city's major story she was at the courthouse to report the escalation the public had awaited. By outward indications, public sentiment remained on Walker's side. Gene Fowler described the scene: "When ruddy-faced Judge Seabury appeared among them a slight, grumbling stir of voices rose in the warm May morning. He paid no more attention to the inimical throng than a lighthouse does to a wave. When the Mayor's black limousine drew up at the curb there was a silence, followed by a buzz of excitement, and then a cheer."[24] In her story for the *Daily News* morning edition, Doris had given a preview of what might be expected in "the biggest show in town." Revealing that three Democratic members of the committee had called on the Mayor the day before but had been told he wanted no help, she observed: "This may mean the absence of those time-consuming wrangles common at recent hearings, which Seabury calls 'obstruction' and the minority protests are developing 'both sides of the picture.'" Followers of her later writing could find a recognizable style, as well as more than a hint of her remarkable sources, as she added that Seabury had been closeted with six aides in his private offices at 120 Broadway. She told readers:

> Although there is only eight years difference in age between Mayor Walker and Seabury they will present a tremendous contrast to one another as their battle of wits gets underway.
>
> The mayor, slender and dapper, looks less than his 50 years, his hair still dark and his sharp eyes seldom veiled with glasses. Seabury is solid and ruddy and his hair is silver. He looks pontifical and his speech matches his dignity except when he flares into sudden rage and barks sarcasms.

If anything was needed to affirm her stature in political reporting, her story of the hearing assured that claim:

> Amid tumult and confusion—the cheers and catcalls of a surging crowd, the sharp, impotent clattering of a gavel, and the raucous bawling of bailiffs for "Order! Order!"—Mayor James J. Walker and his political arch enemy, Samuel Seabury, fought face to face yesterday before the Hofstadter legislative committee. It resembled a battle between an airplane and a tank. Walker swooped on his adversary, deluged him with a machine gun fire of repartee and wit, and soared out of range before Seabury could bring him to earth. But Seabury lumbered steadily forward to the attack, and as night fell, not only he, but Walker, carried scars from the engagement. Walker had admitted that he had drawn profits of $246,692.76 from a joint stock account which he had shared with Paul Block, the publisher—although Walker had not contributed a dollar to the investment. And Walker had held this money, he said, in a safe—"not a tin tox"—in his home in cash, and he had drawn on it as he needed it keeping no book or other record in connection with it.[25]

Within days Seabury delivered fifteen charges to the Governor's desk in Albany. Now seeking the Democratic presidential nomination, Roosevelt faced a dilemma. Republicans were eager to charge his mishandling of the Walker case, but as the chaotic hearing had shown, the Mayor's support was strong in New York. The state's forty-five electoral votes might be crucial. In one account Roosevelt is quoted as asking his intellectual adviser, Columbia University Professor Raymond Moley: "How would it be if I gave the little mayor hell, and then kept him in office?"[26] Just before leaving for the convention in Chicago, however, Roosevelt asked the Mayor to answer the allegations.

New Yorkers now paused in the Walker crisis for the political conventions, the almost back-to-back "shows" to be staged in Chicago, a spectacle veteran journalists would not miss. Henry Mencken and Walter Lippmann were among those converging on the story as Doris, too, left for the scene with credentials of the *Daily News*. She might have been sent to "get" the woman's angle. Although the paper did not outwardly segregate news, its editors were said to follow a subtle formula: page two was given a masculine slant, and page three a feminine tone.[27] The "angle" at any rate, was openly acknowledged. A predictable keynote address generated little enthusiasm as Republicans convened on June 14, adjourning in less than two hours.[28] The real action had occurred outside as Communist lobbyists began a march and Jane Addams led fifty automobiles in a peace parade.[29] Only four sessions were planned for the expected reinstatement of the Hoover-Curtis ticket. But the party faced one emotionally charged issue, as women leaders from throughout the nation rallied to the convention site, both to urge and oppose repeal of the Volstead Act. There were the "wet women," an aristocratic contingent from New York (Mrs. Archibald Roosevelt among them), making their headquarters in the Blackstone Hotel. Mrs. Dolly Gann, sister of Vice President Charles Curtis, led drys including the Anti-Saloon League and the Woman's Christian Temperance Union.

Doris attached herself to the women, whose activities as they fanned out to concentrate on delegates soon enlivened proceedings.

Her dispatches portrayed Mrs. Gann "at the telephone in her suite in the Palmer House, her card index memory, product of years of political striving, functioning at top speed." In the opposite camp was Mrs. Charles H. Sabin directing cohorts "to buttonhole delegates from their respective States, and see what an argument, a bright smile and perhaps a bit of sex appeal—not that they'd admit the last impeachment—would do."

There were vivid differences. "These chic young matrons in their smart print frocks and gay footwear and frivolous hats present an interesting contrast to the soberly attired drys, mostly older," Doris reported. "Mrs. Henry W. Peabody, chairman of the Women's Law Enforcement Committee, had something to say, it's true, at one of her prayer meetings about her side not 'hanging around in hotel lobbies.'"

Although women aligned on either side of the Prohibition issue were the busiest and most conspicuous, members of the National Woman's Party had come on an ERA foray—controversial then and especially among women—pressing an eighteen-word equal rights amendment to the Constitution. While Rebekah Greathouse of Tenafly, New Jersey, cousin of Anne Lindbergh, invoked the support of her aunt, Mrs. Dwight Morrow, wife of Coolidge's Ambassador to Mexico, the effort drew negligible support.[30]

Mrs. Sabin's group for repeal experienced similar dismissal when the party adopted a "straddle plank," the compromise Hoover had been seeking. "Dolly Gann put it over and the lady wets, who didn't, have gone home but they said they weren't mad," Doris wrote. "They didn't wait around Convention Hall today, however, to add their sopranos to the paean of praise for Herbert Hoover, embarking on the Century for New York instead. . . . They will return June 26 to their comfortably iced quarters in the swanky Blackstone—ready to pounce on the delegates of Democracy . . ."[31]

The brief, orderly Republican convention was a prelude to the real show approaching. Arrangements were in place for up to twelve sessions in the Democratic gathering, which held suspense on all fronts: an explosion of the anxiety and bitterness of the Depression, a fight on Prohibition, and a rumored deal to deliver Tammany to Roosevelt in exchange for immunity for Walker.[32] As delegates began to arrive, Doris focused on New York's powerful contingent:

> CHICAGO—JUNE 26—Flaunting bright badges boldly marked "Tammany" and finished off with highly colored medallions depicting a brave in a feathered headdress, the boys from Fourteenth Street steamed into town today. Arriving in two special trains they foregathered at the Drake, where the State delegation was to caucus tonight.
>
> The lobby of the Drake, smart North Shore hotel, was a Tammany Hall in miniature as the beribboned delegates milled about. All were resplendent in new straw hats, the more dashing in panamas and the conservatives in skimmers. Cigars were universal.[33]

In Chicago's midsummer heat, filing dispatches for the *Baltimore Sun*, Henry Mencken was in his element. According to biographer Carl Bode, the great critic of American life complained constantly, but his real regret was that the conventions came only every four years. Mencken's letter to his friend, Jim Tully, expressed his special pleasure in the Democratic gathering of 1932: "The two national conventions almost wore me out, but they were such good shows that I held up until the end. The Democratic show, in particular, would have delighted your Christian heart."

Mencken remembered the awesome heat one evening when Democrats reconvened at eight and stayed in session all night. His seersucker suit began to look like a bathing suit and his necktie "took on the appearance of having been fried." The sessions ground on, with Roosevelt forces pursuing the nomination for which the Governor had directed every effort the past two years. Even Seabury arrived on the scene, monitoring events in case of a deal with Tammany. Al Smith's appearance at the podium delighted Mencken: "The great set piece of the debate was the speech of Al Smith. When he suddenly appeared on the platform, his face a brilliant scarlet and his collar wet and flapping about his neck, he got a tremendous reception and the overgrown pipe organ let loose with East Side, West Side in an almost terrifying manner . . he made some amusing faces, and he got a huge and friendly laugh by pronouncing the word radio in his private manner, with two d's."[34]

The New York women, who had returned to lobby Democrats, were having tea in the Blackstone when news of the platform committee's adoption of a repeal plank arrived. Mrs. Sabin, said Doris, was "electric with the thrill of victory," and Mrs. Carol Miller "will speak for Franklin D. Roosevelt and she was declaring positively that he's 'wet enough for anybody.'"[35] Another bright spot for women was Arizona's promotion of Isabelle Greenway, who had been one of Eleanor Roosevelt's bridesmaids, for Vice President. "We'll get the men used to hearing us nominated by degrees so it won't shock them too much when a woman starts to fight for it," declared a supporter.[36] Many rallied to Caroline O'Day's resolution for public welfare and the protection of children. Among prominent women sitting on "the hard red undertaker's chairs" were Mrs. Woodrow Wilson, Mrs. Condé Nast, Mrs. William G. McAdoo (Woodrow Wilson's daughter) and Mrs. Ruth Bryan Owen (daughter of William Jennings Bryan), a member of the press.[37] For her seconding speech for Roosevelt, Isabelle Greenway received an ovation even from the Roosevelt-hostile galleries. "There are other women seconders, but no Jane Addamses, no Ida Tarbells," noted Doris. "These are women who play the men's game, chosen by the men for their fidelity to it." A light moment amid demonstrations for John Nance Garner for Vice President occurred when a reporter shouted, "I'm for Garner. The only candidate with sex appeal."[38]

In the end it was a deal with William Gibbs McAdoo, leader of the California delegation, rather than the risky bargain with Tammany, that sealed the nomination for Roosevelt. Walker had asked fellow delegates to disregard his problems, and he delighted his old Tammany colleagues by casting his vote for Al Smith. "Good old Jimsie!" Gene Fowler quoted Smith as saying. "Blood is thicker than water."[39]

Roosevelt, feeling the urgency of the Depression and a need for immediate response, now decided to break with precedent and come to the convention to accept the nomination in person.

Doris drew the assignment of covering the candidate's arrival the next day, July 3, at the remote field at 6200 Cicero Avenue, five miles from the Loop. There was tremendous interest. "As early as 10 A.M. crowds were gathering at the airport, nondescript men who wandered aimlessly around and fat women dragging children by the hand," Doris reported. At 12:30, she noted, "the official cars roared up to the door of the airport offices, the city's long aluminum color touring car snorting at their head."

Roosevelt's plane, which had taken off from Albany at 8:12 and stopped in Buffalo and Cleveland, reached Chicago at 5:22. "The huge tri-motored American Airway silver-colored passenger ship, containing thirteen persons, circled the field twice before landing," Doris wrote. "A crowd of at least 25,000 was waiting. . . . The plane made a neat landing at the edge of the crowd."[40]

Roosevelt stirred tumultuous response in Chicago, pledging a New Deal for the American people. From that pinnacle he returned to Albany to deal once more with the vexing matter of Mayor Walker.

Roosevelt was on the brink of launching his campaign.[41] The timing was as inconvenient as possible, and there remained a question of the Governor's Constitutional power to remove an elected mayor. But hearings were scheduled.

Doris was dispatched to Albany for the proceedings.[42] She was on hand to report the "startling spectacle" of Walker's arrival on the evening of August 11, when brass bands, fireworks and a throng of 10,000 greeted him at the station.[43]

An hour before the hearing, crowds had begun to pack the Statehouse corridors, shepherded by State Troopers. In contrast to the Mayor's jubilant arrival, Seabury had "motored in" from East Hampton. Roosevelt, "a pleasant sphinx in white linen," his legal advisor M. Maldwin Fertig at his side, sat as judge. Doris wrote:

> Bulking large in blue serge, the silver-haired jurist sat at

his counsel table on the governor's left, his retinue spread out fanwise on either side.

But when Walker came—their choice! They didn't roar in the intimidating presence of authority but they clapped. The patter of their hands followed him into the sombre high-ceilinged hearing chamber. He wore blue serge, too, but with a different air, and he had a cheerful word for the Capitol attaches, his old friends of Senate days.[44]

The charges against Walker were formidable. It was alleged that he had betrayed citizens for the benefit of friends during a bus company's negotiations for a franchise; that he had failed to explain the sources of nearly a million dollars, including more than $700,000 in cash, all deposited during five years in the name of Russell T. Sherwood; that he accepted more than $200,000 from publisher Paul Block and other citizens who said they made money in the stock market for him merely because he was a friend; that he received $26,000 from a firm interested in taxicab legislation; that he received a $10,000 letter of credit from a promoter of the bus company the day before the franchise contract was signed; that he and Sherwood received $22,000 from a brokerage firm also interested in taxicab legislation; that physicians named for city work split fees with his brother, Dr. William H. Walker.[45]

After two volatile days in the oppressive heat, the hearings recessed late Saturday. By the time the inquiry resumed Monday afternoon the courts had stepped in with a political godsend for Roosevelt, ordering that he could not rule until August 19 and must show cause why he "should not be restrained from rendering a decision." With appeals, the affair might be delayed past the election.[46] At the close of Monday's session, Roosevelt left for Poughkeepsie to meet his running-mate, Garner, for the first time since their nomination.[47]

As hearings continued through the week with one sensation after another, rumors began to fly that the Mayor might resign. On Friday Walker obtained a Supreme Court order requiring Roosevelt to prove his right to continue the inquiry. A wearisome session concluded with a motion by Walker's counsel to dismiss all charges. That Roosevelt declined to do.[48] He then left to launch his presidential campaign in Ohio.[49]

A court ruling in Roosevelt's favor revived the hearings, and they continued for another two weeks before Walker, on September 1, announced his resignation. A few friends who were able to get in to see him the next day in his suite at the Mayfair came out remarking: "Jimmie's himself again. He's back in his old form." Samuel Seabury sailed for France on the liner Paris that night. Roosevelt returned to the executive chamber at week's end to declare the hearings closed.[50]

It was Friday, September 2, 1932, the beginning of the Labor Day weekend, an ironic holiday in the Depression. Between fifteen and seventeen million people were out of work.[51] The First National Bank of Idaho and nine subsidiary banks in central and western Idaho and eastern Oregon had just closed.[52] But in New York, the Walker hearings had been a great diversion, and seemingly the Depression could be denied. Reported one newspaper:

> Edward R. Brevoort, 60-year-old president of F.A. Potts & Co., wholesale coal dealers of 143 Liberty St., plunged to his death early yesterday from a window of his apartment on the seventeenth floor of 55 Central Park West, corner of 66th St. Police listed the death as accidental.[53]

9

~~~

CAPITAL STUFF

Out on the hot airfield on the outskirts of Chicago on July 2, 1932, the party of thirteen disembarking "were happy as larks." As Doris observed them, the Roosevelts chatted with everyone indiscriminately, whether they knew them or not. Their mood revitalized the crowd of 25,000 which had been forming throughout the day, receiving bulletins on the flight from radios attached to NBC automobiles. The Roosevelts, looking fresh, had just ridden out a bumpy nine-hour flight from Albany, after staying up all night listening to the convention. During a stop in Cleveland, Mrs. Roosevelt said she found everything "perfectly marvelous."[1]

Eleanor Roosevelt wrote: "From the personal standpoint, I did not want my husband to be president . . It was pure selfishness on my part, and I never mentioned my feelings on the subject to him."[2] Few, except a small circle of friends, saw the facade as the future First Lady began the campaign, hating to give up the independent life she had created. "If there is anything more dismal than an ordinary campaign biography it is the inanities written about a president's wife," Doris later observed.[3] "Mrs. Eleanor Roosevelt is the rare exception who lived long enough and learned to write well enough to explain herself."[4]

At forty-seven, Eleanor had been a unique First Lady of New York, carrying out the many duties of the executive mansion, while at the same time teaching two and a half days a week at the Todhunter School in New York City. She followed the schedule for four years, returning to Albany on Wednesdays and often arriving at the train station late. As Frances Perkins recalled, Eleanor thought "it odd that a great-tall woman like herself, who towered over everybody in Grand Central Station, would be recognized when she ran for a train and that they would hold the train for her."[5] The private school for girls, of which she was part owner, was one of the ventures she had undertaken in a period she called "the intensive education of Eleanor Roosevelt."[6]

Her troubled childhood was well known. Virtually homeless, she had passed from one to another aristocratic relative during her mother's illness and her father's alcoholism, and after her parents' deaths. She blossomed at Allenswood, the school in England where, at fifteen and six feet tall, she became "almost immediately the school's primary leader."[7] Returning to New York, Eleanor was a debutante at the Assembly Ball, and in the same period she taught at the College Settlement in the Lower East Side. She and her fifth cousin, Franklin, whom she had not seen since she was fourteen, met on a New York Central train going up the Hudson.

She was twenty when they were married in New York City, with the attendance of her uncle, President Theodore Roosevelt, somewhat upstaging the wedding. In the next twelve years, Eleanor bore six children (the first Franklin Jr. died at eight months). It was a period dominated by the matriarchal Sara Delano Roosevelt, focused on the interests of her only child. Eleanor wrote in her autobiography: "In the autumn of 1908 I did not know what was the matter with me, but I remember that a few weeks after we moved into the new house on East 65th Street, I sat in front of my dressing table and wept, and when my bewildered young husband asked me what on earth was the matter with me, I said I did not like to live in a house which was not in any way mine, one that I had done nothing about and which did not represent the way I wanted to live."[8]

Eleanor was remembered as an extraordinary "Washington wife" during the years Franklin was Assistant Secretary of the Navy; before that she had gained self esteem in Albany during his term in the Senate. The shock of Franklin's romance with Lucy Mercer in 1918 was said to be monumental.[9]

Changes in her life began after they returned to New York City in 1920. As a first step she decided to acquire a skill she had never learned. She found a former cook, now married, and went to her home twice a week to cook dinner for her family. She enrolled in a business school to learn typing and shorthand. She also agreed to serve on the board of the League of Women Voters.[10] This was her introduction to lawyer Elizabeth Read and her life-partner Esther Lape, whose influence Blanche Wiesen Cook analyzes in the context of the feminist movement:

> In their company, Eleanor Roosevelt became a "New Woman," a prominent member of that diverse and diffuse group that heralded modernity. Although she lived uptown, in the house that Sara built, which she hated, ER spent several evenings each week downtown, with the women who became in 1921 her most intimate friends. They were among the first generation of college educated women, independent and hardworking, who kept the flame of feminism alive.[11]

The two lived in Greenwich Village in a house at 20 East 11th Street. Nearby, at 171 West 12th, a cooperative building with social feminists, were Marion Dickerman and Nancy Cook. They had lived together since 1909 when they were graduate students at Syracuse University. Eleanor first worked for them on a newspaper for the Democratic State Committee, and she became acquainted with all the women in the building.[12] Eventually the three women and Caroline O'Day formed a partnership which included the *Women's Democratic News*, The Todhunter School and the Val-Kill furniture factory. For the latter, the Roosevelts built a stone cottage along Val-Kill brook on their Hyde Park estate, a project in which Franklin is said to have taken much interest in "the role of concerned and general paterfamilias." He called Eleanor's friends "the girls."[13]

In this period Eleanor began to earn her own money with teaching, writing and radio appearances, and she began to identify with journalists. She liked their style and "their no-nonsense approach to politics and to life," noted Cook. "From then to the end of her life, ER was relaxed in the company of reporters. She enjoyed their jokes, their direct manners. She felt comfortable with them, and they appreciated her unexpected warmth, generosity and good-humored intelligence."[14]

Their paths had touched only slightly when Doris reported the role of the candidate's wife in the newsmaking flight to Chicago. In Albany, while covering the Legislature, she had observed the Roosevelts with their overwhelming entourage and the carnival of life in the executive mansion. Not only did aides and advisors live with the family, but the Roosevelts had numbers of overnight guests in the old gothic quarters. "The Roosevelts seem to have a flair for making intimates of their most competent and most loyal supporters and co-workers," wrote columnist Edith Johnson, noting the residency of Franklin's secretary, Missy LeHand. Eleanor declined a room of her own and "camped out" with the servants or with a friend such as Frances Perkins.[15] When Doris visited Eleanor at Hyde Park in 1950 she found the atmosphere remarkably unchanged. "It is a background familiar to Americans since the early days of the New Deal," she observed. "What is interesting in a return visit is that the traffic in ideas and human problems is undiminished. . . . here is still the broad highway, the Grand Central Station through which flows the main stream of American life and thought. . . ." [16]

In the 1920s Eleanor was associated with every cause in the women's political movement. In an era in which even her husband referred to feminist leaders as "she-males" and President Coolidge denounced women's colleges, particularly Vassar, as hotbeds of radicalism,[17] she was an ideal for Doris and for her intellectual sister, Elizabeth Jordan, who had taught at Vassar. But in 1932 Doris was at the periphery of the journalistic colleagues Eleanor enjoyed.

After covering the Chicago conventions and the riveting Walker case, Doris reported the mayoral contest and the unruly Democratic State Convention.[18] As the Depression advanced, her degree in economics and the insights of her Kansas mentor placed her in a unique position to explain its effect. In early 1933 she was assigned the national banking crisis. Her college major, chosen for the force of her professor's intellect, became an entrée into New Deal circles during the months preceding Roosevelt's inauguration, said her nephew Dick Fleeson.[19]

Following his landslide victory, Roosevelt took office on March 4—the last president to be inaugurated in March. The latest of state bank holidays had brought the economy almost to a halt, but millions listening to radios heard Roosevelt proclaim "the only thing we have to fear is fear itself."[20]

The New York Daily News reported and editorially cheered the First Hundred Days of the New Deal, which by the time Congress adjourned in June yielded the Banking Act and the National Industrial Recovery Act. It was at this point that the newspaper sent John O'Donnell to fill in for two weeks for the vacationing Washington correspondent.

With daughter Little Doris in 1933.

With successes on the domestic front, the administration faced foreign policy issues at an economic conference in London. When Secretary of State Cordell Hull appeared at an impasse, Roosevelt sent advisor Raymond Moley as a trouble-shooter. Hull resented the affront and eventually won out. As Doris told Duke Shoop in 1937: "John was sent here for two weeks to do a Washington column while the regular man was on vacation. He arrived at the moment that Tennessee mountaineer, Cordell Hull, had neatly slit the political throat of the brightest star of that time in the new deal firmament, Prof. Raymond Moley. John wrote a sprightly account of the very amusing turn of the new deal and Mr. Patterson of the News decided to keep him here and sent me along, and the baby, to do our part."[21]

The O'Donnells began their joint column "Capital Stuff" on August 28, 1932,[22] in the newly opened Washington bureau of the *Daily News*, sharing a byline—his name first, and hers as Doris Fleeson. The column appeared at a time of abundant criticism of the American press. Critics were crying for the return of strong, personal journalism. They branded the majority of newspapers "admirably useful and impeccably dull." Those retaining any character of their fighting editors were "small, sparse islands in a sea of gray." The wire services were indicted for conferring a "deathly uniformity" by being calculatingly inoffensive.

There had been columnists since the 1880s, notably Arthur Brisbane, editor and columnist for Hearst, Heywood Broun, and Don Marquis, with his newsroom cockroach and cat, archy and mehitabel. Archy typed parts of the columns without punctuation or capital letters.

The New York *World* was the first to establish a stable of columnists, demonstrating the popularity of the Page Opposite Editorial, or "Op Ed Page."[23] Others who would become stars of the news syndicates were emerging or about to ascend when the O'Donnells began their collaboration.

Frank Kent of the *Baltimore Sun*, writing a column with the name of his 1923 book *The Great Game of Politics*, was syndicated in 1933.[24] Doris' fellow native Kansan in Washington, Raymond Clapper, began his popular "Between You and Me" in 1934, writing, "for the people he knew out in Kansas—being careful not to overestimate their knowledge or underestimate their intelligence."[25] Westbrook Pegler was producing his column by 1935, and Dorothy Thompson, hers, by 1936. Charles Driscoll, the onetime *Wichita Eagle* writer who had contributed the unflattering pieces on his native Kansas for Mencken's *Mercury*, was the successor in 1938 to O.O. McIntyre's "New York Day by Day."[26] A touch of déja vu, sixty years later, crept in when The Associated Press reported on the success of a new kind newspaper, in particular two in Kansas City recognized by the Association of Alternative Newsweeklies (AAN). "Writers aren't trying to take a voiceless, odorless, colorless, pure-news approach," journalist Hearne Christopher Jr. declared. Editor Arthur Brisbane of *The Kansas City Star*, the Hearst columnist's namesake, said that while his newspaper was a constant punching bag for both papers, he did not consider them direct competitors.[27]

For Washington correspondents, the early Roosevelt years offered incomparable access to the President. The intimate group met the President twice or more each week, actually in the Oval Office: Said *NEWS-WEEK*: "Press conference days—Tuesdays and Fridays—see at least 100 news writers jammed against the white lobby door leading to the President's office. If kept waiting five or ten minutes overtime, veterans bang the door with their fists. This is supposed to express good-natured impatience. When the door opens, reporters float through the lobby to The Presence like logs in a sluiceway."[28]

Eleanor Roosevelt immediately began her own press conferences, at the suggestion of her friend Lorene Hickok of The Associated Press. Eleanor was concerned for women reporters, whose positions were vulnerable in the Depression, and sought to give them something to write about.[29] It was an unusual opportunity for Doris and a small group of women to associate with the First Lady, but in truth Eleanor considered them colleagues and enjoyed their "trick" questions.

In 1933 Doris helped found the American Newspaper Guild and was on the committee urging the National Recovery Administration to set a $35 minimum wage for reporters.[30] The O'Donnells, considered a striking Washington couple, settled in Chevy Chase to raise Little

Doris and a second child expected in 1934. Doris' nephews, William and Dick, came that summer from Kansas, where crops had withered in the worst year of the Dust Bowl and Depression. The boys, after stopping at the Chicago World's Fair, visited the Jordans in New Haven and at their summer home in Nova Scotia. The O'Donnells hosted them in Washington, and William stayed on into fall before returning to the University of Kansas.[31]

The baby was stillborn in November; Doris was seriously ill in Johns Hopkins Hospital.[32]
Letters from friends alluded to the loss:

> From Frank and Alice Dains in Lawrence—Elsie has written us of yours and John's disappointment and grief. . . . I feel that as your physical strength returns you will find courage to meet this, and measure all that you have lost. . . . I am so glad you are in that great Hospital. . . . I know you will be prudent about not going back to work until you are completely able."[33]

> From Dr. Mary Halton in New York City—How dear you are—writing to me at this time. I was so glad to hear that you are coming along all right. There was a wild rumor in New York that you were seriously ill. . . . Doris you are a precious beautiful spirit—I remember so many beautiful & poignant things you have said to me in our talks together. Your doctors of John's (sic) Hopkins are the best in the country.[34]

In April, 1935, Doris was in Miami, the only woman correspondent covering the President's Florida vacation. Westbrook Pegler assailed "ink-stained wretches of the Fourth Estate" making the best of things in the Miami Biltmore. They included Mr. and Mrs. Fred Storm of the United Press, Mr. and Mrs. Charlie Hurd of *The New York Times*, Mr. and Mrs. Al Warner of the *Herald Tribune*, Mr. and Mrs. Sandy Sandifer of the International News, Francis Stephenson of The Associated Press, Eddie Roddan of Universal News and Ed Trohan of the *Chicago Tribune*.

"The character of the Roosevelts encourages family parties, except of course, during campaign trips when the expedition must travel light and fast," wrote Pegler. "At Poughkeepsie, the Roosevelts gave a picnic for the correspondents and the wives at their estate and amusing games were played." In Miami, the columnist asserted, the only relief from the grind was "tennis, golf, bathing in the surf, dining on the patio and dancing in the night club."

Of the O'Donnells he commented: "Miss Fleeson and her husband, Mr. John O'Donnell, write a joint column out of Washington and take turns going on the road. Last year it was Mr. O'Donnell's turn. He covered the President's Florida vacation and also went to Poughkeepsie where he played fifth base on the White House varsity bean-bag team in the series with Mr. Lowell Thomas' team from the other side of the mountain. This year Mr. O'Donnell is standing his trick at home, minding the baby and raking the leaves off the crocuses."[35]

Back in Washington, Doris wrote from their home at 800 Bradley Boulevard, Chevy Chase, to her sister Elizabeth, reporting that she was home with a fine tan and feeling rested. The German nurse she had engaged in New York for Little Doris was working out well.[36]

10

CLASH OF KANSANS

In sweltering Cleveland everyone wore summer whites. National Chairman Henry P. Fletcher was "flawless." Ex prize-fighter Warren Barbour, New Jersey's "portly millionaire Senator," was "billowing." Tall Senator Arthur Vandenberg of Michigan, dressed entirely in white, looked especially cool.

Political ambassadors dashed from hotel suite to hotel suite in the steaming city. As a thousand and one delegates gathered for the Republican National Convention, the suspense centered on two men: Governor Alfred M. Landon of Kansas, the favorite, and Senator William E. Borah of Idaho, the "IF" man.[1]

The forty-eight-year-old Landon, whom only a handful had seen and who was virtually unknown outside his native Kansas until the beginning of that year, had ridden a groundswell as the only Republican governor re-elected in 1934. The candidacy had been inventively crafted, first by his uncle, William T. Mossman, a public relations man in Pittsburg, and then by forty-four-year-old national committeeman John D.M. Hamilton of Topeka, former speaker of the Kansas House of Representatives. In January he had arranged for leaders from other states to attend Kansas Day festivities, and for Chicago publisher Frank Knox, the most active candidate for the 1936 presidential nomination, to deliver the main address.[2]

By convention time, the Landon high command was described as dominated by the brains of Editor Roy Roberts of *The Kansas City*

Star, the political reporters of Arthur Capper, the publishing Senator of Kansas, and Hearst "legionnaires." William Allen White was at the convention, with a special interest in chairing the platform committee,[3] and keeping in touch with Landon at the Topeka statehouse with a "fifty-foot telephone cord." In September when Hearst had announced his support for Landon, White had declared: "Doubtless any statesman many times has to ally himself with worse men than Hearst. Probably in my own career I have worked with deeper-dyed villains."[4]

Awaited with an air of mystery was the arrival of Borah, the seventy-one-year-old orator of the Senate. In Washington his deliverances were legendary. Reporters covering Congress did not go to the press galleries unless they heard "Borah's up!" or "Vandenberg's filibustering."[5] Borah's candidacy had enjoyed a boom at the beginning of the state primaries, and he had announced a platform. He was a commanding national figure to oppose the modest Landon, who was being called the Kansas Coolidge from the Dust Bowl.[6] With his liberal Republican views, the Senator from Idaho had been threatening to bolt the party for twenty years, and he offered the best hope of electrifying the convention.

This was the dynamic when the O'Donnells arrived for the pre-convention weekend. Henry Mencken was there, reporting on June 7: "The delegates and alternates to the Republican National Convention are still strung across the country, slowly edging their way toward Cleveland by train, bus, motorcar and oxcart."[7] One of these was Hoover, en route by train and reportedly looming as a "big puzzle," possibly hopeful of a draft in a deadlock. As the convention got under way, Mencken railed that "such hullabaloos, by long usage, have become almost as standardized as baccalaureate addresses or hangings."[8]

The convention immediately placed a focus on Kansas. John O'Donnell wrote of "triumphant, boastful Kansans, who have forced the financially-omnipotent East into the background and now rule the political machinery of the Republican party."[9] Landon and Doris' brother Howard, the Wichita attorney, had been close friends since the Governor's early years as an independent oil producer in southeast

Kansas. And even Borah had a connection with Kansas—in neighboring Lyons ten miles from Sterling. In 1883, at the age of eighteen, he had come from Illinois to live with his sister, wife of attorney A.M. Lasley. He attended Lyons High School; ambitious to become a lawyer he gave orations at local programs. At a time when few credentials were asked of country schoolteachers, Borah was hired to teach in the one-room Wabash School, and while teaching a four-month term he read law with Lasley. The next fall he enrolled at the University of Kansas, where he studied for a year before returning to Lyons. He was admitted to the bar in 1887 and joined his brother-in-law in the firm of Lasley & Borah.[10] The junior partner was said to have left town for lack of opportunity for his far-seeing ambitions,[11] but there also were rumors that he left rather abruptly. Details were said to be locked in Masonic Hall records.

Borah now was a potent national figure, the leading liberal of the Republican Party. "Landon The Favorite, Borah Big G.O.P 'IF,'" the *Daily News* proclaimed on convention eve. The O'Donnells found the Kansans headquartered in the Hollenden Hotel, impressively holding ten press conferences in the morning and five in the afternoon for the dozens of correspondents already on the scene. They presented a coalition not entirely critical of the New Deal. They had supported farm and relief efforts in the early days of the Roosevelt administration, and they favored a Constitutional amendment for state minimum wage laws. They endorsed social security legislation, but with control in the states rather than in Washington.[12] Their platform was expected to be "a New Dealish document."

Borah was barely off the train before he proclaimed that he would not join the anti-Landon drive. But if reporters saw a story fading, they were disappointed only briefly. Doris wrote:

> Five hours after he had turned an icy back on the stop-Landon coalition, bewildering Bill Borah launched a smashing attack at his pre-convention press conference tonight on the Kansas Governor. . . .

In smashing oratorical form, the Senator tossed aside the proposed anti-monopoly plank of Oil Man Landon's forces and defined monopoly as "the power to fix prices which is enjoyed by five great oil companies, some of which are very active in this convention. . . ."

He demanded a complete isolationist plank—one that would not involve us in any way with foreign countries.[13]

Three hundred reporters crowded the conference, straining to hear every word. The Cleveland Hotel room was sweltering. Landon forces, delighted that Borah had concentrated his whole force on the platform, commissioned a messenger to hasten to his headquarters with an olive branch. Furnishing touches of drama and human interest were the arrival of the California delegation, led by Cecil B. de Mille, and the proposal of advertising expert Bruce Barton to find the oldest living Republican and seat that person on the platform. While younger party members were enthusiastic, the plan was shot down by New York National Committeeman Charlie Hilles: "Very interesting idea, but my recollection is that the oldest living Republican is John D. Rockefeller Sr."

The convention opened on Tuesday, June 9, with Hoover hovering in the background, expected to arrive by train from Chicago the next morning. Doris reported:

> The Republican party that nominated Calvin Coolidge by acclamation in 1924, and swallowed Herbert Hoover whole in 1932, reassembled in National convention today in circumstances that recalled vividly the fateful conclaves of both four and twelve years ago. A landslide convention, committed in bulk to Alf M. Landon as it was to Coolidge in 1924, the current assemblance of the Grand Old Party met for a short and platitudinous session in the Municipal Auditorium.[14]

Hoover's advisers had staged a dramatic arrival of the 9:55 from Chicago. "If there had been any doubt that the sage of Palo Alto was ready to make himself the willing victim of political lightning, the circumstances of his arrival wiped it out," O'Donnell wrote. There were bands, banners and flags, and the rotunda of the Cleveland terminal was jammed. Although Hoover could have walked directly from the terminal to the Cleveland Hotel, his advisers had arranged for one hundred police officers to clear the way as a color guard ushered him into Cleveland's public square and then to the hotel.

O'Donnell discerned a change in Hoover, the "high-collared Californian."[15] At the convention he "hurled thunderbolts at the New Deal," and provided the "first taste of savagely jubilant campaigning," when comparing the Roosevelt administration to fascist dictatorships in Europe.

A drama was developing in the wings—a real possibility that Borah might actually bolt. Late in the day, his face grim and "a brown hat jammed on his head," he had stormed off to the anteroom where the resolutions committee was at work, after learning that conservatives were altering liberal planks of the platform.[16] The Landon forces rushed to effect a compromise. O'Donnell wrote:

> Last night saw the prologue—a personal message from Candidate Landon, sitting in Topeka at his trusty telephone with its 50-foot cord, to sub-committee member William Allen White, Emporia editor.
>
> Said Landon:
>
> "By all means, see Senator Borah and do all that you honorably can to satisfy him on the platform and see that his views get the fullest consideration by the committee."
>
> Bright and early with cheerful morning face, the Sage of Emporia toddled up to the cramped little hall bedroom in the sumptuous Hotel Cleveland occupied by his old Bull Moose pal.

Borah, clad in pajamas, graciously consented to give the Landonites a try at conciliating him and agreed to read the planks tentatively outlined by the Kansan's strategists.

His rosy face alight with hope, White gave the precious sheets to Borah's keeping, and returned to wrestle anew with the gold-standard Old Guard in a downstairs room.[17]

By Thursday evening the Landon staff was working against time to obtain a platform it could carry to a first-ballot nomination. "In his little upstairs room," wrote Doris, "the convention Achilles, Senator Borah, was saying nothing. . . ."[18] At about 8:30 the resolutions committee began its report, and after thirty-five minutes delegates adopted it unanimously. Then came an extraordinary development when Landon telegraphed the convention to publicly amend the platform, as a condition of his candidacy.[19] The ballot was a landslide—984 for Landon and 19 for Borah. With Landon leaving the selection of his running mate up to delegates the next day, they unanimously chose Frank Knox, the *Chicago Daily News* publisher who had been an early presidential contender.[20]

The Democratic convention in Philadelphia two weeks later was perfunctory by comparison, but concluded after five days with a dramatic footnote. As he had done in 1932, Roosevelt came to deliver his acceptance speech in person. His son Elliott said that just before stepping onstage, the President nearly toppled to the floor when he reached out to shake a hand and lost control of his braced legs.

A deferential press had aided in concealing the disability, but Doris had not always done so (in covering the opening session of the Walker hearings she wrote that "Roosevelt limped in . . .")

None in the audience at Franklin Field knew of the incident. As the curtains parted, Roosevelt was vibrant, flashing his smile and waving to one hundred thousand spectators. He then began the speech in which he lashed "economic royalists," warned of dictatorships abroad, and ended, "This generation of Americans has a rendezvous with destiny."[21]

11

LADIES OF THE PRESS

HAMLET KNOWS WHAT AN UNCLE IS. H A WALLACE.
The telegram from Washington on September 25, 1936, was addressed:
MISS DORIS FLEESON, NEW YORK NEWS CARE GOVERNOR
LANDONS TRAIN—ARRIVING NORTHGREENBAY WIS 612
PM.[1]

In character, the mystical Secretary of Agriculture ("his feet in a manure pile, his head in the clouds") chided Doris with Shakespeare as she headed southward on the Landon train touring the farm belt. Since the convention she had focused on the Kansan, spending time in the Topeka campaign headquarters, and on September 22 embarking on the Governor's third campaign tour, a weeklong visit through the farm states.

From the beginning of his train trips in August, Landon had drawn criticism for a style that opponents thought "dull, simple-minded, chamber-of-commerce nonsense."[2] Members of the national press were dismayed at his choice of personal friends from Kansas as traveling companions on the first tour. When the special nine-car train reached New York, the Kansans were fodder for Arthur Krock, writing in *The New York Times* of "The Homespun Troupe":

> Less interesting than Mr. Landon's personal and mental exposure to the East, but still very interesting, is the personnel of the Kansas Cabinet which, with a couple of important

exceptions, is accompanying him. These men are supposed to give the general public an idea of the sane, modest, all wool American type of people on whom the Governor will rely if he is elected. . . . .

Roy Roberts, the news magician of the Kansas movement, and Henry J. Haskell, who put his keen brains to work on the Topeka platform, have not come East, for the Kansas City Star requires the services of its managing editor and editor-in-chief. . . . From their profession the Governor is bringing Paul Jones, a Democratic editor of Lyons, Kan., who was a Democrat until his friend Alf was nominated by the other side; and Lacy Haynes, Kansas editor of The Star, who is supposed to know precisely what appeals to the average small-town man. . . .

If what the people want is to see a group of plain folks, acting plainer than usual, they will see it whenever the special train stops, and have nostalgic dreams of the times when Calvin Coolidge pitched hay for the newsreels.[3]

It was a situation in reverse when Landon left on the third train tour, accompanied by sophisticates of the nation's press but traveling in "virtually virgin territory for a presidential nominee."

Crowds had been large and enthusiastic. The Midwest seemed euphoric. Yet when the Des Moines *Register* polled nineteen journalists aboard the train, only six thought Landon would win.[4] Doris shared the majority view, but did not go as far as her husband, who felt that an avalanche for Roosevelt was developing. When she and John considered their joint prediction for "Capital Stuff" the week before the election, her more moderate view prevailed. She regretted the stand once early returns made the stunning Roosevelt mandate apparent.[5] It was a minor misstep in the astute reportage they had produced since early summer, covering the conventions and, by turns, each accompanying Landon and Roosevelt on the campaign trains. Joseph Patterson was appreciative. Two days after the election he wrote managing editor Harvey Deuell: "As of next Monday, November 9th 1936, please raise Doris Fleeson to $100 a week."[6]

As the O'Donnells returned to Washington, the election story gave way to a monumental romance abroad. H.L. Mencken wrote Doris on December 11, 1936, the day of Edward's abdication:

> To my very great regret, I find that December 17th will be impossible. I am enjoying the honor of entertaining a couple of visiting firemen on that evening. I surely hope that you let me come some other time. And I hope too that you and your handsome husband will honor me in Baltimore in the meanwhile.
>
> I continue to deplore your subservience to Heywood Brounism. The Archbishop of Canterbury, in point of fact, had nothing to do with the ousting of Edward. It was achieved by God in person. I predict formally that within another year the name of poor Edward will be the universal symbol for imbecility. Try to imagine a sensible man giving up a good job for a third hand automobile. A third hand wife is obviously much more expensive, and far less consoling.[7]

The sensation overshadowed the O'Donnells' dispatches from Washington, where an attack on J. Edgar Hoover was escalating. An anti-Hoover explosion had been in the making for months, according to "Capital Stuff." Bitterest were the Postal Inspectors and agents of the Secret Service and the Treasury Department, who portrayed a publicity-hungry Director of the FBI double-crossing them at every opportunity to seize the spotlight. Now, in early December, the Hoover story receded as the British story unfolded daily. Free-wheeling editorials with advice similar to Mencken's accompanied the saga in the *Daily News*.[8]

The salary increase placed Doris, who had urged an NRA standard of $35 a week for reporters, in an upper level for women journalists, if not women in general. Missy LeHand, the President's personal secretary, earned $3,100 a year.[9] As Eleanor Roosevelt recognized, it was a precarious time for women reporters, even the tenacious thirty-five or so who had reached the Washington pinnacle.

In the midst of the Depression, young women were finding barriers and disparities they could hardly address in such desperate times. Men generally fared better—some very well. Harvey Deuell as managing editor of the *Daily News* received a salary and bonus totaling $145,000.[10] Arthur Brisbane, Hearst editor and columnist, reportedly earned up to $260,000 a year as the highest paid journalist of the 1920s and '30s.[11]

Eleanor Roosevelt's press conferences for women were as great a novelty as was she herself. All Presidents' wives had shunned publicity, most notably her predecessor, the dignified Lou Henry Hoover. Nevertheless FDR and Louis Howe approved, and on March 6, 1933, Eleanor assembled thirty-five women in the Red Room for her first meeting.[12] Biographer Joseph P. Lash said that she was nervous and brought a large box of candied fruit to be passed around. There was to be a ban on political questions, but that was observed for only a few tentative sessions. The conferences soon were a forum for her passionate causes, targeting sweatshops, child labor, low teachers' salaries, and isolationism.[13] They were "affirmative action" events, in the words of a more recent observer, and they had the intended effect of forcing newspapers and wire services to hire at least one woman to keep track of the newsmaking Mrs. Roosevelt.[14] Said veteran journalist Ishbel Ross: "Never was there such a gift from heaven for the working press."[15]

With the Roosevelts' habit of making intimates of their supporters and co-workers, it was not surprising that Eleanor became close to women journalists—too close in the view of some critics. Wrote Lash: "Most of the correspondents were friendly—too friendly, some of the men grumbled." She considered them colleagues, for she herself had written for more than a decade. By 1936 her annual income from lectures and from her column "My Day" in sixty newspapers approached $100,000. The Ladies Home Journal paid $75,000 for serial rights to her memoirs (her son Elliott said that she gave most away to charity or to the "hopeless task" of Val-Kill Industries).[16]

To detractors, the relationship was too cozy. The women, admiring the First Lady and flattered by her attentions, insisted that they could be friends without losing objectivity. In her generous way, Eleanor offered rides in the White House car, flowers from the greenhouse, lunch at the table, and invitations to Hyde Park. Sometimes she drove herself in her blue roadster to visit them. There were suggestions that friends alerted her to questions and advised her on the answers. But at the conferences, if a reporter cautioned that an answer might get her into trouble, she became especially forthright.[17]

On December 21, 1936, as journalists of the exclusively male Gridiron Club held their annual banquet and skit, Mrs. Roosevelt hosted a White House buffet for the Gridiron Widows, wives of fifty reporters, and other guests, and arranged for the Women's National Press Club to perform.[18]

In 1937 Roosevelt advanced Inauguration Day, for the first time, from March to January. Covering the ceremony on January 20, Doris wrote: "Head bared to an angry sky, his face lashed by the chill fury of a wind-whipped rain, Franklin Delano Roosevelt took the oath of office for his second term as President and pledged his administration to continue the fight against need and poverty, which still are the lot of millions."[19] In his address FDR had penned in the words that would be quoted often: "I see one-third of a nation ill-housed, ill-clad, ill-nourished." Doris and John reported the dramatic beginning of the second term as Roosevelt moved quickly to reorganize the Supreme Court, the unsuccessful "court packing" appeal to Congress, and confronted the rise of fascists abroad and isolationism at home.

The awards ceremony of the New York Newspaper Women's Club in 1937 was significant as the first, but also noteworthy as a comedy of indecision involving the two most prominent women in journalism. As a result, two veterans approaching legendary status shared a prize of $100. Members in evening dress gathered for the Front Page Ball on April 2 in New York's Hotel Astor. A distinguished panel including columnist Heywood Broun and journalist and novelist Ishbel Ross, who had judged entries, announced awards to four contestants.

Doris' coverage of the Republican National Convention was cited as "the outstanding piece of reporting," and she won $100.[20] Eleanor Roosevelt sent a note of congratulations,[21] and Anne O'Hare McCormick wrote: "This thank you has been in storage for too long but it's warm as ever. Your cheer on the Pulitzer prize gave me special pleasure. The ladies of the press are a grand bunch on the whole, and you're at the top of the heap—in every sense."[22]

In 1937 the O'Donnells had moved to a bungalow home at 5400 Connecticut Avenue Northwest. Photos showed John at the piano, Doris at the stone fireplace, and little Doris posing happily. In an interview, Doris credited John as the better journalist, saying that her arrival in Washington had been due to his accomplishments.[23]

Awards began coming in the 1930s. At its award ceremony in 1937 the New York Newspaper Women's Club cited Doris' coverage of the 1936 Republican National Convention as "the outstanding piece of reporting." (University Archives, Spencer Research Library, University of Kansas Libraries)

Doris and John O'Donnell at home in Washington: Helen Thomas remembered: "I think they had a rootin'-tootin' kind of marriage with lots of fights and so forth, but probably had tremendous intellectual rapport." (University Archives, Spencer Research Library, University of Kansas Libraries)

Circumstances had been similar for a few other journalistic couples. When Doris was elected president of the Women's National Press Club in 1937 she found an ally in May Craig, veteran Washington correspondent who had succeeded her husband, Donald A. Craig, as bureau chief for Guy Gannett newspapers in Maine upon his death in 1935. The deceptively prim journalist, described as looking like a small-town schoolteacher, had been a suffragette during the Wilson years and had written for Gannett since the Coolidge administration. She was noted for "dodge-proof" questions and for making Roosevelt uncomfortable. Once when the President launched an attack upon columnists during a press conference, Mrs. Craig reminded him that he had one in his own family.[24]

A profile of Missy LeHand, who in the view of less sympathetic observers was a "second wife" to FDR in the absence of a busy Eleanor, appeared under Doris' byline January 8, 1938, in the *Saturday Evening Post*. It was her first major magazine article, one in which she analyzed the seventeen-year association of the devoted secretary and the "many-sided" leader. Marguerite Alice LeHand was twenty-four when she went to work for Roosevelt in 1920, had lived with the family in Albany, and now held a position of rare authority. Hers was the only door opening directly into the President's office. "For her time is the President's time," Doris wrote. "If there is no formal entertaining being done, Missy dines with the family, and she and F.D.R. will spend the evening at work in his upstairs study. Or he will work at his collections, while she sits near by and reads, ready to lend a hand if need be."[25] (The description was quite different than that offered fifty years later by Elliott Roosevelt in his Eleanor Roosevelt Mystery series.)

Doris received $800 for the article, and a souvenir from her friend Marty Sommers of the *Post*. "Here is the original Missy from the hand of His Holiness," he wrote, enclosing the handwritten memo "Missy—To do This" which had been reproduced for the title.[26] And Eleanor wrote in "My Day": "I have just read an article in The Saturday Evening Post, written by Doris Fleeson about 'Missy.' I think it is a delightful piece of work. It is a rather rare thing for one woman to write such an appreciative and understanding article about another woman. Usually, I think a woman will write with more enthusiasm about some man. . . ."[27]

The University of Kansas *Graduate Magazine* carried Doris' photo and boasted of two 1923 graduates now contributing to the *Post*. Ben Hibbs, native of Pretty Prairie, had authored two recent articles on the dust bowl.[28]

Doris, president of the Women's National Press Club, with Eleanor Roosevelt at the club's stunt party in 1938. (Reproduced from holdings at the Franklin D. Roosevelt Presidential Library)

That summer Doris was the only woman aboard a special train carrying Roosevelt through the states in support of mid-term election candidates. John had started the trip, which began after Roosevelt's fireside chat on June 24, appealing for the election of liberals in the primaries, and interpreted as an attack on party rebels.[29] The address had drawn ridicule: "Hurry To Your Fireside, Folks," said a headline, "Loyal New Dealers Will Light Gas Logs, But Others May Sit By Refrigerator."[30] Together the O'Donnells reported platform stops in Ohio, Kentucky (an accolade for Alben Barkley), Oklahoma and Texas (kind words for Lyndon Johnson). From Fort Worth John took an American Airlines flight to cover preparations for the train's arrival in

Colorado. The *Fort Worth Star-Telegram* wrote of Doris:

> She has twice traveled half across the continent with the President, was on the fishing trip to the Texas Gulf last year, has been on other presidential trips to Florida and Warm Springs—and is thoroughly used to the job now of trailing the Chief Executive.
>
> Miss Fleeson is not really Miss Fleeson, but Mrs. John O'Donnell. She and her husband share the responsibility of covering Washington and Franklin D. Roosevelt for the New York Daily News . .
>
> They frequently argue about stories . . but get along fine in spite of it. She concedes he's a better reporter. He says she's modest.
>
> Their proudest collaboration is a six-year-old daughter, Doris, who is at the beach on Long Island this summer with a French governess.[31]

The contentious spring of 1939 in Washington was highlighted by the unforgettable moment in civil rights history, Marian Anderson's concert before seventy-five thousand on Easter Sunday at the Lincoln Memorial. Following closely was the convention of the American Society of Newspaper Editors, a gathering of two hundred men led by William Allen White and opening its forum to three prominent newspaper women.

Introduced by the Emporian as "lovely little hellcats," the three drew interesting descriptions by James L. Wright in his dispatch for the *Buffalo Evening News*. The speakers were the "ever-gay, though elderly" Mrs. Elizabeth M. Gilmer, known as Dorothy Dix; "the trim modishly-attired" Mrs. Inez Robb, a New York feature writer; and "sulphurous little Doris Fleeson" of *The New York Daily News*. Inez Robb and Doris wore summer prints and flowered hats as dressed for a garden tea, but their words to assembled editors were less genteel.

Robb pounced on two popular columnists: "It has been proposed that we produce a eugenic race, one which will know the answers to all the questions, not just to 95 percent of them. That could be provided by marrying Dorothy Thompson and Mark Sullivan." Doris accused editors of discrimination against women both as readers and reporters. And she could hardly be accused of idealizing the New Deal, as she was in newspaper circles, when she offered an observation of the President: "He is suffering acutely from a suppressed desire to be a managing editor. We see that all the time. He often tells us how we should write our leads, and indicates that if he were not so busy he would be glad to come over and help us get off our stories."

When they had finished, White said from the chair that the "eternal mother has taken us, the eternal child, on her knee, and told us how the world was made."[32]

On the Good Friday preceding Marian Anderson's concert, Mussolini seized Albania. Eleanor Roosevelt was aggrieved at the fall of Loyalists in Spain, Franklin frustrated at the rude dismissal of his appeals to Hitler and Mussolini and his failure to repeal the Neutrality Act. They could, however, focus efforts on the approaching visit of the King and Queen of England, the first visit of a British monarch since the War of Independence, as a symbol of American friendship with Great Britain. For the President, masterminding details for the visit in June became a rare form of escape.[33] Eleanor and her secretaries, overcome with details for the state visit, nonetheless took time to plan a gathering with the colleagues whose company they most enjoyed. Malvina Thompson wrote:

> Dear Doris:
> Mrs. Roosevelt wants to get all the girls together before she leaves for the summer and suggested dinner in the garden here on June 7.
> Will you reserve that night for a while? Something may turn up to change Mrs. Roosevelt's plans, but she hopes for no interference.[34]

Doris sent her acceptance to the White House:

Dear Tommy:
   I shall certainly reserve the night of <u>June 7</u> for dinner in
the <u>garden</u> with Mrs. Roosevelt. It sounds like a grand party.[35]

12

CLOUDS OF WAR

As the cataclysm approached, the O'Donnells and seven-year-old Doris sailed on July 26, 1939, for a "working vacation" in Europe.[1] Tourist travel remained brisk in late summer, with persistent rumors of a five-nation peace deal in the making, and reports that Poland was standing firm. That was the assessment of *Daily News* publisher Joseph Patterson, just back from the Continent and convinced that Germany was unprepared for a showdown.[2]

The unfolding drama was irresistible to journalists, if not for Americans in general, both intrigued by the danger and afraid of missing a last chance to see Europe. Many who could afford to do so had placed themselves in the eye of the storm. Now Britain and France were failing in their efforts to sign an alliance with Russia, whose leaders they had shunned and offended in earlier diplomacy. Russia suddenly announced the resumption of trade talks with Germany, a disturbing development. Negotiations were near collapse on July 29 when Pravda lashed out at the belated offer of friendship, deriding the Western overtures as a sham. If one constant existed, it was believed, it was the enmity of Russia and Germany, and the philosophical opposition of communism and fascism. As further assurance, Sir Thomas Inskip, dominions secretary, was traveling and speaking in Great Britain and declaring that war was unlikely.[3]

Throughout the summer there had been little interruption in the schedules of luxury passenger liners leaving New York harbor. The

O'Donnells sailed on a Wednesday morning aboard the Manhattan, filled with prominent and well-to-do travelers, including U.S. Postmaster General James A. Farley, actress Norma Shearer and singer Gene Autry. Also crossing the Atlantic were Howard and Katherine Fleeson of Wichita, who had embarked in New York on Tuesday for a month's vacation in Europe, planning to meet the O'Donnells in London.[4]

During early August the two couples spent a week in Paris. By the third week, however, when a sense of fear pervaded European capitals, Doris and John placed little Doris in a Swiss boarding school[5] and departed for Berlin.

As diplomacy faltered and Germany pressed Poland more belligerently, British and Russian diplomats met for the last time on August 21. That night German Foreign Minister Joachim von Ribbentrop flew to Moscow. In the Kremlin three days later, representatives of Germany and Russia signed a non-aggression pact that left Western leaders in disbelief.

With a dateline of "Berlin, Aug. 24," Doris and John cabled that German troops "tonight" were poised to strike, with "immediate invasion" of Poland a certainty.[6] The *Daily News* printed the dispatch before a correction could be sent to explain Hitler's sudden, inexplicable change. The attack had been scheduled for August 25.[7] Now seven days elapsed before Hitler ordered the massive strike at dawn on September 1, the opening of World War II.

Joseph Patterson shared one of the current views of Hitler— that he was an ineffectual mystic.[8] A similar assessment by Dorothy Thompson, known as "the Hitler blunder," was an error raised often by her critics, infuriating her at every reference. In March, 1932, *Cosmopolitan* magazine had published her article, "I Saw Hitler," in which she wrote:

> When I finally walked into Adolph Hitler's salon in the Kaiserhoff Hotel I was convinced that I was meeting the future dictator of Germany. In something less than fifty seconds I was quite sure I was not. It took me just about that time to measure the startling insignificance of this man who has set the world agog.

He is inconsequent and voluble, ill-poised, insecure—
the very prototype of the Little Man . . and yet he is not
without a certain charm.[9]

Patterson also had seen Hitler, very recently in fact, during a
ten-day trip he and his wife Mary had taken through Germany earlier
in the summer. He had tried unsuccessfully to obtain an interview, but
could get only a glimpse of the Nazi leader, attired in a smoking jacket
and black tie, at the music festival in Bayreuth. The publisher sized up
Hitler's appearance as an indication of "dolor," and proceeded to discount
the likelihood of a war. A series of three signed articles based on his
observations had just concluded in the *Daily News* when the O'Donnells
began reporting the perilous escalation.

It was described as a week of twilight. John left Berlin for London
while Doris picked up little Doris in Switzerland and took her to Paris.
They booked passage for September 15. Meanwhile in England, their
relatives were among thousands urgently seeking passage from Europe.
Robert and Elizabeth Jordan of New York City had joined Howard and
Katherine Fleeson, but now all were cutting short their holiday. On
August 26 Howard and Katherine sailed from Southampton aboard the
Holland liner New Amsterdam, filled to capacity, with two hundred
passengers sleeping in the ship's gymnasium and children's playroom. The
vessel docked in New York City on September 1, the day war began.[10] In
his dispatch from London September 2 John reported cancellation of the
sailing of the Ile de France, stranding six hundred Americans in France
and three hundred in London. Ambassador Joseph Kennedy had renewed
appeals to the Maritime Commission for vessels to take Americans out of
the danger zone suggesting that freighters also be used. "Only today did
Americans in London take the threatened war seriously," John wrote,
describing the three-day evacuation in British cities to remove children,
pregnant women and mothers with infants.[11]

Robert and Elizabeth Jordan reached New York on Sunday,
September 3, the day Britain and France declared war on Germany.
They had experienced a "hectic blackout trip" aboard the British liner,

the Queen Mary. Almost as though a new tide of immigration had begun, crowded vessels delivered vacationers, tourists, professors, and Americans employed abroad, to the New York piers. Doris and little Doris docked in New York later that month. On the return voyage Doris had looked after Ann Bullitt, daughter of Ambassador to France William C. Bullitt, who remained in Paris.[12]

As a third couple representing the *Daily News*, managing editor Harvey Deuell and his wife Peggy had expected to travel to Europe in the fall. The forty-eight-year-old Deuell died October 29 of a heart attack suffered while driving to the city from his home on the Hudson. A funeral was conducted at Saxony Hall, the couple's fourteen-room pillared mansion at Cornwall-on-Hudson,[13] where Doris and John had been present not long before at the wedding of their friends Tex and Blake O'Connor. Doris, John and Harvey all had arrived at the *Daily News* in 1927, and the O'Donnells' careers had flourished as Harvey rose from city editor to assistant managing editor, and finally managing editor in 1935. And Doris and Peggy, women with uncommon journalistic credentials, had an additional tie in having both grown up in Kansas. Peggy, born in 1889 in Bennington, had begun her career on the *Junction City Sentinel*, but soon left the state in a restless desire for adventure. As Peggy Hull, she had flamboyantly covered the Pershing expedition against Pancho Villa on the Mexican border in 1916–17, becoming the first woman accredited as a war correspondent by the United States War Department. She had reported on the training of U.S. soldiers in France for the *Chicago Tribune* in 1917, on the Siberian Intervention at Vladivostok for the *Cleveland Press* in 1918–19, and on the Japanese attack on Shanghai for *The New York Daily News* in 1932. Now fifty, Peggy had lived since her marriage in 1933 on the estate fifty-six miles north of New York City. With its ten acres, a lake, an eight-room gatehouse and an 1840 hall with an observation cupola, it was an impressive manor in which Harvey left behind the more sordid details of tabloid journalism for the life of a country squire. He was more suited to the life than was Peggy, who restlessly pursued cooking, needlepoint, rose gardening, and writing a book, *Beyond This Post* (never published).[14]

Shortly before Harvey Deuell's death, John returned to Europe as a foreign correspondent for the *Chicago Tribune*, accredited by Great Britain. An Associated Press photo of October 22, 1939, shows him in British uniform, with the caption: "O'Donnell calmly lights his pipe as he prepares to leave London for the Western Front."[15] Doris was among friends who rallied around Peggy, visiting at Saxon Hall in the weeks following Harvey's death. Another was Kay Hawkins, wife of W.W. Hawkins, general manager of Scripps-Howard newspaper syndicate. Peggy and Kay were listening when Doris appeared as a radio panelist on Sunday, December 10. Peggy wrote Doris from her cupola the following Wednesday—a letter from her pica typewriter, its style revealing her years as a journalist:

> Kay and I were going to send you a telegram Monday morning after listening in on your broadcast but we had to hasten to the city and in the meantime it was put off.
>
> We are now sitting up in the cupola and there is a beautiful snowstorm outside. Kay is embroidering a petticoat and I am trying to catch up with my correspondence.
>
> To get back to the broadcast . . . I suppose everyone has told you by this time that you walked off with the show . . . which you did . . . you were so clear, concise and persuasive that your colleagues sounded like thoroughly befuddled old men . . . they hemmed and hawed and couldn't quite make up their minds . . . then you would come on with that direct, thoroughly confident way of yours which is very impressive and our living room rang with applause. . . . [16]

To the Pattersons' 1939 trip to Europe was traced the beginning of an isolationist pattern and opposition to the president the *Daily News* had ardently supported for eight years. The days following the invasion brought forth an "America first" sentiment not limited to Charles Lindbergh, who broadcast to his fellow citizens while visiting Japan: "If we enter fighting for democracy abroad, we may end by losing it at home."[17] Newspaper editors wrote unequivocally for neutrality, perhaps none more pungently than William Allen White who called Poland "a duplex apartment—a couple of illicit love nests for the Germans and Russians." He proclaimed: "A brave, gay, lovable, cantankerous people are the Poles, with long visors on their soldiers' caps. They are getting the hot end of the international poker. Freedom is about to shriek again. But the United States of America should be looking after its own affairs."[18]

The shift in *Daily News* policy divided Doris and John; he could follow the publisher's new direction but she could not. As the war moved through the first year, the paper credited Roosevelt with keeping the nation out of "Europe's War," and supported him for a third term. But soon after he was inaugurated it turned against him bitterly over the Lend-Lease Bill, which it called "the Dictator Bill." In October, 1941, Patterson first used the expression "Roosevelt's War." Even conservative editors began referring to the *Daily News*, the *Chicago Tribune* and the *Washington Times-Herald* as "the axis," and to Patterson, McCormick and "Cissy" Patterson as the "three furies of isolationism."[19]

In Europe, Germany and Russia had split Poland as the spoils of a blitzkrieg that was over before the end of September. There were no major land battles for the next seven months, as the French waited behind the Maginot Line and the Germans behind the Siegfried Line. Tension mounted with the anticipation of a spring offensive. In February, Roosevelt decided upon a bold initiative, announcing at his Oval Office press conference on February 9 that Under Secretary of State Sumner Welles would travel to Europe on his behalf. Welles would make a personal survey of conditions in Italy, France, Germany and Great Britain, and although it was emphasized that the visit would be "solely for the purpose of advising the president," one official speculated that if the diplomat found conditions ripe for a peace move, one could be undertaken upon his return. The authority emphasized the timing of Welles' visit, observing that a spring military offensive "might end for a long time whatever slight chances for peace may now exist." At the same time Secretary of State Cordell Hull announced that the United States had undertaken peace conversations with neutral nations and that the talks might be extended to belligerent nations.[20]

Welles was among the most patrician of public servants, with old family ties and old school ties to open doors. A great-nephew of the abolitionist Senator Charles Sumner, he had been a page at Eleanor and Franklin's wedding in 1904. Eleanor felt especially close because their mothers had been friends and Sumner had been a classmate at Groton and Harvard of her only sibling, her brother Hall. Welles and his wife Mathilde, sons Benjamin and Arnold, their horses and a dog, Mr. Tobey, led an aristocratic life on their estate, Oxon Hill Manor, in Maryland.[21] Among adjectives used in describing the Under Secretary were "tall, correct, disciplined, aquiline of feature, erudite, urbane, coldly handsome." In his 1975 book, *A Rendezvous With Destiny*, Elliott Roosevelt wrote: "Welles seemingly had all the necessary qualifications for a distinguished diplomatic career: brains, the right Eastern Establishment background, a rich wife in the former Mathilde Peake. There was, however, a flaw in his character which Mother could not recognize and Father ignored. Sumner Welles was bi-sexual." Welles was said to be a thorn to Secretary of State Hull, and hated by diplomat William C. Bullitt, who had been Roosevelt's ambassador to Russia and to France before the outbreak of war.

Welles today is a footnote in history, but he remained at the forefront of U.S. diplomacy as the nation declared war and entered the battlefields of Europe and the Pacific. His career ended abruptly on September 25, 1943, when Roosevelt announced his resignation. The Undersecretary, FDR said, had advised him "of his desire to be relieved of his heavy governmental duties in view of his wife's health." The President did not want to make public the letter of resignation or the text of the acceptance, as was generally done. Contacted that night in Bar Harbor, Maine, Welles told the press: "Whatever the White House has to say concerning my resignation as Under Secretary of State covers the situation." He refused further comment, but said that his wife's health had improved and that they hoped to leave their estate in Maine soon for their home in Maryland.[22]

"The facts of the situation remained obscure tonight," The

Associated Press reported. Actually, details were hidden for thirty-five years, apparently the result of a gentleman's agreement in the media of the kind that shielded public figures in that era. Two accounts given since 1975 contain conflicting information. According to Elliott Roosevelt, Bullitt set up Welles for public disgrace, "knowing of the sexual duality of this fellow member of the Eastern Establishment." In Roosevelt's narrative, Welles had an appointment in "a Midwestern city," and booked a pullman on an overnight train. Police were waiting when the train stopped in the morning, having been alerted by a porter who claimed that the Under Secretary "had enticed him into the compartment to make homosexual advances." Elliott wrote: "Father believed Welles' version of the incident—that it was the porter, bribed on Bullitt's behalf, who had made the overtures. The outcome, no matter what, was that in ' September, 1943, Welles resigned."[23]

Another version is that of Geoffrey C. Ward in his 1989 book, *A First-Class Temperament.* According to Ward, the incident occurred on September 17, 1940, as Welles traveled on a special train carrying mourners back to Washington from the Alabama funeral of Speaker of the House William Bankhead. The author contends that Welles' "alcoholism and his private sexual habits" were common knowledge among his social and professional peers. The Under Secretary, said Ward, "reeling from far too many whiskeys, propositioned several black porters whom he had summoned to his special compartment. All of them turned him down and one lodged a formal complaint with the Southern Railway Company."[24]

Welles had held immense diplomatic responsibility in the European peace attempt. For journalists, the possibility of accompanying him on his survey offered a rare chance to cross the Atlantic, virtually barred, and to enter the closed borders of Germany. With John now in France, still working as a war correspondent for the *Chicago Tribune,* Doris obtained credentials to represent the *Daily News* in the Welles entourage. The elegantly printed First Class Passenger List of the Italian liner Rex, sailing from New York February 19 for Gibraltar, Naples and Rome, named:

Fleeson O'Donnell, Mrs. Doris
de Caraman-Chimay, Prince Alexandre
de Caraman-Chimay, Princesse Alexandre and Maid
Duchess of Leeds
Mr. and Mrs. Walter Lippmann
Welles, Hon. Sumner and Valet
Mrs. Sumner Welles and Maid[25]

Also with the Welleses, in a blueblood touch, was their constant traveling companion, Mr. Tobey. They doted on their pet as did the Roosevelts on Fala, but escaped criticism of the indulgence.

British authorities, now making contraband searches, detained the Rex for about four hours at Gibraltar. On February 27, Welles met at tea in Rome with Hans Georg von Mackensen, German ambassador, conducted a press conference at the American Embassy, and boarded a midnight train for Berlin. A thousand Swiss citizens cheered the Welles entourage as members left Zurich, Switzerland, the next afternoon. Arriving in Berlin at 9:30 in the morning, the group went to the old, grand Hotel Adlon, three doors from the American embassy.[26]

The Adlon had been a favorite of Dorothy Thompson, and it was here that she received her expulsion order from the Gestapo in 1934. Thompson appreciated the hotel's amenities: a bartender who welcomed her with a martini and a manager who asked about her family and remembered the room number from the last visit. It was "all the courtesy, all the cleanliness, all the exquisite order which is Germany," she wrote.[27]

Other journalists knew the Adlon. Walter Trohan, traveling with the Welles party for the *Chicago Tribune*, found the ballroom changed. In earlier years, he recalled, it had been a long place on the roof, where "on hot nights, while they played their sentimental tangoes(sic), the glass ceiling would roll back to show the stars."

On the morning of March 2, Welles, accompanied by Alexander C. Kirk, American chargé d'affaires´, both in formal morning clothes, entered Hitler's chancellery. A company of honor saluted the Undersecretary, in unusual protocol for one who was not a state visitor. Then Hitler delivered his message of "lebensraum"—living space—that Germany would fight until Britain and France recognized a "German Monroe doctrine for central Europe." Welles and Kirk left after a ninety-four-minute conference in the Fuehrer's study.[28]

Despite the old elegance of the Adlon, Doris found an atmosphere of regimentation and austerity in Germany. "Life flows like chilled molasses, dark, slow and sticky," she would write in her first article after leaving the country. It was not the impression the Third Reich sought to convey, as was demonstrated with unexpected developments at a luncheon arranged by Paul Joseph Goebbels. Doris, Trohan and several other journalists joined four of Goebbels' men for luncheon in a private room of a restaurant. Waiters produced Scotch whiskey, French champagne (not the more common Ribbentrop manufactured by the Foreign Minister's family) and an enormous, browned turkey which they basted and kept warm over a flame. But when the head waiter began to carve the turkey, it bounced off the sideboard and landed under the table. Waiters scurried to clean gravy off the guests' shoes as the bird was carried out, washed, and brought back.[29]

Doris accompanied the Welles entourage as it left Berlin for Switzerland. Across the border in Basel, Switzerland, beyond German censorship, she filed the first of her articles offering *Daily News* readers an inside view of life in the closed regime. "Keeping up one's standard of living is a continuous and grim game of hare and hounds," she wrote. As one example, she noted: That when the government found citizens buying ski suits to eke out the winter with meagre clothing rations, it increased the points needed for the purchase.

With fats and fuels affected by the Allied blockade, citizens had been left with a substitute for soap. "Incidentally," Doris wrote, "the American Embassy has taken notice of the rationing of hot baths—the ordinary German householders can have hot water only on Saturday and Sunday—by adding two staff bathrooms, one for men, the other for women, to its spacious office in Pariserplatz. It is considered quite good form to excuse oneself from work for 15 minutes to make use of these." Doris found wine and liquor "scarcely to be had," and beer sinking "perilously near" 3.2 percent. "Never have Berlin's theatres, cafes and night clubs been more crowded," she reported. "Their homes cold, their spending for other things curtailed and not caring to save for fear of inflation, Berlin has turned to the artificialities of night life, which booms despite the blackout."[30]

A prolonged winter and shortage of coal had left citizens disconsolate, longing for spring. Working all day in hat, coat and gloves was common in many offices, while women stood for hours in cold, dark markets, returning to chilly homes. "Movies? There are loads of them," wrote Doris, citing the Berliner's choices. "He can see Marlene Dietrich again in 'Blonde Venus,' although she has fallen from Nazi graces. 'Honolulu,' 'On the Avenue' and 'Shanghai Express' are other American films showing."[31] In an odd mockery of the clothing allowance, fur coats were "free" but scarce and expensive, since the fur business had been in the hands of Jews, excluded from citizenship and deprived of property rights in the decree at Nuremberg in 1935. The fur business had not flourished for several years.[32] Doris described a threat hanging over the unmarried childless German woman of twenty-one or older, who might be drafted to work in the harvest or in munitions factories. "I was assured repeatedly that the upper class of Germany, if any, would not hope by wealth or influence to dodge the work camp," she wrote. "Dr. Hans Dieckhoff, former Ambassador to the United States, smilingly told me that his daughter, Charlotte, an ex-pupil at the swank Madeira School outside Washington, is in a labor camp near Munich, as is also Field Marshal Goering's niece."[33]

A more chilling duty for women had been bluntly charged in December by Heinrich Himmler of the Elite Guard, coldly acknowledging a need to replace the present generation of Germans who would die in the war. As Himmler presented the order, it would be a high duty beyond laws and customs for German women and girls who were not yet married to bear children of soldiers going to the front. The government promised to care for all children, legitimate or not "but of good blood" if their fathers died in action. There were mothercraft schools training women in fundamentals of housekeeping, cooking, sewing and infant care. "Undoubtedly, so far as they can be under war's stern necessities, mothers are the favorites of National Socialism," Doris wrote.[34]

During the time they were in Berlin with Welles, Doris and other journalists tried to confirm a report that the Wilhelmstrasse near the Chancellery and Foreign Office had been cleared of snow the previous day by forced labor of Jews and Polish prisoners. Sources discounted the rumor, explaining that forced labor generally was exacted of Jews only in Austria. Doris reported, however, that an apparent new policy of sudden, forced emigration to the East was a cause of intense anxiety. Recently, Nazis had evacuated twelve hundred Jews from Stettin on a few hours' notice on an unheated train to Lublin, Poland. Jews in Germany, facing new difficulty in obtaining even transit visas, feared that if they were transplanted to Poland they would never get out. The declaration of war had closed not only British and French frontiers, but those of small neutral nations. The war also made exchange problems more acute, Doris noted. Even with relatives or friends furnishing money in the United States or South America, it was difficult to make arrangements to leave. More than two hundred thousand Jews remained, ninety thousand of them in Berlin. "The war's restrictions, as might be expected, bear heavily on them," Doris reported. "Many stores forbid them to enter at all, and they cannot shop in any market until after 12. This is to insure German housewives having first call on the day's supplies."[35]

Welles had gone from Berlin to Lausanne, Switzerland, and then to Paris on the Simplon-Orient Express. With France insisting that any attempt to make peace now would be premature, he met new President Lebrun in the Elysée Palace, and conferred with leaders of the Polish government in exile.[36]

Doris had decided to return to Berlin for the Memorial Day Parade on Sunday, March 10, the day Welles planned to fly to London. Witnessing Hitler's speech and laying of a wreath on the Unknown Soldier's tomb, she reported that "Black Shirts, Brown Shirts and regular army men lined Unter de Linden shoulder-to-shoulder for block after block. To one who has followed parades many times with President Roosevelt in cities where a few perspiring not-very-efficient police kept back the crowds, the spectacle came with great impact."[37]

A legend remains in the Fleeson family that following the ceremony, Doris spoke out, "You buried the wrong man." Knowing how direct Doris could be, close family members believe it is true.

As Welles traveled from Paris to London and back to Paris, Doris and John, whom she had met in Berlin, proceeded to Rome for the Under Secretary's final conference. Although the arrival of German officials and the announcement that Pope Pius XII would grant an interview caused a flurry of excitement, the O'Donnells reported on March 19 that Welles had washed his hands of Europe's diplomatic efforts, "disclaiming all connection with the present mess of peace and anti-peace rumors over Europe."[38]

They sailed the next day from Genoa for New York with the Welles party aboard the Contte de Savoia. Two days later the O'Donnells cabled a dispatch from Gibraltar reporting a thirteen-hour detention as a British contraband control crew searched the ship for Dr. Hjalmar Schacht, former German Finance Minister. The noted financier was one of the men Welles had interviewed in Berlin. With the captain protesting the delay, three British officers questioned seven hundred thirty third class, two hundred twenty-five second class and one hundred seventy-five first class passengers—everyone on board except Welles and his party. The O'Donnells and other American journalists were questioned at length about their German visas. "Through diplomatic courtesy, the passports of Welles and his party were set aside," Doris and John wrote. "None of this group, including the diplomat's valet (or his dog Tobey), was questioned." The Savoia carried a large group of Polish, Hungarian and Russian Jews, they reported.[39]

In New York, at the time of the incident at Gibraltar, the British liners Mauretania and Queen Mary were sighted moving out to sea after being tied at piers for months. Now painted slate gray, with windows darkened and no signs of identification, they were sailing under sealed orders amid rumors of their missions. Still behind at the New York piers were the Queen Elizabeth and the Normandie, the world's first and second largest ships. The 85,000-ton Queen Elizabeth had arrived March 7 after a secret dash from England, while the 83,423-ton Normandie had been there since the outbreak of the war.[40]

A quickening of maritime activity was evident as Doris and John docked on March 29, photographed by the *New York Times-Herald* in conversation with Sumner Welles.[41] By 3:09 that afternoon the Under Secretary was being conveyed into the Oval Office by Cordell Hull to report on his failed mission.[42]

13

DARK HORSE

The dark horse of the Republican Party had been placed in a hay wagon in the stockyards and hauled about Chicago on a flatbed truck. His Friday the Thirteenth visit was crammed with appearances—four speeches in the industrial areas, competing against the winds coming off Lake Michigan. As a consequence, the day of rest planned for the campaign train in Kansas City on Sunday, September 15, 1940, faced uncertainty.

Wendell Willkie had punished his voice on numerous stops through Illinois and eastern Iowa and now could hardly speak. There was a possibility that his epic tour, planned to cover thirty-one states and eighteen hundred miles, might end before it could begin. Journalists learned that Dr. H.G. Bernard, throat specialist from Beverly Hills, was on hand and might hospitalize the candidate.[1]

As her brother Will and nephew Seward arrived in Kansas City, the quiet Sunday Doris had planned to spend with Kansas relatives was becoming a frenzied news watch.[2] Among the forty-eight journalists aboard the train were the nation's top political analysts, and they had not seen a tour such as Willkie's. His entourage of thirty staffers rivaled the size of the press contingent,[3] but the candidate was micromanaging the campaign. The "simple barefoot Wall Street Lawyer" who had become president of a giant utility holding company would take orders from no one, especially doctors. "Uncoached, apparently trying to manage every detail of his campaign personally, this man Willkie is a fire horse that answers all calls," wrote Doris' friend, Kansas political columnist A.L. "Dutch" Shultz. The same momentum had swept convention strategists off the floor in Philadelphia, in a "smashing short hand drive" by the dark horse. "Now the strangest of all campaign trips is starting with Wendell Willkie, an admitted political novice, traveling into the great open spaces without a campaign compass," Shultz observed.[4]

He would remain hoarse throughout the tour, ignoring instructions to stay in his drawing room, slipping through the train to join journalists in the club car—"for a little off the record visit with the boys and girls—and to finish a cigarette before some specialist grabbed it."

As Willkie vowed it would, the train left Kansas City for the formal opening of his tour—a major speech in Coffeyville, Kansas, challenging the third-term bid of Franklin D. Roosevelt. He launched his candidacy at the school where he had taught history in 1913 and '14 after receiving a law degree from the University of Indiana.[5]

It was a wild, intensive three weeks, one of the toughest assignments veteran journalists had faced. There was such chaos on the train that columnist Raymond Clapper, an early Willkie enthusiast, began to question whether the candidate could run the country. The plumbing failed, and according to speechwriter Marcia Davenport, "everything related to physical order and cleanliness, including laundry, was a nightmare." Staff members were on the verge of mutiny,[6] but reporters were assigned for the duration. The whistlestop proceeded through Tulsa, Amarillo, Phoenix, San Diego, Los Angeles, San Francisco, Butte, Fargo, Omaha, Madison, Philadelphia and New York.

However unorthodox Willkie's quest for the presidency, it incorporated a phenomenon of American politics—restoration of a discarded wife to the candidate's side. Willkie's long affair with *New York Herald Tribune* literary editor Irita Van Doren was widely known but never exposed in public print, in an era of media accommodation. Willkie believed that his private life was his own, and declared to friends that "everybody knows about us—all the newspapermen in New York."

The romance was a classic attraction of opposites—Willkie the rumpled, self-made corporate executive, and Irita the talented, sophisticated book editor. Willkie lived with his wife in their apartment at 1010 Fifth Avenue, and with Edith and their son, Philip, a student at Princeton, spent holidays on their farm in Indiana. He traveled on weekends to Irita's farm in Connecticut,[7] an arrangement not likely to draw understanding in the Midwest where there was anticipation of a groundswell of support.[8]

Edith Willkie was willing to aid her husband's political fortunes. Willkie biographer Steve Neal quoted Theodore H. White: "Campaigning in America is done with wives. Wives are on public display. The code calls for their participation however unrealistic that code may be."

During the seven-week whistlestop, Edith shared her husband's private car at the rear of the train, appearing at his side at every public appearance.[9] In Chicago she wore a fur-trimmed coat with an orchid, tossing roses to the crowd while riding in an open car through the financial district. In contrast to Eleanor Roosevelt's cloth coat, she wore a fur "thrown over her shoulders" in San Francisco.[10] Shultz, by now exasperated with Willkie, convinced that "nobody on the personnel staff ever saw a presidential campaign train before," found Edith a particular solace. "Mrs. Willkie's presence on the train is a big help to the candidate," he wrote. "Troupers aboard the 14-car train adore Mrs. Willkie for her constant evidence of devotion and care in protection of her husband from abuse of his energies without becoming conspicuous at her task."[11]

Doris was intrigued with the public wife, and was apt to write a burning defense if she thought one had been unjustly criticized. She was especially sympathetic toward the candidate's wife: "The general theory of her place in the cosmic scheme seems to be that she should be a mirror which reflects her husband only in the most flattering light. And yet she is the person who knows him best!"[12]

Columnist Shultz found Willkie "alert and curious, and as constantly concerned about everything as a small boy at a circus." Willkie's intellectual curiosity struck correspondent William Shirer as an attribute not often seen in politicians. He was an independent thinker who had joined the Republican Party only two years before he ran for

President. "Other prominent Republicans were clumsy in their dealings with the press, but Willkie had a magic touch," observed Neal. "While his cultivation of the press worked to his political benefit, it was not contrived. He genuinely liked reporters and they liked him."[13] Journalists in their most critical moments may have considered the Willkie Special a runaway express, but sessions in the club car with the candidate, a fugitive from his advisors, were a compensation.

Citizens returned Roosevelt with a vote of 27.3 million to 22.3 million. Willkie, who had received the largest popular vote in Republican history, soon reiterated his support for Great Britain in the war and stressed national unity. From his office at 109 East 42nd Street, he wrote on November 16:

> My Dear Doris:
> Now that the pressure has let up on me a little, I want to tell you before I leave for a few days rest how much I enjoyed having you on the campaign train. I do not know of any one on the train with whom I enjoyed debating with as much as I did you, as the voice of the opposition. On the few occasions when you were able to join us, you brightened the train no end.[14]

Willkie, a registered Democrat until 1938, occasionally addressed supporters in 1940 as "you Republicans."[15] His political shift was one example of national ambivalence rising with the crisis in Europe. Another was that of The New York Daily News, fervent supporter of Roosevelt for eight years, now turning against the President. Germany's spring offensive had torn Kansas editor William Allen White from the isolationists to urge support for aid to the allies, declaring the war "no longer a battle of empires but a battle of ideals."[16]

Debating political issues had been a way of life for Doris and John in seven and a half years of producing a daily column, writing sometimes under a joint byline and at other times individually. Joseph Patterson's turn down an anti-Roosevelt, isolationist path soon after the 1940 election divided them sharply. In a position that startled moderates, the *Daily News* suggested: "Britain could probably make peace with Hitler fairly soon, save itself from invasion and keep its empire, if Britain were willing to recognize Germany as the dominant power on the European continent."[17] John Tebbel wrote in An American Dynasty:

> There have been one or two serious attempts to analyze O'Donnell, trying to determine why he is what he is, and why he turned against Roosevelt, with whom he was so friendly earlier in his career on the *News*. These students point to his Irish-American background in New England as an explanation for his isolationist, ultraconservative attitudes, which emerged at a time when some Irish-Americans were fighting for neutrality and most of New England was a hotbed of Roosevelt-hating.[18]

John drew Roosevelt's wrath when he reported impending charges in the Senate that U.S. Naval vessels were secretly convoying British ships. Detailed information would be made public the next day, he said, to show that Roosevelt was permitting the Coast Guard and Navy to escort British munitions ships from Baltimore, Philadelphia and New York to "a rendezvous determined by the British Admiralty."[19] White House Secretary Stephen Early quoted Roosevelt as describing the story as "a deliberate lie." The following day publisher J. David Stern, in an editorial in the *Philadelphia Record*, called O'Donnell a "Naziphile." (A jury in 1943 awarded $50,000 from the *Record* for libel.)[20]

At the age of seventy-two, William Allen White had reluctantly undertaken leadership of the Nonpartisan Committee for Peace, seeking revision of the Neutrality Law, believing that the nation could avoid war by aiding its allies. He began two years of strenuous work at a time when his health was failing, when he still edited the *Emporia Gazette*, and when he hoped to devote spare time to writing his autobiography. Instead, he became a propagandist, writing the copy himself, a volunteer lobbyist, and a liaison with the White House, traveling a circuit from Emporia to New York to Washington. Reprints of his editorials filled newspapers. After Dunkirk and the fall of France, the organization changed its name to the Committee to Defend America by Aiding the Allies, and by now its members were becoming divided on the nation's course. Many began to feel that the only hope was for the United States to convoy its own ships, virtually an act of war. White could not bring himself to give a full endorsement to war, and amid criticism that he was inconsistent he resigned as chairman in 1941.[21]

White wrote Doris on May 13, telling of Sallie White's illness, an attempt to find relief in Arizona, and a trip to Rochester, Minnesota:

> We went to Arizona last winter hoping that it would clear up a sinus difficulty that she had. It didn't get better and we went to a perfectly good conservative doctor who took some Ray pictures and thought she had a brain tumor. So we skedaddled to Rochester to the Mayo Clinic and they took a lot more pictures and said she had no brain tumor, but she did have an irregular blood pressure . . .
>
> We may come East in June and hope to see you, but if you come West, please, dear, dear child, drop in and see us. You are a great comfort to our declining years.

He wrote below his signature "over," continuing on the back of the page:

> Tell me, Doris dear, what about the President? Why doesn't he speak out? The tide is at the flood. I am terribly afraid that unless he takes it now it will begin to ebb and it may ebb with a rush if Great Britain has many more tragic losses. Is he tired? Is he worn out? Does he fear that we are not ready—I mean short of powder, shells, planes, ships, equipment, men, or what not? Or has the spark of life and joy and buoyancy been dying in him since election? Would you mind writing me in confidence what you think is the trouble?

I should like to help if I can.[22]

The *Daily News* headlined Doris' article "Lindy Stands Where Father Stood in 1917." Doris portrayed Charles A. Lindbergh, Jr. as "cast today in almost the identical role as was his Congressman-father during World War I years." An economic reformer, arguing that financial interests were drawing the nation into war, the elder Lindbergh had taken a stand that ruined his career. Doris wrote:

> Reporters once asked the late Speaker Longworth about a photograph of House colleagues that he was prominently displaying and in which they saw no familiar faces. Longworth replied that he kept the picture for the sake of the little boy sitting on his father's chair. They were the Lindberghs, and the speaker reminisced about how the studious Minnesota Congressman used to bring the boy to the floor of the House to hear debate.
>
> Undoubtedly it would come as no surprise to Longworth to find young Charles now associated with Mrs. Longworth and others in the anti-war Save America First.[23]

Six weeks later the *Saturday Evening Post* carried a reminiscence by the elder Lindbergh's former law partner, Walter Eli Quigley. The reformer, he wrote, still turned away cases that did not come within his standards of ethics or justice, and occupied a $3.50-a-week room in the St. James Hotel, run by the federated churches of Minneapolis.[24]

Doris wrote her *Saturday Evening Post* friend Marty Sommers: "My attorney, Mr. Wendell Willkie, will be in touch with you regarding my suit against the SEP for one million dollars for plagiarism. . . . Had you notified an expert you were interested in this topic I could have helped you out of the mail I received after the publication of my masterpiece. One correspondent avers that the Colonel resembles his humanitarian father about as much as Goebbels does Johnny Weismuller."[25]

Friends had known of stresses in the O'Donnell marriage. Helen

Fleeson, Doris' niece, said of John: "He was such a romeo. He liked the bottle and he liked women. But he was very charismatic. Everybody liked him." The family in Kansas enjoyed John's visits, although he was a challenge to their prohibitionist habits. Robert Fleeson recalled: "When he came to Sterling he brought his own liquor and brought a very generous supply and he used it all." Doris and John often traveled on long assignments, engaging nurses and governesses for little Doris. In addition to their hectic life, personality conflicts were obvious. Doris was neat and punctual. John, the bon vivant, was frequently absent. With an organized, systematic mind that could grasp the facts of a situation quickly, Doris could be hot and cold, according to Helen. Political differences beginning in 1940 were magnified in their profession. Yet the O'Donnells remain vivid in the minds of their colleagues as a dynamic Washington couple. "I think they had a rootin-tootin kind of marriage," Helen Thomas said, "with lots of fights and so forth, but probably had tremendous intellectual rapport."

Three months after the nation declared war, Doris took the final step of establishing residence in Reno, where she wrote Eleanor Roosevelt from Apartment 6, 429 Virginia Street. Eleanor, now with her daughter, who had undergone surgery, sent a long, handwritten letter from Mercer Island, Washington:

> Dear Doris,
>
> I am glad you wrote me and I am more glad that your decision is made. I have long feared it could not be otherwise and you tried so hard to prevent the break that I know it must cause you suffering. . . . and when it's over peace will come again and in time the zest for living which I associate with you. You will be back early in May, I imagine, and please come see me for I am really fond of you and would be so happy if in any way I can help. I'm not making light of what you are going through. I know how desperate a time this is for you but all things pass. We all have to tell ourselves that these days.[26]

Doris responded:

> I am treasuring your letter. Of course I shall see you when
> I return which I expect will be the last week in April. . . .
> You always inspire me with confidence and courage and
> never more so than now—perhaps I never needed them so
> much. And I am truly grateful.[27]

14

'HENRY MY LOVE'

Doris returned from Reno to find that John had reorganized the bureau without her. "I hated leaving Washington but it seemed best to fall in with whatever plans were made for me for the present," she wrote Eleanor Roosevelt, giving the location of her new apartment, 180 East End Avenue, at the corner of 88th Street, Manhattan. In February 1942 the *Daily News* had expanded into radio broadcasting with round-the-clock, five-minute hourly reports on the popular New York dance music station WNEW.[1] It was to this "rip and read" department that Doris came in the aftermath of the divorce, as Joseph Patterson pondered what to do with his star reporter. John inevitably was the partner who would stay in Washington as bureau chief and would continue the popular "Capital Stuff" column.[2]

"I have been too busy getting settled. . . . But of course I miss many things in Washington. There is virtually no news worth writing except the news from there," she added in the letter.[3] In support of an application for little Doris to the Brearley School, Patterson wrote the registrar that he had known Doris for fourteen and a half years and that she was "generally considered one of the ablest newspaper women in the country."[4]

Doris remained for several months on the radio desk, where she was unfailingly gracious, according to copy boys Ed Quinn and Frank Holeman.[5] Eleanor wrote back in less than a week, inviting Doris and daughter to lunch at her apartment (29 Washington Square West,

Apartment 15-A). "I will have Diana Hopkins and a friend of hers, so Doris would have young company," she advised. Diana was the daughter of Harry Hopkins, FDR's Works Progress Administration director and Secretary of Commerce. When Hopkins' wife died in 1937, Eleanor took five-year-old Diana into the White House. Her response was immediate and overflowing to children left unsettled as she had been, or to adult friends whose childhoods had been disrupted. Eleanor's solicitude for Doris and little Doris during their adjustment was typical. They traveled with her on Monday, June 29, on the 5:23 train to Poughkeepsie, staying at Hyde Park until Wednesday morning.[6]

Working on the radio desk on July 7, Doris received an Associated Press report of a gas explosion in the *Baltimore Sun* composing room, which had rocked the block-long newspaper building, blowing out windows and injuring seven employees. She slipped the bulletin into a letter to Henry Mencken, in which she wrote: "Can't you control yourself better than this dear? I don't like a lot of things myself about the way the world is going—or even that my revered employer is doing—but I control myself!" Doris said that she would like to see Mencken and asked that he call her if he came to New York. She gave her new address, adding, "I suppose you know I went to Reno."[7]

Doris first became acquainted with Mencken at national political conventions in the thirties. He was by that time a celebrity. In 1923 Mencken and George Jean Nathan had founded the *American Mercury*, the most influential magazine of the twenties. Written for "the urbane and the washed," it became a powerful influence on a generation of educated people, and made Mencken, as editor, an institution as the arch critic of American mainstream society. A favorite topic was the small-town puritanical mentality, for which he seemed to find Kansas with its "hayseeds, moralizers and Methodists" the perfect example, despite the fact that students at the University of Kansas voted it their favorite magazine. Socialist Norman Thomas observed that "this generation of college students has shed all illusions but one: that they can live like Babbitt and think like Mencken."[8]

Reflecting Mencken's fascination for trivia was a column titled

"Americana," a collection of "splendidly asinine" quotations from contemporary life, divided by states. Beyond its satire, the magazine was a true literary journal in which Mencken assembled a new school of writers. One was Edgar Lee Masters, the author of *Spoon River Anthology*, who was born in Garnett, Kansas, and practiced law in Chicago before moving to New York City. Mencken was credited with discovering Joseph Hergesheimer, James Branch Cabell and Sinclair Lewis, and with championing F. Scott Fitzgerald.

Henry Mencken, "the man who hated everything," was fond of Doris. For a period in 1942–'43, following her divorce, they were in constant communication. They arranged frequent nights out in New York, to which his letters referred, variously, as "Gotham", "Gomorrah" and "Nineveh". (University Archives, Spencer Research Library, University of Kansas Libraries)

Mencken considered himself a practicing newspaperman, with his native Baltimore (he was born there in 1880) and the *Sun* as his base. He might outrage moralists, but he was acclaimed by scholars for three editions of his treatise *The American Language*. Other books included memoirs of newspaper work, *Happy Days*, *Newspaper Days* and *Heathen Days*, and his 1922 classic *In Defense of Women*, portraying a superior female sex in which women are realists and men mere sentimentalists, easily led. "A man's women folk, whatever their outward show of respect for his merit and authority, always regard him secretly as an ass, and with something akin to pity," he wrote. "His most gaudy sayings and doings seldom deceive them; they see the actual man within, and know him for a shallow and pathetic fellow."[9]

Mencken and Doris were among journalists covering the Republican convention in 1936. The death of his young wife, Sara Haardt Mencken, had occurred the previous year. According to his assistant, Charles Angoff, Mencken was always attracted to women, and came close to marrying half a dozen. His public declarations created a certain confusion in what he found appealing. On one hand he described his ideal as a buxom German waitress, sufficiently mature. "I like my women a little moldy, and I like a generous supply of beef around the entrances and points east and west, and north and south," he told Angoff.[10] Biographer Carl Bode dismissed his pronouncements as mainly rhetoric, noting that women he favored had been pert, trim and bright, and that Mencken had written to Fielding Garrison commenting, "I like the little ones."[11] It did seem apparent that women with literary talent held his interest, and he often encouraged and counseled them on details of their "art."

When Doris invited Mencken to an event after returning from the conventions in 1936, he declined, pleading an engagement with "visiting firemen." He demurred several months later when she invited him to address the Women's National Press Club, which she headed as president. For this he cited a "long-standing rule against addressing women's clubs: I made that rule nearly fifty years ago and have kept it resolutely."[12]

However, the two continued corresponding. Doris, knowing Mencken's delight in small-town minutia, sent items from the *Sterling Bulletin*. A mortuary advertised: "Service measured not by gold but by the golden rule. Member, The Order of the Golden Rule. To Serve Humanity Better Is Our Aim—It Costs No More."[13] Responded Mencken: "I am leaving orders that I be planted in Sterling when my time comes. Or more accurately, that Brother Porter be given the contract to stuff me for the National Museum."[14]

The O'Donnells and Mencken developed a closer friendship during the next few years, drawn together by coverage of the political conventions and presence on campaign trains. Mencken enjoyed Doris' company and became more and more complimentary about her work.[15]

Doris had been out of touch with Mencken when she wrote in July, on the day of the Baltimore explosion. He responded the next day: "You concealed the Reno visit from me for a very good reason: I'd have prohibited it on penalty of the bastinado. The news of it in the papers was really a tremendous surprise and shock. I had always thought of you and John on the best of terms." Adding that he was en route to Johns Hopkins for minor surgery, Mencken advised: "If the chiropractors murder me let it be known that I died with the name of Coolidge on my lips."[16]

He wrote again, saying that he was "hot for Miss Dorothy," but that if Doris' maternal duties permitted, he might look in on her. Soon he planned an evening at Luchow's restaurant in New York, with Doris, Edgar Lee Masters and his wife. Thereafter visits and letters became frequent, and continued for eight months, although complicated with Doris' new assignment to interview prospective candidates throughout the country for the 1944 presidential race.

What the relationship with Mencken was remains ambiguous. One of Doris relatives denies that it was romantic, while another says that Mencken proposed marriage. Passages in Mencken's letters seem rather ardent, as when he declared, "If your art takes you to Chicago on the 19th I shall go into the river with a low moan." Or when he wrote, "I kiss both your hands with loud and ostentatious smacks. What a gal you are!" Doris expressed her fondness: "Henry you are a joy forever to me and I weep over your kindness."

Mencken, now sixty-two, with thinning hair and hunched shoulders, had resumed communication with actress Aileen Pringle and other women with whom he had been romantically linked before his marriage. His biographers, attempting to interpret his relationships with women, have found them simply "not simple." In any case, the correspondence and meetings of Doris and Henry for a period in 1942–'43 are intriguing to ponder:

August 3

I now discover that I won't be able to get to New York until the week of August 17th. What of having dinner with me on the evening of that day? I suggest No. 21. It is air-cooled, and the victuals are not bad. . . .

August 10

It will be a pleasure and an honor to victual you on the evening of Monday, August 17th. I hesitate, as a Southern cavalier, to ask a lady to meet me at a restaurant. Can't I pick you up at your house or your office?

August 14

Yes, General Lee, you may pick me up here at my home. About seven or thereafter?

August 18

Despite the uproars of that Japanese woman it was a grand evening and you will be rewarded throughout eternity for being so nice to a poor old war hero . . . If you don't let me see you the next time I am in Gotham I'll start telling people that you are writing editorials for PM. . . .

August 20

I can think of no comparable threat if you neglect me except that I might forge your name to a letter to The Times endorsing Henry Wallace and the people's war. . . . As proof of my devotion I shall send you shortly a copy of Cissy Patterson's published view of Drew Pearson. . . .

August 21

I'll be delighted to see any and all of La Patterson's diatribes. They are magnificent pieces of invective, and I only hope that she never turns her guns on any really honest man. . . .

August 30

It was grand to have your letters on my return from the bat-and-Republican-ridden vistas of the Grand Union hotel in Saratoga. . . . I had a refined letter from Dr. Boyd. He sent it to The New York Times. I hope I have not tarnished your fame by pointing out to him that I am on The News.

September 1

If La Cissy busts out again you must certainly let me hear of it. I have made various efforts to get copies of her fulminations from Washington, but they always fail. The Brethren in the Sun bureau never read any papers at all. Some of them, in fact, can hardly speak English. I apologize in the name of Boyd for his error. At Princeton, of course, the Times is the only New York paper heard of. A few members of the faculty may read the Daily Forward and one or two bootleg PM, but the rest stick to the Times. It has been fooling them for so many years that they are now used to it.

September 3

September 15 is duly noted and nine rousing cheers. . . . The city editor thinks it is my duty to go see Thomas E. Dewey—Buster to the correspondents and Tommy Dewey to the Democrats.

September 4

Swell. I'll wait on you on September 15, which is a Tuesday, at some time between 6.45 and 7 P.M. and we can then consider the matter of an eating-house. I am in favor of some place that is luxurious and expensive, but free from female F.B.I. operators. . . .

September 17

You are probably still yawning at the Algonquin but I have a word or two to say to you so I think I had better get it into the mail before MacLeish closes his desk for the week-end. . . . My research discloses that three weeks from today will be October 8 and I shall bear it carefully in mind. I shall be taking to the road with one of the aspirants for Governor about that time. As soon as I get their schedules I'll check in with you.

Monday

I surely hope you let me cast eyes on you before you make off with those political hoboes. Will you be in New York on Tuesday of next week and free for a dish of victuals? If so, then I crave the honor of squiring you to the trough. Let me know as soon as you can. I am invited to a war rally at Oheb Mazuma Temple on that night, but I'll duck it if you will watch me eat.

Thursday

How can a gal weighing 118 lbs. expect to survive beefsteaks weighing 9 lbs. and fit only for longshoremen? The next time you give me the felicity of seeing you I shall feed you on breast of guinea hen . . I hope the safari with Dewey is not too onerous. If he proposes to harry the back settlements in motor-busses, tell him that that was what ruined Willkie. . . .

Monday

God will reward you for that telephone call. I rejoiced to hear that you are still alive, despite all the horrors of field service in the upstate Solomon's Islands. I rejoiced to hear that Tom is wearing down his enemies, who are also the enemies of our Christian civilization. I rejoiced to hear that you are loaded with a good story, and that my avid ears will hear it. I rejoiced to hear that the campaign is dam nigh over. But most of all I rejoiced at the news that we are to victual together on November 4. . . . I am writing to Masters, proposing a session at Luchow's on November 5.

October 9

All week I lie here upon my bed of pain and from you I receive a lithograph of Harlem's hero which, as I am not Eleanor fails to console me. . . . I'm not even interestingly ill—just a cold. . . .

Saturday

I assumed that you were out in the wilds with Dewey, miles from a postage stamp, and now comes your news that you have been ill. I am sorry to the point of blubbering, and I only hope the chiropractors let you up and out anon. . . . I am sending you two books, and shall follow with 200 or 300 more as soon as I find out which ones you have. . . . The new book was finished night before last, and the MS. is now on its way to the Knopfs. It is full of idealistic stuff, some of it relating to God and some to the Flag. . . .

October 11

You were sweet to respond at once to my caterwauling and now that I have wrung this attention from you, I naturally feel better. . . . I find it tiresome sitting around the city room here but I can't go back to Washington for The News. So? I hope I can see you soon.

October 12

    . . . When we meet Masters and his lady let us adjourn early and so have some time for a palaver. I want to hear more about your situation on the News. Two more books go to you today . . My new one is called Heathen Days. It hops and jumps from 1892 to 1936, and is full of inspiring ideas. . . .

October 13

    Next to the inscriptions I like the books best. In my pride I shall probably out-insufferable your candidate with whom I leave for—of all places—Niagara Falls in 45 minutes. . . . I must not miss that train—after all it isn't every girl who gets to go to Niagara Falls with Mr. Dewey!

October 15

    No busier gal than you are exists on God's green footstool. . . . I note your schedule, and surely hope to come up with you before you are as old and gray as I am myself. I have no head for figures, but gather that you will be back in Gotham by October 29th. If so, why not let me round up Masters and lady, and blow you to a swell dinner on October 30?

October 16

    Well, thank God, I have a home to go to and the mailman, while slow, does come around. And I suppose Oct. 30th will arrive eventually and I can hardly wait. It will be grand to see you. . . .

October 17

    October 30th, as I figure it, will be a Friday. Shall I ask Masters and his lady to meet us? Let me know. He turns in early and we can proceed on our own. If you object to victualling so far downtown, then I'll say nothing to him. He seldom gets above 34th street. . . . I'll be so glad to see you that I may actually bust into tears.

October 17

Hold everything. Buster has just announced that he will speak six nights in the metropolitan area—and of course one of them is Oct. 30th. . . . The Oct. 30 speeches will be in Westchester which means that I cannot get back into the city until nearly midnight.

October 21

I have stuck a flag into November 5th on my calendar. I hope and pray to God that we'll both be alive by then, and that the Republic will still survive. Maybe we had better not round up Masters and his lady. I leave it to you.

November 1

Tuesday will be Tom's big day but mine will be Nov. 4—and I am happy to note, Nov. 5 also. . . . Henry, I am going to have your testimonial to my skill framed. Actually it convinces me that I am not too bad in other departments if you know what I mean and I think you do.

Thursday

You will wallow in Heaven for 750,000,000 years for being so nice about the Masters party. If you hadn't rescued it, it would have fallen to pieces, and I'd have poured in alcohol, and got back to Algonquin Palace Hotel in an advanced state. It was the end of a hard day, including a newspaper meeting lasting 3 hours. But when you pranced in all was well. . . .

November 9

Masters writes that Alice was ill the night we victualled

at Luchow's, and I believe it is true. Certainly she looked very pale and wobbly. The old boy himself was hardly able to sit up. His trouble is that he is in the hands of chiropractors who have warned him against alcohol. It is bad advice. At his stage of life a couple of shots of rye in the evening would do him more good than all their baking and rolling.

November 11
 I depart tomorrow at 4 p.m. for Ohio. I'll write at length later. Henry you are a joy forever to me and I weep over your kindness.

Columbus, O.
November 18
Henry my love:
 If you had had a letter from me every time I have thought of you and wanted to share a joke with you, you would have (been) doing little but attending to your correspondence with me. . . . I leave here tonight, spend Friday with Alf in Topeka—your ears will burn, dear, but I shall never give you the worst of it—and so west. . . .

November 20
 Your dispatch from the Columbus front took two days to reach here, so I am not too sure that this will get to you in Los Angeles before your art carries you to San Francisco; hence the complicated address. . . . If you knew how you are missed you would abandon those quacks and hustle home. I have not been in Gotham since you departed, and shall keep away until you return . . I envy you the chance to see Stassen. He is a true demagogue, and will go far. . . .

November 24
 I needn't tell you that I was touched by that beautiful

picture of the <u>Tribune</u> Tower. I am having it framed in gilt, and shall hang it on my office wall, between views of the Vatican and Sing-Sing Prison. I have been unable to write to you since San Francisco because I simply don't know where you are at. . . . Are you likely to cover the trial of the A.P. case in New York? It will probably be called in January. If you can wangle the job I may meet you at the press table, and you will have the honor of sharpening my lead pencils and shooing flies off me. . . .

December 4
St. Paul was 6 below last Wednesday and had your letter not been there to warm me I should have perished.

December 7
I wired to you at St. Louis this morning, and with my hand on my heart. The Bricker and Warren pieces were really first-rate goods. I couldn't help setting here and trying to figger out how many of the Washington princes of the press could have done as well. Answer: not a damned one. It is not often that our Heavenly Father is decent enough to endow one and the same wench with both female loveliness and talent, but now and then He throws them together, maybe just to show off before the other gaseous vertebrata. . . .[17]

For the next four months the two were in frequent communication. On April 1 a pronouncement from the unpredictable Patterson stunned Doris. She wrote:

I need your help. Mr. Patterson informed me today that I can't cover politics for The News any more—my heart is not in the right place for it. He said I would always have a job here and things would be found for me to do.

15

❦ ❦

Behind the Lines

After she left the *Daily News*, Doris credited its pungent journalism with influencing her career, and continued to refer to Joseph Patterson as a genius. But in the spring of 1943 the publisher's harsh order and the prospect of returning to the rip and read desk made her departure inevitable. That Patterson was capable of sizable errors in judgment had been demonstrated in his assessment of Hitler. His termination of Doris as a political correspondent was also a notable blunder, for she retained remarkable connections to the nation's political life, especially at its epicenter, the White House.

This was evident in the memorandum Press Secretary Stephen Early sent FDR's secretary Grace Tully on April 10 concerning Patterson's action. "There was something providential about our thought of Doris Fleeson this morning," he told Miss Tully. "I called her in New York at the phone number you gave me and found her nursing a sick baby and grief stricken. Because she did not report that the South was filled with Roosevelt haters, she was called to New York, relieved of her assignment and fired. She took her dismissal rather than continue to serve the Daily News and write in accordance with the dictates of her bosses. Thought this would be of interest to you."[1]

Doris resigned from the *News*, the historic first tabloid on which she had worked for sixteen years, gathering honors as her stature grew. It was with obvious ease that she surveyed new possibilities, including an offer from *Woman's Home Companion* magazine to accompany the first WAC contingent (the name had just been changed from WAAC—Woman's Army Auxiliary Corps) to Europe. However, eleven-year-old Doris was still recovering from a siege of illness.

At this point Doris was again single, with a child, without family wealth, and essentially as dependent on her talent and drive as she had been at age twenty-six. Although by now her credentials were impressive, and the offer a worthy one, it was a slight contradiction that the magazine deriving its very name from woman's role in the home did not necessarily mean that role for its staff.

"I am strongly against the English trip but God's will, not ours, be done," wrote Mencken. "I hope you can get your papers quickly. If there is any undue delay, and even Barney Baruch can't help you, call in Frank Kent, who is thick with the White House, and likely to be made a lieutenant general and military governor of Greece."[2]

Expecting to leave about May 25, Doris accepted an invitation for what possibly would be her last weekend at home. She wrote Mencken: "Jane Hamilton (wife, John-ex-Rep. chairman) has asked Doris and me to their farm at Paoli near Philadelphia for the week-end May 21–23. She suggests I bring a friend. Do you ever visit the Main Line? If you would on this occasion I'd like it. The house in swell, ditto the plenishings."

The invitation draws an interesting interpretation in Fred Hobson's 1994 biography *Mencken A Life*. Characterizing Doris as a "divorcee and prominent newspaperwoman," and the Mencken-Fleeson correspondence as filled with "genuine affection and sexual playfulness," Hobson elaborates:

> Fleeson, a former president of the Women's National Press Club, was too public a presence and besides—a lusty, good-humored, tough-talking woman with a "healthy Kansas appetite"—too much one of the boys. Although he enjoyed seeing her in New York, when she invited him for a weekend at a friend's farmhouse outside Philadelphia, he preferred to remain in the safer precincts of Baltimore.[3]

This reluctance, however, does not appear in Mencken's reply, which contained an example of the ethnic slurs cited by critics, and not included by Hobson. Whatever his excuse, he wrote Doris: "Unhappily, I am barred from the Main Line by the military. No Japs are allowed nearer to it than West Chester, Pa."

In an ironic turn, Doris was scheduled to receive the New York Newspaperwomen's Club's award for best reporting in 1942. "No ceremonies this year—a radio program," she told Mencken. "I hope Mr. Patterson is listening."[4]

Mencken sent compliments and suggested a resounding ceremony after the war with a speech by Nicholas Murray Butler, president of Columbia University. "God knows, I hope you let me see you before you go." he wrote. "May 25 seems only a few days off. I am still as rocky as a man of 90, but I am hoping to get to Gotham. Damn the war!"[5]

The radio award program focused on women journalists who were becoming war correspondents, with commentator Edwin C. Hill telling of Doris' resignation at the *Daily News* and her new assignment. Sonia Tomara, club president, cabled a message from an air base in South China where she was covering the Asian front for the *Herald Tribune*. "I hope there will be many more women in such assignments before the war is over," she said, "and am confident they will do as well as men, if not better." Linked up in the international broadcast were Tania Long of *The New York Times* and Ruth Cowan of The Associated Press, speaking from London.[6] Cowan, the veteran journalist who had started her career in the twenties, writing under the byline R. Baldwin Cowan to get better assignments,[7] had just returned from the North African front. Among the judges was William L. White, son of William Allen White, and author of two recent books of wartime experience: *Journey for Margaret* and *They Were Expendable*.

"Was the award based on any specific stuff?" wrote Mencken. "If so, what? I hope it was the Western series on the super Willkies."[8] The entry was, indeed, from Doris' series on Republican presidential prospects, written after her tour of cities deemed "political nerve centers."

In portraying Wendell Willkie as a man without a party, but not without a country, she had written:

> He is probably second only to President Roosevelt in his ability to command a nationwide—and an international audience. He speaks, writes, debates, discusses, is interviewed, dines out, incessantly. . . .
>
> His energy is prodigious and his industry titanic.
>
> Some years ago, when the late banker-philanthropist, Otto Kahn, was at his zenith, a wit remarked that whenever you found as many as three people dining in public, one of them was bound to be Otto Kahn. The modern version would substitute the name of Wendell Willkie. Alice Roosevelt Longworth, who is bitterly hostile to Willkie's Internationalist views, put it another way. She said it was no longer necessary to invite Willkie to a party—you just put a lighted candle in the window and he would drop in.[9]

Doris answered Mencken: "The prize was based on my Willkie story. The Captain assured me at the time it was a masterpiece. It is only when I venture to assert that Roosevelt falls somewhat short of Judas in the estimation of a few voters that he thinks I can't write politics."

At the White House on May 20, Eleanor Roosevelt's secretary, Malvina "Tommy" Thompson wrote Doris that Eleanor would be in New York City on the 23rd and "wants very much to see you." Doris was invited to come to supper at the Washington Square apartment at 7:30. On a typed draft of the letter, Miss Thompson instructed her assistant: "Look up address in NY telephone book—it may be under Doris Fleeson O'Donnell and the address is East End Ave." The assistant replied in a memo: "Miss Thompson: No success in locating New York address for Miss Fleeson. However, she is in Washington today at Carlton Hotel. Should this letter be sent to her there, by hand ?" This piece of information may have reflected enterprise, but Miss Thompson advised tersely: "Please readdress envelope—It is in NY Tel. book under Fleeson O'Donnell."[10]

Well known was the fact that the Carlton was headquarters for Bernard Baruch and that a variety of visitors came to his "rather shabby" suite, decorated with faded brocades, a chaise longue and a grand piano in the style of the hotel's past grandeur.[11] Mencken had written Doris on May 19: "What is your address in Washington? I hate to call you up at the Baruch seraglio, for both Frank Kent and the F.B.I. listen in on all calls."[12] On that day Doris had been in Washington on the second of three trips to obtain credentials and to take inoculations before leaving for Europe.

Returning to New York on her forty-second birthday anniversary, Doris found little Doris, now at home after three weeks in the hospital, failing to recover. She called John O'Donnell to come for a conference. "It may be that I shall have to give up my new job before I start it," she wrote Mencken. "I want to see you but I warn you that I shall probably blubber. Today was my birthday—and what a day."[13]

In the *Companion* offices at 250 Park Avenue, editors planned lunches, conferences and photo sessions—"command performances" in the view of Doris' sister Elizabeth. Although she held the important position of education secretary of the National Tuberculosis Association, with offices on Broadway, Elizabeth often dropped what she was doing to aid Doris in her career. She believed strongly in women's achievement—in fact both were ardent, early feminists. Their niece Helen Fleeson observed: "Today as far as women's rights were concerned, they would be the champions."[14]

Mencken's strange style of compassion continued to flow from Baltimore: "What wretched news. But please don't forget that even if it turns out that there is a t.b. infection the safest place to have it is in a gland. There are plenty of ways of dealing with it, and they work. I hope Doris is reasonably comfortable and that the doctors give you such a report that you can see the sweating Motherland. You will regret it, but it will at least cure you of Anglomania. You will come back howling for Hitler and the Irish."[15]

At this point the *Companion* learned of the imminent departure of a WAC contingent for Europe. "So, with small Doris being taken to the doctor for dressings, to the hospital for x-rays, given sun lamp treatments and being looked over with tests by the pediatrician, Doris had to assemble a complete WAC uniform," Elizabeth wrote relatives. The sisters went to Saks and other stores, but had to search the city for the required shirts, gloves, shoes, shoulder-bags, ties, and finally for alterations because of Doris' small size. "But Doris in a uniform is a knockout," Elizabeth wrote. "For some strange reason, the color and the fit is more becoming than anything she has worn for years. We, at once, called her 'the General' and she does look it." Another member of the family, Doris' sister-in-law Eva Lynn Fleeson of Sterling, offered to come to New York to help care for little Doris.

Doris was the first of three top women journalists to become war correspondents for national magazines. After accompanying the first WAC contingent to Europe in 1943, she covered the war for *Woman's Home Companion* magazine.

When Doris' orders came, she, Elizabeth, Bob and little Doris went out for a steak dinner, stopping at the neighborhood drug store to buy lipstick, soap and powder for gifts in Great Britain. They packed at Doris' apartment until 3 a.m. Her departure the next day was delayed, and that evening all helped take her luggage to Grand Central Station. She left on the last train possible at 9 o'clock.

The next morning Elizabeth returned to the station to meet Eva Lynn, but in the wartime congestion could not find her. "It is easy to understand when you see the crowds that come in on every train," she wrote, "but it still seems strange to me that we should be within a few feet of each other and neither of us spot the other. By telephone we finally met at East End Avenue and I left her there, to meet the problem of small Doris while I looked in at my office which had been sadly neglected during all this time. That afternoon late when I telephoned, John had come down to see little Doris so I felt better that we were going to the country."

Upon her return, Elizabeth called Eva Lynn. "To my surprise, the 'General' answered the telephone," she told the family. "Her first act as a WAAC had been to ask for a furlough and in true Doris fashion, she had gotten it. Doris has apparently hit it off very well with the Companion staff and looks and acts like a different person. It was a very difficult decision for her to make and there were many times when she regretted this step when little Doris was so sick, but I think she realizes that this was the time for her to go and I am sure Doris (j.g.) will do as well as she has during the past year. After all, Doris has been away from her child for long periods and it is no new thing for small Doris to adjust to strange surroundings."

Doris, leaving in June, was the first of three top women journalists to become war correspondents for national magazines.[16] Martha Gellhorn, correspondent of the Spanish Civil War, soon was covering the war in Europe for *Collier's*. She had left Ernest Hemingway in Key West working on *For Whom the Bell Tolls*. He complained of her departure, of "having a goddamned wife try to put you out of business when you are writing the best book you ever wrote." Hemingway later decided to go to Europe as a correspondent himself, wrote to *Collier's* and was hired in his wife's place. It ended their marriage.[17] The third to leave was Dorothy Thompson, famed for her expulsion from Germany in 1934.[18] She had divorced Sinclair Lewis for "willful desertion" in 1942,[19] the same year the O'Donnells divorced. With her new husband, artist Maxim Kopf, she covered the war for the *Ladies' Home Journal*.[20] For Doris the assignment lasted nearly a year and a half, including coverage of the air raids in London, the invasion of Italy, the wait before D-Day in Great Britain, the second blitz, and the liberation of France.

Under an information blackout while traveling, Doris could tell friends little more than her APO address. The account of her voyage and arrival in England with the First WAC Separate Battalion appeared in the *Companion* of October 1943. "We take pride in announcing that Doris Fleeson, widely known newspaper reporter, has been named the exclusive war correspondent of the *Woman's Home Companion*," the magazine told readers. It described Doris as a homemaker and mother of an eleven-year-old daughter as well, and noted that American women "are entitled to up-to-the-minute coverage of events abroad by one of their own sex."

In the account Doris told of the WACs' voyage aboard a once grand British ocean liner that had been converted to a troop ship. She and eighteen others slept in one space, the cabin, she speculated, "where Lady Gotrocks once soothed jangled nerves by taking the salt sea air." Sailing such a ship was an enterprise that would pay off in manpower, but she was sensitive to the risks: "It was strange to realize," she wrote, "that this transport of good-tempered friendly people was actually a task force and as such a rich prize inviting to the enemy, that the sea was a haunt of killers who would destroy us instinctively as wolves tear dogs in the forest."

Reading it today, one is struck by the difference in Doris' writing on the war front. The articles are reminiscent of wartime newsreels and sentimentally scripted war movies. They may reveal a skilled writer's adaptability to a publisher's expectations. In any case, her colorful, irreverent political coverage for which she became known and which

Mencken kept citing as her forte, was on a back burner. Also striking, and comical from this brief period, is the contrast of stiff, stilted letters written to Eleanor Roosevelt, and the sarcasm, occasionally targeting Eleanor, that she happily exchanged with Mencken.

Five companies of WACs arrived in England to serve as clerks, stenographers and telephone operators for the Army Air Corps. "We are grateful for all that American women have done for our children through the Red Cross, Bundles for Britain, et cetera," said the RAF commander in a welcome. "Englishmen are particularly grateful for the visit of Mrs. Roosevelt." That thought, said Doris, must have been in the mind of an elderly Englishwoman who said amid tears as the WACs stepped off the tender, "Young, pleasant, strong—I have not been so moved since Dunkerque."[21]

From the White House, Eleanor Roosevelt wrote: "I have just read your first article in the Woman's Home Companion on the WAC's trip, and it is a swell story."[22] Because Eleanor herself had contributed a page in the *Companion* before she became First Lady,[23] the magazine made its way regularly to the executive mansion. But the recruitment of Doris as war correspondent brought new readers from unexpected quarters. "I bought a copy of The Companion, which is not a part of my usual reading matter, but apparently they decided to delay your piece because it wasn't there," wrote Wendell Willkie. "Perhaps I should demand a rebate."[24] What was undoubtedly the most unusual order came from Baltimore: "I have entered my subscription for the *Woman's Home Companion*, and shall read you with popping eye," wrote Mencken.

Checking into the Ritz in London,[25] Doris felt as if she had run into a convention of the American Newspaper Publishers Association. "All the lords of the press are here to give their blessing to the war effort," she wrote Mencken by V-Mail. She related that U.S. Senators were plentiful, and officers of the Eighth Air Force were holding forth amid celebrities at the Savoy. She found old friends among the reporters, many trying to move on to North Africa and Sicily.[26]

In her letter, Eleanor Roosevelt mentioned Lady Stella Reading whom she had known since the years in Washington when Franklin was Assistant Secretary of the Navy and Lord Reading was the British ambassador. When Eleanor went to Great Britain in 1942 in response to urging from the Queen and as an emissary of her husband, Lady Reading helped the Queen plan her itinerary and guided her to universities, factories, and estates turned into nurseries for evacuated or wounded children.[27]

She added:

> Now I have a letter from Lady Reading saying how much she was impressed with you. She thinks you are going about getting your material in the right way. I gather you are going to live in homes all over England and she is going to help you. I think she can do it better than anyone else.
>
> It is wonderful you have so many friends over there so you are never really lonely, though I am sure you miss Doris. Be sure to let me know if you get home for Christmas. If you don't and you would like me to try to have Doris come to us, let me know. Perhaps you will arrange for her to go to someone in your family.
>
> The trip I took was very interesting, but most exhausting, emotionally as well as physically. . . .
>
> I went to New Zealand and Australia and made seventeen island stops. I never got to New Guinea because General MacArthur was too busy to bother with a lady. I did get to Guadalcanal and met the Senators on their return trip. They must have had an interesting experience.
>
> Take care of yourself and write me how things go. I will continue to read your stories.
> Affectionately
> Eleanor Roosevelt[28]

Eleanor had made the goodwill trip to the South Pacific, again on behalf of her husband, but because of criticism at home when she went to Britain, she arranged to travel as a representative of the Red Cross. Her dislike of MacArthur was longstanding, having begun with his command of the attack on Anacostia Flats.[29]

Doris applied to visit one of the Army Eighth Air Force bases from which Flying Fortresses were attacking Germany. It was by happenstance—the offer of a hut—that she witnessed the staging of the raid on Regensburg and the Messerschmitt plant in Bavaria. An acquaintance who was adjutant to Colonel B. "Chick" Harding, former West Point football star, solved a problem of housing (there was none for women) by arranging the use of the small Red Cross headquarters on the base. And the wait in London had not been entirely tedious, Doris told readers: "All bomber groups have particular advantages, which they boast of. At one you may see Clark Gable himself. I've met Captain Gable twice with air force officers in London where he is working on a government film. The first time we sat in the center of a lounge in a fashionable hotel where he was the center of all eyes and I was thoroughly self-conscious. He looked very handsome. . . . At the second meeting the group was smaller and included newspaper friends of both myself and Gable. He talked well and appeared to enjoy himself. I was told that Gable much prefers a bomber job. He has been on several fortress raids and is popular with his colleagues. The present task is not his idea."

On leaving London, Doris reported to the Wing Headquarters Bomber Command to which Harding's group was attached. She then traveled to the base, a former English brewer's country estate which the RAF had developed for its use and then given to the American force. Her hut was without electricity when she arrived. At one point she had encountered some derision, having been told by an Eighth Army major that "there is no woman's angle on a bomber." But Harding's command was accommodating, sending a corporal the next day to connect electricity, and placing a jeep at her disposal.

"I quickly found the small world of the bomber base to be organized with utter precision toward one end—to get those planes off the ground, over the target and home," she wrote. "One mission follows another and everybody knows exactly what to do or is told. Outwardly it is calm. . . . When the planes are out on a dangerous mission voices get shriller, the bar more crowded, and men appear reluctant to abandon one another's company."

The athletic Colonel Harding already was much decorated and had led bombing raids, as did all the Air Force commanding officers. Months before Doris arrived, bomber crews at the base had been given unnamed maps of Schweinfurt and Regensburg and had practiced formations over and over, according to reports. Everyone on the base ultimately knew of the targets and their significance. The German command, in hiding factories in Bavaria had calculated that Allied fighter planes could not carry enough fuel to protect invading bombers facing Nazi fighter fire for hundreds of miles. The B-17 Flying Fortress, with firepower to protect itself, weakened the strategy. Its precision daytime bombing was a unique American contribution to the war. Doris related that a time was set for the raid, but weather cancelled the mission. Security was so important that Harding restricted every man who attended the briefing to the post, ordered that they were not to discuss it among themselves and cut off telephones.

Finally, with clear skies, Harding gave orders and again instructed the airmen. "I asked him what he said," Doris wrote. 'I told them to stay in formation,' he answered. 'I reminded them that missing faces usually belong to forts that weren't in formation and I mentioned names. It's brutal but that's the way the boys can get home.'" The planes were to land in North Africa before returning. Doris found everything at the base outwardly the same, the waiting "undramatic, but very wearing." The appearance of Major John C. Egan wearing his oak leaf on a red fez heralded the return. Doris wrote:

> Then from all mouths tumbled out stories of the man-made hell they had been through, beginning hours before the target was reached. All agreed that nothing like it in size, venom and duration was ever before experienced in aerial warfare. All around were fighters, forts blowing up in flame, and the thunder of guns without end. The Nazis arched

strings of blinding new rocket shells across the forts' path, but still our bombers moved toward the target.

The fortresses battled German fighters for two and one-half hours—the longest engagement in the history of heavy bombings. . . . The final score proved it to be the biggest day of the war with three hundred and seven Nazi fighter planes knocked out of the sky near the burning ruins of the factory which can no longer replace them, although for this victory we paid a price—fifty-nine fortresses and fifty-five crews.

A group of laughing boys—the Wolf Pack—had been in a plane piloted by Second Lieutenant Robert H. Wolf. How could they be in such high spirits while giving awful accounts of death and destruction, Doris wondered. "You should have seen us when we hit Africa," Major Egan told her. "We leaped out of our ships, laughing, slapping each other on the back. We were lucky to be alive."

As Doris left the base to return to London, many of the airmen were leaving too. The loss of companions was vivid when they returned to barracks, and "to cut the mood," the commanders had arranged leaves or a change of work.[30]

Doris received a letter from Mencken, deploring the state of journalism and admonishing Doris to be careful, that there would be much to do after the war. "Many persons now conspicuous in the public prints will have to be hanged," he said. His home front seemed little changed, as he described an evening with old colleagues from the *Mercury*:

I was at Luchow's with Edgar Masters last week. He moaned and blubbered over your absence, and urged me to send you his kindest personal regards, with his best wishes for your continued success in your chosen art. I should add at once that he had hardly got the message into my ear when George Nathan popped in with his girl, Julie Hayden, and that thereafter Edgar devoted himself assiduously to admiring Julie. I tell you this simply to show you that poets are not to be trusted.[31]

From London Doris wrote long letters to Mencken and to Eleanor Roosevelt. Her sister Elizabeth had enrolled little Doris at Miss Choate's school in Brookline, Massachusetts. "My sister wrote that she gave your name for a social reference," Doris told Eleanor. "I am sorry I did not have the chance to ask your permission for this. Of course, my sister and her husband are wonderful influences for her. Both are Ph.D's from Yale and I have entire confidence in their choice of schools . By the way, if you are ever in Boston and have a moment, would you be kind enough to call Doris and say hello? I know she would deeply appreciate it and so would I."[32]

Eleanor answered that, of course, she was delighted that Doris' sister used her name.[33]

"I know nothing of Miss Choate's," wrote Mencken, "but assume from its address that it is a respectable place, and that its instruction is based upon Christian principles."[34]

16

⊗∂ ⊂∂

INVASION OF ITALY

By fall the world's attention was focused on the Allied invasion and surrender of the Italian government. Doris was the first woman correspondent to reach Italy, where she traveled with the 15th Evacuation Hospital unit to the battlefront on the Volturno plain. Events had moved swiftly since a dramatic radio announcement on September 8: "This is General Dwight D. Eisenhower, commander in chief of the Allied forces. The Italian Government has surrendered its armed forces unconditionally. . . ."[1] Landings at Salerno and Taranto preceded an advance up the Adriatic coast, with a great air base at Foggia falling on September 27. Within a week the Fifth Army was beginning its assault on the German line along the Volturno River. Doris had gone from England to North Africa, and there arranged to cover the nurses, presenting credentials to Lieutenant Colonel Bernice Wilbur, the thirty-three-year-old chief nurse of the North African theater. She flew to Sicily but learned in Palermo that the unit had started for the front. Early the next morning she left with a dispatch jeep, traveling north over the island's damaged highways and through towns taken in the summer warfare. From the Messina Straits she accompanied an antiaircraft battery being ferried to the mainland to join a convoy.

In her account appearing in the *Companion*'s January issue, Doris described "a deep night of war blackouts which America cannot envision." She ate with the battery, then continued with a jeep and driver over roads in "total blackness, but straight to where I wanted to go—how, I shall never quite know." At ten o'clock she arrived at the nurses' staging area. She slept on blankets on the ground until the unit was roused before dawn. To the loud cry of "Four o'clock, girls," Doris, while half asleep, cried out indignantly, "Do I hear correctly?" It brought ripples of laughter and served as her introduction, she related. Trucks carried the nurses toward the battlefront over bombed-out roads and pontoon bridges, partly through mountains with a view of Mount Vesuvius. The hospital site, Doris wrote, was "damp and cold, cut by a swift brook and ditches." A complete tented hospital was in place within a few hours, and Army ambulances flying Red Cross flags began to arrive. "I saw tired soldiers lifted down on litters. Many of them—the German prisoners of war—were hardly more than boys. Some were seriously hurt. All were quiet, terribly quiet. They did not weep. They did not smile. The nurses explained the utter exhaustion of the soldiers, who probably had slept only when they dropped in their tracks, possibly lying in fields for hours before help came. Whether Allies, co-belligerents or prisoners of war, all the wounded received the same care."

Of the nurses, Doris observed: "Their home is an unfloored tent. . . . For the wonderful luxury of a hot bath they huddle on boards under a tented spray. . . . There are no corner drugstores, no Macy's. And yet their faces, so often bent above the wounded, are smiling, fresh with make-up and crowned with curled hair. The lipstick is their red badge of courage. . . . Their reward comes when exhausted boys look up from the stretchers and with heartfelt simplicity exclaim: 'Gee, it's good to see an American girl.' On bivouac, precious cosmetics were dug out of the deepest recesses of kit bags. I even saw one girl soberly and determinedly wielding an eyelash curler."[2]

Companion articles were headlined "cabled" from Europe, but letters to friends apparently had a slower delivery by the Army Post Office.

Doris found the front sprawling everywhere in the mountains of Italy. After the Fifth Army crossed the Volturno River, Allied reconnaissance troops used horses and pack mules to bring supplies along muddy roads. Engineers worked on bridges destroyed by German forces which had blown up even those chiefly scenic. It had been raining heavily at Thanksgiving time, when Doris spent the day with Rangers in their hill station named "Morass." Abundant holiday food had arrived under the order of General Mark Clark. A mess sergeant, a Southerner, wrote the menu of southern fried turkey, baked onion dressing, mashed potatoes, creamed corn, blueberry cobbler, fresh olives, bread, butter, coffee with cream and sugar, apples and walnuts.

Following the Fifth Army up the boot, Doris and a driver were heading toward the summits of the Appennines when they encountered the worst morass yet. They found a Red Cross clubmobile at the bivouac of an infantry battalion withdrawn from the fighting line to give the men a rest. At the head of a chow line were the "doughnuts," passing out doughnuts and coffee. Finding the girls so far forward was no surprise in Italy, where Clark had declined to put up barriers, Doris wrote. "If the Red Cross girls with their portable snack bars wanted to contribute to the morale of his men at the front they had the green light."

The clubmobile had moved up all equipment in a weapons carrier. For its headquarters the Red Cross had rented an ancient stone house in one of the towns the Fifth Army had taken a few weeks earlier. Although the Red Cross liked for the girls to be feminine, they had abandoned skirts and impractical fleece-lined boots the agency had issued, and wore pants and GI footwear. The Red Cross was putting a machine and crew, plus girls, with every division and an extra one or two with each corps of the Fifth Army, attaching them to units permanently. "I have had a two-star general ask me wistfully when I thought he would get his doughnut machine, and ask me to use my influence," Doris wrote.

In addition to the young women, Doris found men workers, often veterans of World War I, in the field. One had rented a vacant house in the hill city of Venafro, and with the help of the Army special service and chaplains had established a Red Cross club "right under the guns." Bill Fine was a New Yorker receiving a pension for being permanently disabled at Argonne. "The sight of an old house in the town that no one was using reminded him how cozy the YMCA huts had felt to boys who served in the mud of France," Doris wrote. "I spent the night at that club. I saw men sleepwalk in from the peaks, dirty, exhausted, their nails black-ringed and broken, their feet dragging shoes that had not been dry for weeks. No one pushed a word against them. Quietly a chair would be put forward and another pair of boots would join the arc of boots already around the fire. Sometimes the cheerful conversation of others who had rested long enough to regain easy speech would bring the newcomers into the circle of talk. But oftener, after the fire had soothed them, they would shuffle off silently to an adjoining room, where for the first time in days a bed awaited them—only a pallet of straw with blankets, but a bed. See the same men twelve hours later and what a difference—bright, cheerful, wisecracking—each the typical American soldier."[3]

Doris, hoping to return home by Christmas, was unable to do so until February. During a brief, troublesome visit, she accepted Eleanor Roosevelt's invitation to attend one of her White House press conferences, and to describe her experiences on the Italian front.[4] Little Doris was ill again, and Doris and John O'Donnell's separate concerns became a confrontation as they disputed whether the child should have surgery. When John had a relative appointed temporary custodian, Doris hired a lawyer in Boston to fight the order. "Now a doctor chosen by John's lawyer advised the operation, so it is going through," she wrote Malvina Thompson at the White House. "But due to the delay I have to take off and can't be present." On the letter, Eleanor left a memo: "If you can get little Doris' address send her a book & some flowers. What an outrage!"[5]

A message was sent to Mencken on the *Companion* letterhead advising that Doris had hoped to get in touch with him but had received orders to leave for England within twenty-four hours. "Your letter to her came this morning just as I was about to write to you explaining her hurried departure," wrote *Companion* staff member Virginia Floyd.[6]

Even to members of her family, the nature of Doris' and Mencken's relationship remained puzzling.[7] During the spring and summer of 1944 the correspondence between Mencken and Doris and Doris and Eleanor Roosevelt began to mention a wartime romance.[8] The man was William Clark, a judge serving in the U.S. Army, a member of a wealthy family in

New Jersey. Mencken wrote that he was up to his ears in his supplement to *The American Language*—"a dull, pedantic job, suitable to my years and learning," adding that once it was off his hands he probably would do four or five bawdy sketches for *The New Yorker* and *Esquire*. "I miss your illuminating conversation very much, and I miss your superb general's uniform even more," he wrote. Mencken said that he had decided not to go to the conventions although "the shows will probably be as good as usual. The Democrats, for one, can always be trusted to make an uproar, even when they are unanimous."[9]

In her May 10th response Doris mentioned the judge to Mencken: "I have not heard from Miss Doris for two weeks. I am hoping it is the fault of the post office. Judge William Clark of New Jersey has helped me to draft some directions for the shysters in case of trouble. Of course in the end I should have to return and bury my own dead."[10] And mention of the romance is found in Ben Bradlee's memoir *A Good Life*, in which he retells an account of his friend Blair Clark: "Blair remembers having breakfast with his father one morning during the war, when Doris showed up at the table, saying, 'Okay, Judge, I'm packed.'"

As she waited for the invasion, Doris wrote Eleanor acknowledging her kindness to little Doris: "Again my thanks and love to you. It is hardly stop press anymore that you are a wonderful friend but I am in a position now to appreciate it more than ever."[11] Eleanor seemed to welcome a chance to confide worries and frustrations, writing that she felt as though a sword were hanging over her head, dreading its fall to end the war. "Martha Gellhorn has gone back to London and I hope you two will meet," she said. "Life keeps on being busy—everyone in the world seems to be holding some kind of convention and I am asked to all of them!"[12]

Doris felt that there were enough correspondents in England to form a beachhead, and told Mencken that the National Press Club must be strangely deserted. Sitting in a nearby armchair, she said, was General W.A.S. Douglas, who sent his best regards. Duke Shoop of *The Kansas City Star* had spent several days at a bomber base "collecting" Kansas and Missouri heroes. He was in a near state of collapse, she wrote, "it having been some time since the Kansas City Star could not buy better than a Nissen hut and an Army cot."

"I'll put this in the mail forthwith and more later," she told Henry. "You are my dream prince."[13]

And Mencken continued to encourage Doris in her art, as he called it, declaring that she had "the gift." He said it had become impossible to make out from the newspapers what was going on in Europe, with the front pages filled with feature stories, and "little sediment of fact."

"I certainly hope the Woman's Home Companion decides to bring you back and restore you to politics," he wrote. "It is your natural habitat, and you'd certainly be happier depicting the Washington buffooneries for the ladies than trying to cover the war."[14] Just before the invasion, Doris wrote Eleanor (on May 29):

> I am expecting to move with a hospital early in the invasion so you can imagine what life has been for me of late. But I have wonderful news that will not wait. I want to tell you myself.
>
> I am going to be married to Judge William Clark of New Jersey and I am happier than I have ever been in my life. Bill is here in the Army now. We cannot be married for two months due to Army regulations but we shall be married as soon as possible, meanwhile I shall continue working as usual.
>
> Doris and I are going to have a most lovely life from now on and I know you will rejoice with us. . . .
>
> Tell Tommy and Mrs. Helm that I shall give them a faithful report on my return and let them admire my beautiful diamond and pearl ring!
>
> Much love as always to the truest friend in the world.[15]

Doris' letter to Mencken six days later, two days before the invasion, was a puzzling contrast; there was no rush to tell him the news and no mention of the judge. She spoke of the Liebling treatise, the

Luce publications, and the conventions.[16] And she responded to his advice for her career: "Of course you are right that I would be much more in character in Washington but I should not want to miss this story. Whatever I must do to get in on it, I am willing to do. When we talk it all over I do not think you will find that I have failed to profit thereby." While she might speak candidly with Mencken, she wrote a more altruistic thought to Eleanor: "I do not believe my conscience will let me rest if I don't always keep trying and working to avert another such war."

Doris' article on England awaiting the invasion, "Men With A Date," appeared in the Companion's June issue. London, she wrote, was "like a woman badly battered in an accident who had collected her wits, straightened her clothes and gone about her business with dignity, but naturally hadn't taken the time to buy new clothes, get a hairdo or make up her face." The women just wore what they had, she explained, and even the queen reportedly shared the wartime rationing, using her clothing coupons to buy gloves (she wore them out so quickly shaking hands).

Doris made it a point to talk with hundreds of servicemen and women as she traveled through England and Northern Ireland. She found them playing darts in the pubs, confiding in "motherly barmaids." She told of a vastly different scene in Northern Ireland, shrouded in mist every day. The Belfast pubs were cheerless, the city "scrimped for fuel, short of liquor, drenched in dark brown stout." Her article reached readers just as Operation Overlord finally began.

On the morning of the invasion Doris traveled by air taxi from London to the command field where the airborne infantry was to take off. As she flew over picturesque fields, the ground appeared as a great striped rug. Aircraft, their wings painted with blue and white stripes, stretched across the acres. In North Africa and Italy, Doris had seen fields in which effort was made to conceal and blend weapons of war. "Here our planes were marshaled out in bold ranks," she wrote, "the most lethal sight I have ever seen."[17]

It was only a week after the Normandy invasion that Germany

began a new siege of air warfare, sending the first flying bombs over London. It was their secret weapon, the Vergeltungswaffe (Vengeance Weapon), or V-2. To the British, it was the buzz bomb, a new threat with a supernatural quality. An argument prevailed throughout London: Which was worse, the old blitz or the new?

One evening Doris was near the docks when she heard the characteristic humming. Seeking the nearest shelter, she found herself in the basement of a warehouse. "I expected to stay there a minute or two," she wrote. "Actually I could not tear myself away until after midnight. The buzz bomb had driven me into the very parlor, bedroom and bath of that Thames-side Cockney community. More than a thousand men, women and children were there, settling in for a sociable chitchat before bedtime. They made me welcome, poured me tea and talked. I can't remember a pleasanter or more interesting evening." Those in the shelter had heard it before, but they listened as the borough councilor explained the particular dangers of the new explosive. It reminded Doris of a Kansas tornado sucking out doors and windows and flattening buildings.

As Doris left, the councilor invited her to go with eight hundred children who were being evacuated to Leicestershire the next day. She arrived as children were boarding buses for a trip to the railroad station, with gas masks over their shoulders and bags and bundles under their arms. They were saying goodbye to their "mums" quite matter-of-factly, Doris thought, and she found when she asked for a show of hands on the bus that almost all had been evacuated before. "Certainly the children showed no signs of weariness on the journey to Leicestershire, and it was a tiresome one," Doris wrote in the August issue of the *Companion*. "They clamored to know their destination and hoped it would be the seashore, which it wasn't, and eagerly gulped cups of milk with the usual accidents, munched buns, hung out of windows identifying every plane that passed and in general behaved with utter normality."[18]

It was not until June 19 that she wrote Mencken a letter similar to that sent to Eleanor. Victorian in tone, it was quite unlike any she had sent him:

Dear Henry,

I have wonderful news. I am going to marry Judge William Clark of New Jersey. I know you will be glad with me that I have found such happiness.

Bill is in the Army attached to a British outfit. They are about to leave for France as am I so we hope to meet there and be married about mid-July, the paternal Army forcing us to wait for 60 days after asking its permission.[19]

Three days later she wrote an unusually personal letter to Eleanor, although retaining the customary "Dear Mrs. Roosevelt." It ranged from Judge Clark ("He has already gone. For the first time I am really sharing the anxieties so many others have known.") to John O'Donnell ("John has remarried. I don't know the girl . . ." Little Doris, she told Eleanor, would be spending the summer in Kansas with her family. "Kansas isn't exactly a summer resort but I am sure she will be loved and cared for and the change should amuse her." (Doris, however, did not spend the summer in Kansas.) Any chance of accord with John O'Donnell seemed remote: "My sister tells me that John has not paid Doris' bill for her operation this spring and is two months behind in his support payments. That suits us. I called her to pay all Doris' bills at once and never to ask John for money. Bill fortunately can take care of us both and John's position will certainly be untenable unless he keeps up his end. He has never paid more than $100 a month for Doris and of course I didn't ask for alimony. I rather fancy that when the new bride finds out I am marrying Judge Clark she will be reluctant to let go of $100 a month for Doris anyway."[20]

As Doris waited in London to accompany a University of Kansas evacuation hospital unit to France, her wedding plans were abruptly sidetracked. At the same time, the confrontation with John O'Donnell escalated to the courts, and Doris' self-confidence appeared shaken as seldom before. To Henry Mencken went details, in a letter less than a month after her announcement of future plans:

I have attracted so much bad news lately I am beginning to feel like Typhoid Mary. It is not precisely the kind of glamour girl I set out to be. Perhaps I should return to Sterling Kansas and begin all over again.

Soon I shall be home and tell you All. My child has sent an S.O.S. John, despite a new and I am assured young and blonde bride, spent his honeymoon in the courts at Dedham Mass. trying to upset our custody agreement—so sporting in my absence of course. Doris tried to talk her way out of it but wasn't wholly successful, hence the cry for help. She did manage to get to camp for the present so I have a few weeks grace during which I hope to continue to France. . . .

I wrote you that I was going to marry Bill Clark— well, it transpires that Mrs. Clark didn't get the divorce she wrote two years ago to say she was getting so that is in a state of suspended animation so to speak. Bill is in France. I understand the gossip columnists at home are having a field day with me and that has brought out all the Kansas in me—I Hate It! You don't suppose God is getting back at me for having worked so long on a tabloid do you?

We got the news about Bill's un-divorce just before he left. He assured me of his thorough annoyance but admitted he couldn't help being reminded of the song: "You may tempt the upper classes with your villainous demi-tasses but heaven will protect the working girl." Or will it?

Yours

Doris[21]

Before her return to the United States, Doris crossed the Channel, along with correspondent Tania Long. According to Nancy Caldwell Sorel's book *The Women Who Wrote the War*, the ship was stalled by fog for three days and the two spent the time mending signal flags. Finally, as they approached France, a tiny boat was sent out, and the women climbed down a rope ladder, Long carrying her typewriter.[22]

Doris visited Normandy and the mushroom caves at Fleury in which twelve thousand refugees from the bombing of Caen were huddled. "The children, still fearless and inquisitive, came running toward me," she wrote. Evacuation of the caves began the next day.[23]

17

LAUNCHING A COLUMN

A chronicle of society then, as now, *The New York Times* on September 21, 1913, spared no detail in describing the event of the previous day at Blairsden, the estate of Mr. and Mrs. C. Ledyard Blair at Peapack, New Jersey.

On that day, in a floral Grecian temple set amid boxwood trees on "velvet" terraces, one of the Blairs' twin daughters married William Clark, student at Harvard and son of Mr. and Mrs. J. William Clark.

Six hundred guests had come from Hoboken on a special six-car train, arriving at Peapack to be taken in buses, motorcars and horse-drawn carriages up the winding mile-long drive. The mansion sat on a ledge overlooking the region, with a sharp one hundred-foot fall to the Peapack River and valley.

As related by the *Times*, the guests gathered on terraces as choir boys from the Cathedral of St. John the Divine in New York sang the *Lohengrin* "Wedding March." The bride, Marjorie Bruce Blair, descended the circular stairway in the main hall, crossing the drawing rooms to an outside isle of white stanchions and flowers.

The aura of the age of innocence was complete. As described by the *Times*, bridesmaids were attired in white satin, their lampshade overskirts edged with lace and tiny rosebuds. Bands of fur trimmed their hats, and frills of lace cascaded over the wide brims. Marjorie's twin, Florence, wore a flounced white satin skirt and coatee of silver-white satin brocaded in tiny pink flowers.

The bride, as she appeared with her father, wore a satin gown with long square train. A voluminous veil of Brussels net and point lace came far down the train, and a short veil also edged with lace fell over her face, the *Times* reported. She wore a short string of pearls, and another of diamonds from which was suspended a huge star sapphire pendant.

During the ceremony the choir took its place on the terrace to sing the Sevenfold Amen, and as the couple left the altar it rendered "O Perfect Love."

The reception took place in the large salon overlooking the terrace. Conrad's Orchestra, stationed in the wide hall running the length of the house and decorated with American Beauty rose trees in bloom, played during the reception.

After the wedding breakfast served on small tables on the covered verandas and pergolas, the newlyweds "dashed" to one of Mr. Blair's limousines, as guests showered them with rose petals.

The couple was en route to a honeymoon cruising on Mr. Blair's 254-foot yacht, The Diana, described as one of the largest of the New York Yacht Club. They planned to live in Cambridge where the bridegroom was completing his law degree at Harvard.[1]

William Clark, an heir to the Clark Thread Company fortune, was born in Newark, New Jersey, the elder son of Mr. and Mrs. J. William Clark. At the time of his marriage, the family divided its time between homes at 51 East 74th Street in New York, and Morristown, New Jersey.

William spent two more years at Harvard, and was admitted to the New Jersey bar in 1916. Like Doris' brother Howard, he returned from World War I a decorated officer, having risen to the rank of captain and having received the Silver Star for gallantry in France. He joined a law firm upon his return, and in 1923 was appointed a judge of the New Jersey Court of Errors and Appeals. Two years later, at age thirty-four, he was one of the youngest men to reach the federal bench when he was appointed to the U.S. District Court in Newark.

In 1930 Clark gave an indication of the flair for controversy that would become his hallmark, especially in increasingly confrontational years after World War II. He would be known for his ruling in 1930 that the Eighteenth (Prohibition) Amendment was invalid, and that the ratification by state legislatures had been improper in transferring power from state governments to the federal government. Although hailed by opponents of Prohibition, the ruling was reversed by the Supreme Court two months later.[2]

Judge Clark had resigned his place on the federal bench and was serving as a colonel in the U.S. Army, following service as a liaison officer with the British Eighth Army in North Africa, when he and Doris met in London.

By 1945 the romance was decidedly off course, its outcome foreshadowed by Mencken's diary notation on January 2: "Lovette told me that he met Doris Fleeson's fiance, Judge Clark, in London, and was not favorably impressed. He said that Clark is a very sour fellow and he predicts frankly that Fleeson will find him dull. He has, however, plenty of money and that may help."[3]

Clark's problems multiplied as he prepared to leave the service and marry Doris, with the discovery of his "un-divorce" and his efforts to regain his seat on the United States Circuit Court of Appeals. Ultimately he sued the government on grounds that he was entitled to the position under the GI Bill, but the courts ruled against him.

By that time he and Doris had broken their engagement, after a suggestion that he might be named in a new custody suit by John O'Donnell. It was not until 1947 that he obtained a divorce from Marjorie Blair Clark. The judge, however, remained attracted to journalists. In that year, in a ceremony in the Russian Orthodox Church in Rue Montevideo, Paris, he married foreign correspondent Sonia Tomara, exile from Russian aristocracy and noted foreign correspondent.[4] Six years earlier Sonia and Doris had been prominent figures in the annual awards program of the New York Newspaperwomen's Club—Doris honored for her article on Wendell Willkie, and Sonia, president of the club, cabling greetings from her assignment in South China for The New York Herald Tribune.

In 1948 Clark was appointed a civilian member of the legal staff of

General Lucius D. Clay, commander of the occupation forces in Germany. In August of that year he was named Chief Justice of the Allied Appeals Court in Nuremberg, but he remained at the center of controversy. After several clashes with the office of the United States High Commissioner in Germany, he was notified in 1953 that he would not be reappointed chief justice because of a diminishing amount of work for the court. He refused to step down and challenged the State Department to remove him. He was forced to return to the United States when his diplomatic passport was withdrawn. From that time until his death he was engaged in a running verbal and legal battle with the government. He died of a heart attack at the age of sixty-six on October 9, 1957, in Ceylon while traveling with his wife.[5]

Doris flew home from France in August, 1944, staying temporarily with the Jordans in their apartment at Sutton Place South in New York City as she concluded her work with the *Woman's Home Companion*. She traveled to Chicago to make a speech for the magazine. "Well, I am home, thanks to Mr. O'Donnell, he planned it that way," she wrote Mencken. "Jobless of course. . . . There is no immediate prospect of my being in your vicinity. I hope you will be coming to New York. All free meals will be even more appreciated than usual! Will you get the waiters to put up a box lunch that I can bring home to Doris? I have missed you and will be enchanted to spend one or many evenings with you. Make it soon."[6]

Mencken had just finished the first volume of his supplement to *The American Language*, and was working on the second, the two expected to run to more than 700 pages, he told Doris, as he proposed a meeting in New York in mid-October.[7]

One year earlier Wendell Willkie had written Doris that he would hold her to her promise of "getting back in time to get in with us next fall," confidently expecting to again be the Republican candidate.[8] But events had taken a remarkably different turn. With his pledge of support and his increasingly useful role in the Roosevelt administration since the declaration, and the publication of his book *One World* in 1943, there had been an indication that Willkie might return to the Democratic fold and replace Henry Wallace as Roosevelt's running mate. Although Roosevelt had allowed a trial balloon with Democratic leaders, and Willkie's name had appeared frequently in press speculation, the President ultimately rejected the prospect. Willkie then entered the Republican primary in Wisconsin, and when he was defeated he announced his retirement from politics.

In his letter he had proposed that Doris join his campaign train, beginning in Rushville, Indiana, as it had in 1940 when he had enjoyed her company. By September Willkie was gravely ill, the result of his characteristic intensity and of his refusing to be hospitalized immediately after suffering a heart attack. He died that October at the age of 52.[9]

Mencken and Doris met in New York on Sunday, October 22. "It was grand to see you," he wrote. "Please don't forget that you once promised me to tackle a book on your political adventures."[10] Doris, however, had begun to think pragmatically, acting on Henry's old advice that her place was in Washington, depicting the "buffooneries" of its leaders. "I start hunting a job next week in Washington and will advise you of what luck I have," she wrote. "Between the gyrations of O'Donnell and the uncertainty regarding His Honor's moves, I am mildly confused."[11]

Franklin Roosevelt had just won re-election as Doris returned to the capital to assess its possibilities. She was there when a letter from the White House arrived at the Jordans' apartment in New York. "Mrs. Roosevelt hopes that you can dine with her on Tuesday, November twenty-eighth, at seven-fifteen o'clock," wrote Edith Helm. "After dinner Mr. William Courtenay, British war correspondent, will show a film of the South Pacific landings. Mrs. Roosevelt hopes that you will arrange to spend the night with her. If you will let me know the hour of your arrival in Washington, a car will meet you."[12]

Doris accepted the invitation, then returned to New York to move into an apartment at 219 East 81st Street. "I had such a nice visit and appreciated to see you all," she wrote Eleanor. "I tried to telephone you the good news that Bill was home but you and Tommy were en route to New York."[13] William Clark had arrived December 6, and Eleanor now invited the two, along with little Doris, to lunch at her Washington Square apartment on Saturday, December 16. "I am delighted your Bill arrived safely and looking well," she told Doris.[14]

On the day after Christmas, Doris wrote to thank Eleanor for a photograph, relating that Bill and little Doris "are getting along together splendidly" and that they all "felt fortunate to have each other at this somber Christmas."(The Battle of the Bulge had begun on December 16). Clark planned to see his wife's lawyers that day to begin proceedings for a divorce, she said. Perhaps as an indication of the separate lives the Roosevelts led, Doris informed Eleanor of her effort to obtain FDR's influence in restoring Judge Clark to the federal bench. "I explained the situation about the Third Circuit vacancies to Pa Watson (FDR aide Edwin Watson) and he promised to speak to the President about it," she wrote. "Pa very sweetly said he thought the President should do it for me!"

The campaign to save her engagement was obviously a race against time, for the Allied Crimes Commission also beckoned Judge Clark.[15] Doris wrote Eleanor on January 1: "We had a quiet time here with my sister. John was in town only briefly and interfered very little. His new wife telephoned to express a hope for peace and his lawyer seems moderate and sensible. There are absolutely no indications that he intends even to raise the question of Bill."[16]

John had married Betty Potter, a staff member in his Washington bureau.[17] Clark, said Doris, had promptly accepted his wife's conditions for the divorce. "She returns to New York this week and then her action will get underway in Virginia."

When Doris called on Edwin Watson personally, she found that he was not in, but had left a message that he had spoken to the President, but that FDR said it was a matter to be decided by the Attorney General. Watson would within a month die at sea while returning with the President from the Yalta Conference.[18]

Clark's lawsuit against the government under the GI Bill was the final result of the unsuccessful effort. Doris wrote Eleanor on January 9.

To my great distress the President has left the matter of Bill's return to the bench entirely to the discretion of Attorney General Biddle. Biddle in turn has refused to recommend him. . . .

However I am not content to let even the Attorney General decide what the country owes its returned soldiers on the basis of his personal likes and dislikes and neither is Bill so our story is not yet ended.

I then asked Harry Hopkins if I might see him about the situation and he said he would see me Thursday. . . .

My best to you as always. I hope the "simple" inauguration isn't too much of a strain.[19]

Doris had obtained an assignment from the *Saturday Evening Post* to write an article about Anna Roosevelt Dall, but told Mencken: "So far have not caught fire. No dogs in it." She said that if he would let her know when he was to be in town she would "unveil His Honor for you if you wish it."[20] Mencken's visit in early May finally afforded a meeting with William Clark. "The judge is a grand fellow and I offer my archepiscopal blessing," he wrote after returning to Baltimore. "I was delighted to observe that he is wholly free of that tendency to riotous and insensate lushing which has been the curse, historically, of the American judiciary."[21]

But the romance was faltering, and William Clark's return to Europe appeared inevitable. Doris wrote Malvina "Tommy" Thompson that her situation was "suspenseful." She had given up the East 81st Street apartment and now was with the Jordans at their Sutton Place South residence. She had tried to write the article about Anna Boettinger, but was so dissatisfied that she had withdrawn from the *Post* assignment. The magazine, however, had asked her to reconsider. "Would Mrs. Roosevelt let me talk to her about it, do you think ?" she asked Tommy. "Since they seem bent on having it, I shouldn't want it to fall into unfriendly hands." Eleanor penciled on the letter in her sprawling hand (the letter found in her papers at the FDR Library): "Yes of course."[22]

A photo of Roosevelt being wheeled out to greet villagers on election night at Hyde Park, a black cape draped over his shoulders, had dramatically suggested his failing health. In February, the President who had taken care to conceal his disability throughout his public life, was willing to address Congress sitting down, upon his return from the draining Yalta Conference.

Word of his death at Warm Springs on April 12 traveled across news wires as a stunning bulletin. After the state funeral, although the Trumans urged her to take her time, Eleanor wanted to vacate the White House quickly. "I rode down in the old cagelike White House elevator that April morning of 1945 with a feeling of melancholy and something of uncertainty," she wrote in her autobiography. She told of going to New York, to the apartment on Washington Square which she had taken "a year earlier," thinking it would be "just the right place for my husband and me when he left the Presidency."[23]

Doris, now in Washington, received a letter from Eleanor on April 27 (the apartment address the same as in 1942) saying she would be in Washington from Monday evening, the 30th, until Friday morning, staying at Secretary Morgenthau's apartment. "I would particularly like to see you while I am there," she wrote, "so if you will call Tommy through the White House, I will let you know the best time."[24] By summer Eleanor was in Hyde Park clearing out the big house which the family planned to give to the government. She wrote Doris on July 6: "It has been such a long time since I had any word from you I am wondering how you are and what is happening in your life."[25]

Mencken had written: "I hope your difficulties pass off quickly, and that I live to see you a contented wife, sitting beside His Honor and blowing spitballs at the lawyers."[26] But the engagement was over, and as Doris assiduously sought a job Mencken offered help. He wrote Paul Palmer, Senior Editor of *Reader's Digest*, and John N. "Jack" Wheeler, whom he described as operating both the North American Newspaper Alliance and a private syndicate of his own. Palmer replied that he had written Doris, and Wheeler wrote that his general manager, Henry M. Snevily, would contact her.[27]

Doris' reception at the *Reader's Digest* offices on Lexington Avenue in New York City was less than cordial. "The R Digest people seem to think I'm an imposter because Palmer has quit them to write a book for Knopf which is a fact they think you surely know!" she informed Mencken. "I saw Palmer about a second—he said he was rushing to his train." Wheeler was out of the city, she wrote: "His stooges talk kindly but indefinitely. It looks there as if first I'll have to get a foothold myself in Washington and then try to get them to do a sales job."[28]

Doris was "parked" for a few days with Inez Robb at her apartment on East 82nd Street when Eleanor wrote on July 25: "I want very much to see you and as I will be in New York next week, how about lunch on Tuesday, the 31st?"[29]

Eleanor also was at a crossroads, sometimes receiving unsolicited advice on what she should do with her life. One day that summer Major Henry Hooker, a friend, asked if he and theatrical producer John Golden could call at her apartment. They had appointed themselves as a committee to scrutinize offers that came to her, considering which were in her best interest. Major Hooker would pass legal judgment while Golden would provide showmanship, if necessary. She did not know whether to interrupt their presentation, or burst into laughter.[30] Undoubtedly she enjoyed talking with Doris and comparing frustrations of moving one's life in a new direction.

As Eleanor was writing to invite Doris to lunch, Mencken responded on the *Reader's Digest* chill: "Unhappily, I have been out of contact with magazines and their editors for so long that I simply don't know how to advise you. In most cases I don't know the present editors at all, and in nearly all of the remaining cases I am convinced that they are idiots. Have you ever thought of the *Saturday Evening Post*? If you could offer it a profile on Eleanor you'd find the door wide open for you."[31]

Ben Hibbs, the native of Pretty Prairie, Kansas, with whom Doris had served on the staff of the *Daily Kansan* at the University of Kansas, was now editor of the magazine. Acting on Mencken's suggestion, she immediately received an assignment for an article on Eleanor. "One word from you and I arrange with the S.E. Post to do a 'Whither Eleanor' piece," she told Mencken. "It's in work. I had tea with her Wednesday—a chill windy day—we had iced tea and cheesecake." Doris mentioned that the North American Newspaper Alliance was making "tentative, a trifle nebulous offers."[32]

"I am certainly glad you are tackling the portrait of Eleanor. I trust you make it plain that she is a Christian woman and a sincere lover of humanity," Mencken responded.[33] Now, along with the *Saturday Evening Post* work, Doris received an offer from NANA, its affiliate Bell Syndicate, and *The Washington Star*, proposing a three-month trial for a column. "Do you think it a risky enterprise?" she asked Mencken. "Would it be better for me to try to get a more permanent job with one newspaper? The Star will keep me only as long as the syndicate does. Having no private income and with John refusing to help support Doris, I must look for security in a job."[34] Doris had consulted Eleanor that summer on schools for Little Doris,[35] but with the uncertainty of job prospects had considered sending her thirteen-year-old daughter to high school in Sterling, Kansas. Ultimately she chose a school in Littleton, New Hampshire.

She sent Mencken a copy of the Bell Syndicate contract ($150 a week for three months) and asked his opinion. Although he deemed the trial period too short, he advised against making a point of it, for he thought she would quickly satisfy her employer. "It seems to me that the chances of the column are excellent," he wrote. "All the existing Washington columnists have turned statesmen, and are filling their space with mere opinion, mainly vapid."[36]

Which, essentially, was the criticism against Dorothy Thompson, the "most celebrated oracle of her sex," according to author Charles Fisher. In her home-office on East 48th Street in New York, she wrote furiously, with the newspaper journalist's habit of crowding deadlines, producing her column "Off the Record" three times a week. With books, lectures, a radio program and a monthly article in *Ladies Home Journal*, she was a grande dame of theatrical dimension. Her long association with the *New York Herald Tribune* had ended as the result of her abrupt shift from Willkie to Roosevelt in 1940. In 1941 the newspaper "bounced" her column and she moved to the *New York Post* and the Bell Syndicate. Of her column, which appeared in one hundred twenty-five newspapers, critics complained that she had grown tired of reporting what happened, as she had done so brilliantly as a foreign correspondent, in favor of lecturing on what ought to happen.[37]

"I am returned to the salt mines. Let me have your prayers," Doris wrote Mencken on September 23. The trial period seemed inauspicious as she moved to a studio apartment on Connecticut Avenue in Washington.[38] But there was nothing tentative in the colorful writing she produced for *The Washington Star* that fall. It set her course as the first nationally syndicated woman political columnist, a career in which she would write some 5,500 columns in the next twenty-two years. "Have you any idea what a term of hard labor you have committed yourself to?" Walter Lippmann had written Dorothy Thompson when she began her column next to his in the *Herald Tribune* in 1936. "When I see people sign up to write columns I can understand why young men, in spite of all the horrors of war, still enlist when the drums beat."[39]

By the time Harry Truman launched his sweeping program for peace, Doris was again a member of the White House press corps, and revising her estimation of the man she had dismissed as a tame little haberdasher. Truman had not wanted to wait for a state-of-the-union message. Within days of the Japanese surrender he sent Congress a comprehensive domestic program that was a "rude awakening" for Republicans and conservative Democrats who had concluded the New Deal was over.[40] "Truman has chosen a course which is more liberal, more pro-labor, than that of Congress," Doris wrote. "And Congress is finding it hard to take seriously the man they knew so well for ten years."[41]

Mencken read her first columns, offering advice every few days. "Avoid mere opinion as you would the pestilence," he declared. "The customers, I believe, are tired of it, but they always fall for the inside stuff. There is plenty of it in Washington, and you know precisely where it is. You have already got a lot of it into your stuff; all I ask for is more."[42]

There was every indication that Doris took Mencken's words

seriously, cutting through official statements and press agentry as she had learned to do on the *Daily News*. It was a style that became the distinguishing feature of her column, the hallmark that drew allegiance from readers. Her clientele grew with her reputation for beats and "tough analysis," as Mary McGrory described it.[43]

For months members of the press had sought an interview with New York Mayor Fiorello LaGuardia on charges that the United States was reneging on promises to Italy. During the war LaGuardia had made regular broadcasts to the Italian people urging them to overthrow their rulers in return for U.S. aid. The mayor's role had been unofficial, but the broadcasts from an Office of War Information facility appeared to have had Roosevelt's approval.[44] LaGuardia's decision to tell his version of events brought Doris back to New York in late October, and she and Mencken arranged to meet there for an evening at their old haunts.[45]

The visit coincided with the unexpected arrival of Doris' nephew Dick Fleeson, sent "home" from Westminster School in Connecticut because of a polio epidemic. Since his home was a Kansas farm, he was adrift for an indeterminate vacation with relatives in the East. Doris and her sister Elizabeth, since inheriting an aunt's Pearl Beer profits (these went only to female descendants) had decided to use the fund in educating the next generation of Fleesons.[46] Four nephews from Kansas eventually benefited—a Yale medical graduate, a Yale scholarship recipient, a Harvard lawyer, and Dick, a graduate of the U.S. Naval Academy.

Doris thought Dick's holiday a windfall and an opportunity for him to see Washington. They met at Penn Station the next morning, after her session with Mencken, to travel to Washington. After they had boarded the train Doris went to sleep, and Dick had the impression that she was "hung over." He stayed at her small ground-floor apartment with screened-in porch at the back, at 5406 Connecticut Avenue, N.W., and was given a job with Doris' friend Tex O'Connor Leggett, former Canadian journalist and native of Texas, who had been buying and refurbishing apartments during the war.[47] Dick would continue his periodic odd jobs for "Tex"'s enterprises throughout his school years.[47]

The column by now had picked up the *St. Louis Globe Democrat,* and *The Wichita Eagle*—"family pressure," Doris told Mencken. She was mailing her own copy in "bales of envelopes" provided by the syndicate, and was considering the purchase of a duplicating machine and a name for the column.[48] Should she follow the general practice of using simply the columnist's name?[49] "The customers are running my stuff as a column under headings to suit themselves," she explained.[50]

From the beginning Doris gave unprecedented coverage to the roles of women in political life. "The woman who knows more secrets of the war than any other member of her sex is in this country exploring the possibilities of becoming an American citizen," she wrote on November 6. The visitor was WAC First Lieutenant Kay Summersby, Gen. Dwight D. Eisenhower's receptionist and administrative assistant. "At present," wrote Doris, "the attractive British WAC is in New York City, presumably replenishing her wardrobe with those essentials which are virtually nonexistent in the depleted areas where she has held a central post since her first assignment to drive Gen. Eisenhower in the spring of 1942. Her friends, however, say she has long talked of her desire to become an American citizen, and they are confident that whatever first steps are now possible she will be swift to take." Doris explained that Eisenhower was expected to return to become Chief of Staff and that "presumably, like other secretaries, Lt. Summersby is eager to take steps in time to hold on to her good job when and if her present employer changes stations." Doris reviewed the secretary's role since the invasion of North Africa, including the fact that she was not replaced though jobs like hers were from then on filled by WACs. She had been inducted into the American WAC with the rank of first lieutenant. "Just how this was managed WAC headquarters here cannot say and they have no record regarding it," she added.[51]

"The Summersby piece stops short at the most interesting part, but nevertheless it tells a good story of a poor working girl's rise in life," wrote Mencken. "What is the rule in Kansas about such interlopers? Do wives shoot them, or only slander them?"[52]

"We shoot those interlopers of course," Doris responded. "I also hear Ike has decided to become Ambassador to the Court of St. James so maybe Mamie can't shoot that far."[53]

Again considering the woman's role in politics, Doris gave Bess Truman her personal nomination for woman of the year for having the courage in Washington to give a small dinner party. "The usual practice followed by Washington hostesses of taking various capital lists as long as the roster of General Motors stockholders and inviting every one of them lest a vote from Dubuque be lost was not followed," she reported.[54]

At year's end Doris told readers of the new direction her friend, Eleanor Roosevelt, was about to take. Truman was ready to name the American team to the United Nations and Mrs. Roosevelt was expected to become one of five delegates. "Mrs. Roosevelt will serve as the voice of the women of the United States who, in increasing volume and without regard to politics, have protested against exclusion from the peacemaking machinery," Doris wrote. She noted that Eleanor would receive a salary of $12,000 a year.[55]

18

GEORGETOWN

In 1953 when her husband came to Washington to advise John Foster Dulles on international oil problems, Mrs. Herbert Hoover Jr. took a fancy to Georgetown. Her husband vetoed her on the ground that too many New Dealers lived there.[1] The area was closely associated with Democrats after their twenty-year era, and Republicans pouring into the capital with the Eisenhower change of command may have been charmed by the brick sidewalks and walled gardens,[2] but generally turned to the northern suburbs. Symbolic of wealth and power, the ten-by-twelve block square neighborhood had a lingering identity with the "thinking rich," old-fashioned upper-class liberals. According to writer Martha Sherrill, Georgetown was largely a working-class neighborhood, 30 percent black, slowly becoming fashionable for upper- and middle-class whites.

They were attracted by its antiquity. It began in 1751 as George Town, an earlier settlement than Washington. Its fortunes surged with construction of the C&O Canal in the 1820s, and ebbed with its decline in the 1890s, the towpath along the canal degenerating into a slum. The few distinctive mansions and characteristic Federal town houses represented a prosperous period in the mid 1800s when the area was a center of commercial activity and the home of upper middle-class whites.

To writer Susan Mary Alsop, Georgetown was "a small, ramshackle southern city."[3] In a less guarded time, the public could see the interiors of twenty houses on the Old Georgetown House Tour, a popular event in early spring which raised money for social welfare projects of St. John's (Episcopal) Church. Visitors could ride a streetcar from Washington Station for tea served in the parish hall of the church on O Street.[4]

Such was the ambience in 1946 when Katharine Graham moved into an imposing home on the height of the Rock of Dumbarton. Her husband, Philip L. Graham, had succeeded his father-in-law, Eugene Meyer, as publisher of The Washington Post, and the Grahams with their boys led a fashionably shabby life, with a grassy lawn encircled by a front entrance drive. Becoming a newspaper legend herself as publisher of the Post following her husband's suicide, Mrs. Graham maintained the elegant home, taking it through "many incarnations" over the years. Her dining room, epicenter of Washington society, had been the shredded-wheat room once floored with linoleum and filled with tricycles and bicycles, in which she ate breakfast with her children before driving them to school.[5]

While coping with inconveniences with the period architecture, many in Washington aspired to down-at-the-heels Georgetown chic. Journalist and author Sally Quinn, wealthy Georgetown resident, has said with apparent seriousness that "shabby is the operative word."[6]

Constance Casey, writing of her childhood in the 1950s, remembered a friend's mother who had been yearning to move to Georgetown, and finally, in 1960, moved the family from the suburbs to P Street. Casey's essentials of "Georgetown Comfortable": "Authentically child-worn slipcovered sofas, squashed pillows and books heaped on 120-year-old tables." The Georgetown mothers, she said, were warm, sometimes plump and noisy.[7]

In 1946, the year the Grahams acquired their home, Doris was enjoying success with her column, which the Bell Syndicate had sold to fourteen newspapers in the first four months.[8] Doris had by this time tasted the Washington suburban life, and unlike Mrs. Hoover Jr., could follow her fancy in choosing a home. The one hundred-year-old Federal town house at 3344 P Street, two blocks from Georgetown University, had a desirable exposure on three sides, with steps and front entrance on a brick sidewalk. It was typically small, with clapboard siding and shuttered windows. A living room, dining room and pullman kitchen occupied the first floor, two bedrooms and an office, the second. In back was a garden, surprisingly large enough for entertaining as many as thirty guests. The interior doorways were low and the rooms uneven, with a step up or a step down between each.[9]

Doris furnished the house "mostly in books,"[10] and with antique furniture from her friend Tex O'Connor's swap shop. There were brocade chairs, velvet-covered stools, oriental rugs, and a baby grand piano for Little Doris.[11]

Also living on P Street were Dean and Alice Acheson, and among other residents of the village were Drew Pearson, John Sherman Cooper, Ralph Yarborough, Christian Herter, and Senator and Mrs. Prescott Bush.[12] As an Episcopalian, Doris worshiped at St. John's, along with the Bushes and others more representative of the denomination which sometimes was called "the Republican party at prayer." In the late 1950s Jack and Jackie Kennedy bought their narrow red brick house on N Street two blocks away.

Little Doris arrived from New Hampshire to spend the holidays in the new P Street home. "You will be properly impressed I know that I have been invited to make the annual Kansas Day address January 28 at Topeka," Doris wrote Mencken. "Advice and suggestions gratefully received. Probably not since Carrie (sic) Nation has a woman been thus honored in the state. Of course I am her natural successor." She said that Little Doris had just departed and asked if Saturday, January 19, would be a suitable day for Mencken to entertain her.[13]

"It doesn't surprise me to hear that you have been invited to harangue the Kansas intelligentsia on January 28th," Mencken responded. "If you can run over for lunch on January 19th, I'll be delighted. There is a train leaving Washington on the Pennsylvania Railroad at noon, precisely. If you will leap aboard it, it will put you into Baltimore at 12.45. Give me notice, and I'll be at the Pennsylvania Station here to meet you. We can lunch at one of the luxurious dumps in the vicinity. Let me know about this as soon as possible. I may be able to make some wise and prudent suggestions for your speech."[14]

He wrote again on January 16 that he would look for Doris "as the noon Cannonball from Washington disgorges its hordes. . . . There is a good lunch-wagon quite close to the station, with backs to the bar-stools. The liverburgers are well spoken of."[15]

For Kansas Day, the eighty-fifth anniversary, Doris planned to address fellow Kansas on "The State of the Union," stopping first in Kansas City to see the Jackson County Courthouse in Independence, Missouri, of which Truman was proud. He was presiding judge during the remodeling, when his brother-in-law, architect Fred Wallace, transformed the building with porticoes inspired by the Greek Temple of the Winds.[16] Arriving a day before the Topeka event, Doris told The Kansas City Star: "In Washington, we call Truman's proposed addition to the White House the 'Jackson County Gothic.' I want to see the courthouse he built." She sent Henry Mencken a picture postcard, advising, "Now you know how the White House will look." In reply Mencken observed that the courthouse seemed to be "a cross between Independence Hall at Philadelphia and the #2 mill of the Carnegie Steel Company at McKeesport, Pa."[17]

Every war had its letdown, historians warned. As Truman faced the "frightening peace," Henry Wallace estimated the drop in gross national product and foresaw a possibility of seven or eight million unemployed by spring. Workers who had pledged not to strike during the war felt it was time for catch-up pay raises. "Sudden peace," observed Truman biographer David McCullough, "had caught the country almost as ill-prepared as sudden war." Some two hundred thousand meatpackers were on strike, a walkout by electrical workers, with rippling effect, had paralyzed Pittsburgh, and on January 19, eight hundred thousand steel workers had abandoned the mills.[18]

This was no time for her to be out of Washington, Doris told the Star. In the ballroom of the venerable Jayhawk Hotel, wearing a sequined dress she had purchased for her role as toastmistress to the Trumans at a coming Women's National Press Club dinner,[19] she rose to address her audience. A few Democrats were sprinkled among the diners, but in general the group represented the state's conservative Republican elite. As she began, it appeared that Doris might have taken a text from Kansas Populism, evoking the aura of Mary Ellen "Yellin'" Lease and Kate Richards "Red Kate" O'Hare as she viewed the labor crisis. "There won't be another golden age such as grandpa knew," she declared. "The man who lives by the sweat of his brow will keep his social gains and his improved standard of living. The employer will give it to him and like it—or the once underprivileged will take it by force." She chastised a "do-nothing Congress—a bunch of puddie-wuddies sitting on their thumbs without a thought in their heads and lacking courage to act if they thought of something." And she proposed that now labor was being permitted to use too much power, as had business.

"Miss Fleeson writes and talks like a tarantula walks," *The Topeka State Journal* observed.[20]

Doris also touched on a recent embarrassment. Although Kansas remained dry under a state constitutional amendment, five hundred seventy of its citizens held federal retail liquor licenses. Wet forces had begun a major effort for repeal. With the echo of William Allen White's pronouncement—"Kansans will vote dry as long as they can stagger to the polls"—it was an uphill battle.

For the abstemious reception following the banquet, the third floor of the executive mansion near the Statehouse was opened for the first time in many years. Governor and Mrs. Andrew Schoeppel greeted guests amid palms festooned with sunflowers.[21]

A letter to the editor in the next week's *Sterling Bulletin* assessed the speech:

> On January 29 I tuned in my radio to WIBW, thinking to get in on some of the Kansas Day speeches and perhaps hear "Okie" Moore scalp the Democrats. What I got instead was a rebroadcast of Miss Fleeson's address given the night before to the Natives. However, I didn't know this at the time, and at the conclusion of the broadcast didn't get her name. I sat there that night thinking I was listening in on the banquet speeches, and after listening awhile concluded some heretic

had certainly gotten by the program committee. And I knew my suspicions had to be confirmed when she made a half complimentary remark with reference to Eleanor. I thought her speech one of the fairest appraisals of the mess we are in. It should have been heard not only by the Natives, but by our congressmen in Washington. On the other hand, the tomblike silence that followed many of her remarks made me wonder how well the Natives took it. To me it was tops.[22]

Back in Washington, Doris found the rest of the capital suffering little from the Trumans' example of frugality in the White House. "Washington Parties are Serious Business" she titled an article for *Nation's Business* magazine. The famous trio whose invitations still were greatly prized were Evalyn Walsh McLean, Alice Roosevelt Longworth and Eleanor Patterson. Doris portrayed the oft-ridiculed Mrs. McLean as an anachronism of hospitality practiced on a grand scale in a past era. "Her parties are fewer this year," she related, "because every Saturday she throws Friendship open for the amputees from Walter Reed hospital and their girl friends. She feeds them the same dinners and champagne that she gives the Cabinet. They neck happily among the antiques gathered by the Walshes and McLeans from every city of Europe and the girls take turns wearing the Hope Diamond, the Star of the East, the 100 carat rings and the inch-wide diamond bracelets. Mrs. McLean calls all the lads what she calls the President and Supreme Court Justices: 'Darlin' boy.'"[23]

Doris had more than a passing acquaintance with the aging chatelaine, who had grown fond of her, and was in the habit of sending her telegrams. One she had addressed To Miss Doris Fleeson, Democratic Headquarters, Chicago (during the convention in July 1940): GOOD FOR YOU DORIS. WAS PROUD OF YOU LAST NIGHT WE WERE LISTENING IN AND YOU CERTAINLY HELD YOUR OWN WITH THOSE MEN AND THEN SOME. And in February, 1942: DEAREST DORIS HOW SWEET OF YOU TO WRITE THAT LOVELY ARTICLE ABOUT MY PARTY ITS THE FIRST CHEERFUL RAY OF LIGHT

THAT I HAVE HAD IN THE PAST WEEK AND YOU WILL NEVER KNOW HOW IT HELPED ITS JUST LIKE YOU DEAR CHILD YOU KNOW HOW I HAVE ALWAYS LOVED YOU.[24] After she had gone to New York following her divorce, Doris stayed with Mrs. McLean when she visited Washington. "I shall stay at Friendship and attend one of Evalyn's small informal dinners for 150," she once had written Malvina "Tommy" Thompson.[25] At the time of Mrs. McLean's death, Doris wrote: "To a worried wife she would quietly whisper: 'Stay here tonight with me.' Counsel, help would be quietly bestowed, and the social protection of being received always at Friendship, no matter what steps had to be taken."[26]

In the case of Alice Roosevelt Longworth, Doris had written the article in *The New York Daily News* on June 24, 1940, including the now famous quote that Franklin was "one part mush and three parts Eleanor." Mrs. Longworth denied to New Deal historian Joseph Lash that she had made the statement: "Never, I never said that. I'm so glad you asked me about it. It wasn't true. . . . I think what happened is that I ran into a friend, Bill Hogg, and he said, 'Have you heard what Jim Reed said about Franklin and Eleanor?'. . . 'Mush' is a bad, a silky word. There's no ring to 'mush.' How nice to have you ask me if I said that."[27] A widow for fifteen years, Mrs. Longworth lived in her home near Dupont Circle amid zebra and tiger skin rugs and mounted animal trophies of her father. Her caustic wit, Doris wrote, was increasingly confined to an inner circle "since the dual advent of Cousin Franklin and the war of which she took an equally dim view. Her party's candidates are not spared. Of the ubiquitous Willkie she said: 'It's not necessary to invite him to your house. You just put a lighted candle in the window and he will drop in.' Of Tom Dewey: 'How can you vote for the man who looks like the bridegroom on the wedding cake?' Anybody who can talk like that will have an audience in Washington."

Doris viewed Eleanor Patterson as wielding enormous influence as a hostess and publisher: "Cissy can walk down a staircase better than any woman in Washington. She can also make you feel that she has that white marble palace on Dupont Circle so that you could come there.

The lulled recipients of these attentions sometimes are jerked awake by a whiplash of Cissy's Times-Herald but they never find her dull."

The per capita consumption of liquor in Washington might be the highest in the nation, but social life at the White House was much subdued under the Trumans, compared with the Roosevelts' "Grand Hotel," Doris reported. Neither was diplomatic society what it had been in the old days. When the Russians first reopened the old Czarist Embassy in the 16th Street mansion, "their decor was dazzling and the guests shoveled in the caviar with teaspoons. Since the war a morsel on half a hard-boiled egg is the rule, but the vodka remains ample."

Embassies of nations seeking American aid faced a dilemma in the postwar period, knowing that social functions yielded results, but also aware that public opinion would question their expenditures. The French and Chinese had erred disastrously. Fearful of hurt feelings and sensitive to any charge of snobbery, they had issued thousands of invitations that fall. The guests felt free to bring others. "Kindly darkness finally engulfed the shambles where well-fed Americans were wolfing proffered turkey and champagne as if they expected never to eat again," Doris observed. "The best people in Washington will go anywhere to a respectable address if the drinks are free."[28]

The Trumans, who had lived in a modest Connecticut Avenue apartment, saw the effect of surtaxes on the presidential salary. Without private means with which to supplement the White House operating budget, they discharged eighteen of the staff and cut entertainment to a minimum. Others, however, were willing to relieve the austerity. Mrs. George (Pearl) Mesta who had recently given a "gilded" debut for her niece in Newport, planned a lavish dance for Margaret Truman in her new home, the former Herbert Hoover residence on S Street. Eighty-year-old Representative Adolph Sabath wrote Truman a letter of "paternal remonstrance," Doris revealed. The hostess, it seemed, had confided to society reporters that she planned to fly an orchestra to Washington from California, a touch which might, Sabath suggested, seem a bit excessive to men on the steel picket lines.

In Pearl Mesta, Oklahoma oil heiress, Doris saw the successor to Mrs. McLean and the late Mrs. Jacob Leander Loose of Kansas City. Representative Sabath, she wrote, would "get short change from Missourian Truman, who is strictly southern in his reactions to any criticism of his wife and daughter."[29]

Truman's popularity rating, according to pollsters, had dropped from 80 to 67 percent by early 1946, and Doris' assessment displayed ambiguity. Joining frequent criticism of White House Kitchen Cabinet cronyism, she wrote, "He gives no inkling that he is aware of the great power of the White House and proposes to use it."[30] She felt that in dealings with the press Truman was ill served by aides who discouraged an easy give-and-take. Press Secretary Charles Ross permitted little to escape that had not been published in the World Almanac, she complained.[31] And as labor unrest mounted, she suggested that Francis Perkins, "hoisted out of her job as soon as decently possible," was comfortably ensconced to watch the passing show.[32]

Characteristically, she was attuned to news involving women. Clare Boothe Luce, whom she did not like, fascinated her nonetheless. She wrote on February 8, 1946:

> When Representative Clare Boothe Luce announced that her reasons for deciding not to seek re-election to the House would "become abundantly clear in time," the hidden meaning experts of the capital—a busy group—went into a trance and emerged with the whispered conclusion that Mrs. Luce is going to have a baby.[33]

Two months later she reported that Mrs. Luce was not leaving politics, but was about to run for the Senate against Chester Bowles—a race by two Washington prima donnas. "Should Mrs. Luce continue her political career in the Senate, there will be a boom for her for vice president in 1948," Doris wrote. "Nearly 43, Mrs. Luce still has the faculty of making other women look as if they hadn't quite finished dressing."[34]

On February 9, Joseph Stalin made the stunning declaration in Moscow that another war was inevitable. He predicted that a confrontation with the capitalist West would come in the 1950s, and he ordered tripling the production of materials for national defense. Consumer goods must wait.

Within three weeks Winston Churchill, introduced by Truman, delivered his Iron Curtain speech at Westminster College in Fulton, Missouri. A few weeks later General Eisenhower was making arrangements for a visit from Marshal Zhukov, confident that friendship between Russians and Americans could be cemented and save the peace. Eleanor Roosevelt, in her role in the United Nations, planned to spend the summer traveling in the Soviet Union, learning of working conditions and the life of women and children, issues to which she had devoted her energies.

With contradictory signals, winds of the Cold War were fanning suspicion. Doris portrayed the State Department as "plagued with its own Red troubles here in Washington."

"A kind of civil war is raging between it and the House over allegations that Communists are infiltrated into the various bureaus and agency under Secretary Byrnes' control," she wrote. Individual members of the House had begun to voice accusations of communism against the Byrnes lower level, she reported. "No one who attends a gala at the Russian embassy can doubt that they have many sympathizers among the lower-level bureaucracy, but no facts have ever been offered by an inquiry to support any conclusion."[35]

There was much to inspire discourse when editors gathered in the capital, but Doris, unimpressed, told Mencken: "I went to the editors dinner last week and awarded it the international, all-time prize for platitudes. However the evening was not without its excitement as a very young lady in our party had a peek-a-boo gown that brought sight to the allegedly sightless eyes of Joseph Pulitzer among others."[36]

Trouble on the Supreme Court came into view when the American Bar Association openly charged the tribunal with disarray under the loose rein of aging Chief Justice Harlan Stone. It was an unusual denunciation, adding to the nation's other vexing problems. As was their custom, the justices did not answer, but their reaction in Washington was evident, Doris said. "In capsule, their 9-0 opinion regarding the bar association's stricture is: 'The same to you and many of them.'"[37]

The elderly Stone was seen as ineffectual in molding a united front as had his predecessor, Charles Evans Hughes. The justices, with an average age of fifty-six and a half, were individualists, and separate ambitions fueled by awareness that Stone's retirement could not be far off played a part. And Truman had impulsively removed Robert Houghwout Jackson from the court to conduct the trials at Nuremberg, increasing the burden on the rest. Then came the dramatic death of the Chief Justice during a court session. "In selecting a new shepherd for this unruly flock, Truman needs to make a most discriminating choice," Doris declared. Every member of the court had been appointed by a Democrat and only one was a Republican.[38]

Even before Stone's death, Jackson had been considered the heir-apparent. But there was an undercurrent in the situation which only added to Truman's lament that everyone in Washington wanted something at the expense of everybody else. Readers were shocked to learn that the latest antagonists requiring the President's attention were two Supreme Court justices—Jackson, now sitting in judgment in Nuremberg, and Hugo Lafayette Black, former Senator from Alabama who had served on the court since 1937. Details of the feud broke in Doris' column on May 16:

> Although it escaped public notice at the time, the blood feud raging on the Supreme Court which has caused the court's anxious friends to urge an outsider as Chief Justice was embalmed in the judicial archives by one of the protagonists, Associate Justice Jackson, on June 18, 1945.
>
> In a virtually unprecedented statement attached to the court's denial of a rehearing in the controversial coal case, Justice Jackson all but told his senior colleague, Associate Justice Black, that Justice Black ought to disqualify himself, as the coal company had asked so that a new trial might be had.

The basis of the coal company's request, Doris explained, was that Justice Black's former law partner was attorney for the United Mine Workers' local to which a five-to-four majority awarded the decision. She continued:

> Concurring with Justice Jackson in the unusual commentary was Associate Justice Frankfurter, who is now surreptitiously booming him for Chief Justice.
>
> Justice Black reacted with fiery scorn to what he regarded as an open and gratuitous insult, a slur upon his personal and judicial honor. Nor did he bother to conceal his contempt. An already marked coolness, especially between Messrs. Black and Frankfurter, froze into impenetrable ice.
>
> The inside story of the clash of strong wills has been laid before President Truman. The harassed President, a Southerner himself, was quick to perceive the affront which Mr. Black feels he suffered. He has confided to a Senator: Black says he will resign if I make Jackson Chief Justice and tell the reasons why. Jackson says the same about Black.[39]

On June 6 Truman unexpectedly announced the appointment of Secretary of the Treasury Fred Vinson to succeed Chief Justice Stone. He trusted and respected the workhorse Vinson, who had left the federal Court of Appeals bench during the war to direct the Office of Economic Stabilization and later the Office of War Mobilization and Reconversion. Yet the choice, to many, seemed "singularly uninspiring," and to have been made in haste. In fact, when asked when he had made up his mind, Truman replied, "About an hour and a half ago."[40]

In Germany on June 10, Justice Jackson summoned American correspondents to his office in the Nuremberg courthouse at 10:30 p.m. to release a six-page statement he had cabled to chairmen of the House and Senate judiciary committees. In it he said that he had been unable to defend himself while the appointment of Chief Justice was pending, even to the President, "without being in the position of pleading for the post." There was more.

Congress was said to be dazed by what The Associated Press termed "a blast worthy of the atomic age against his colleague Justice Hugo Black." Charging that confidence in internal matters of the court had been broken, Jackson intimated that Black was behind "attacks" in the press.

The message fairly sizzled toward the end. "Bombshell" seemed to accurately describe the situation. Official Washington wondered how the two could ever serve together on the court. Press Secretary Ross declined at his daily conference to comment, saying that Truman had not discussed the matter with Chief Justice-designate Vinson.

Ben Reese of the *St. Louis Post Dispatch* cabled Doris that day: "Renewed congratulations on your scoop are in order because new developments in Jackson Black row. Reprinting your story in its entirety today so readers will understand your part in this big news."[41]

19

MR. AVERAGE MAN

Harry S. Truman had more difficult, far-reaching decisions in his first months in office than any president, according to biographer David McCullough.[1] The next two years could not have been a more exciting or more important time, said Truman aide Clark Clifford.

For the insatiable press, the story moved from crisis to crisis. As labor turmoil subsided, Truman stumbled into an embarrassment which led to the firing of Secretary of Commerce Henry Wallace and the resignation of Secretary of State James Byrnes. The debacle of a sweeping Republican victory in the mid-term election placed the GOP in control of both houses of Congress for the first time since before the Depression.

Rejected by the Republican Congress, Truman was repudiated by southern Democrats over civil rights. The British economic crisis and pullout in Greece shocked the West. With the issue of Palestine and the threat of war over Berlin rising, Truman was urged to step aside as the Democratic nominee in 1948. There was a boom for Eisenhower, a boomlet for McArthur, and not only a third, but a fourth party candidate had entered the arena—Wallace for the Progressive Citizens of America, and Strom Thurmond for the Dixiecrats. Journalists knew no slow news days.

Colleagues and readers noticed that they often found a "scoop" or details of a "secret" meeting in Doris' column. She broke the story that Wallace was about to make a foreign policy speech approved by Truman which contradicted the foreign policy of Secretary of State Byrnes.[2] On September 12, 1946, Wallace addressed an audience of twenty thousand in Madison Square Garden, advocating Russian and American spheres of interest. Condemning British "imperialism," he departed from his text, declaring, "I realize that the danger of war is much less from Communism than it is from imperialism." At a press conference that afternoon, reporters who had been given copies of the speech read Truman a notation that he had "read these words" and approved them. He said that he had. The next day, a Friday the 13th, State Department officials were reported to be stunned.[3] The episode proved a major blunder, with Truman acknowledging later that he had skimmed the speech while dealing with other matters, and had trusted "Henry to play square with me."[4]

Now official pressure for a Big Three meeting was increasing in view of worsening relations with Russia. Truman had twice invited Stalin to Washington and had twice been rebuffed. Doris noted:

> At Potsdam Truman informally invited Stalin to visit us. To his amusement the theoretically godless Communist replied that God willing, he would. Someone's good memory later recalled that Stalin once studied for the priesthood, at which time he probably picked up the Latin Deo volente.[5]

Doris received the European Theater Ribbon for her work as a war correspondent, at a ceremony on November 23, 1946.[6] The list had omitted her friend May Craig until she wrote Eisenhower, now Chief of Staff. His response included a penned postscript in keeping with Doris' assessment of the Eisenhower prose ("at best pedestrian, at worst involved and repetitious.")[7] The General wrote: "I am truly grateful to you for the opportunity to correct a mistake in advance! DE."[8]

With the mid-term election over, Doris found Republican presidential rivalries the hottest politics in town. On the Democratic side, Clark Clifford was "the hunted social lion in Washington" by reason of his eminence as leader of the palace guard. Clifford was a young St. Louis lawyer who had "jumped" to captain in the Navy eighteen months earlier and who had become Truman's naval aide, "thereby causing all

Annapolis acute pain."[9] The handsome, graceful Clifford, no longer wearing a uniform, was clearly a rising star in the Truman administration.

Senator Robert A. Taft was seen as using the chamber as a springboard for the presidency and creating hard feelings. A world tour including Russia was providing visibility for the young former governor of Minnesota, Harold Stassen. New York Governor Thomas E. Dewey, who had presented a strong challenge to Roosevelt in 1944, was an apparent front-runner. Would people be fed up with all of them and "ready to welcome a fresh and spirited dark horse ?" Doris wondered.[10]

Editor Ben Reese of the *St. Louis Post-Dispatch* called upon another of Doris' admirers, Roy Roberts of *The Kansas City Star*, to second his nomination of her story of the Jackson-Black Supreme Court feud for a Pulitzer Prize.[11] He pressed Henry M. Snevily, manager of the Bell Syndicate, to promote the column sufficiently, suggesting that he get some letters from editors.[12] In response to Snevily's request, Editor B.M. McKelway of *The Washington Star* wrote: "She is doing an outstanding job, in my opinion, and for these reasons: She is a great reporter with access to excellent sources of news in Washington. She knows news and what to do with it. She works hard to find out what is going on and she usually knows. She writes one of the newsiest and best columns out of Washington."[13]

Joseph Pulitzer, complimenting Doris on one of her columns, wrote: "Accept my most cordial congratulations and try to reserve a few minutes for a drink with me when, if my plans materialize, I hit Washington for the Editors' meeting April 17th."[14]

Doris delivered an address on "Women in Politics" for the Kansas City Advertising Club on May 12,[15] entering the hospital soon after her return for dilation and curettage (D and C) surgery. "I just heard from Ruth Cowan that you had to have that very unpleasant operation," wrote Eleanor Roosevelt on June 6. "Having gone through it myself, I know just how painful it is. Do take time to get entirely strong."[16] Eleanor wrote again on June 24 to say that she would be in Washington on the 29th for the NAACP rally, and inviting Doris to lunch at the Women's National Democratic Club. "I am asking the other girls too," she advised.[17]

Center of attention in a man's world. (University Archives, Spencer Research Library, University of Kansas Libraries)

Senator Joseph McCarthy, bachelor ex-Marine from Wisconsin, had been busy that spring as co-sponsor of a bill to de-ration sugar, and as sponsor of an amendment to remove fur-trimmed coats from the 20 percent excise tax.[18] Now from Washington he anxiously watched developments in Wisconsin, where he had agreed to manage the Stassen primary campaign. A presidential preference vote at the midyear state convention buoyed Stassen's hopes with two hundred eighty-six votes, only thirty-five less than Thomas E. Dewey's first-place total. General Douglas McArthur, Wisconsin native, drew one hundred fifty-seven. "Rumors of a triumphal MacArthur return at an opportune time are a hardy perennial of the cocktail lounges here," Doris noted.[19]

If a columnist wished to observe a future president, there was no better place that a governor's conference, Doris believed. At the gathering in Salt Lake City that July, Secretary of State George Marshall spoke in "an atmosphere laden with presidential politics," she reported. "The tough talk came along in the aggressive pro-preparedness remarks of Governor Thurmond of South Carolina which one colleague described as 'the speech Marshall ought to have made.' An ex-paratrooper, wounded in Normandy on D-day, Thurmond will contest with Senator Johnston for a United States senate seat next year."[20]

Eleanor Roosevelt, living in New York City and serving as a delegate to the United Nations at Lake Success, wrote Doris from Campobello Island in late July with a motherly request: "If you happen to go to the hearings at which Elliott appears before the Brewster Committee, I wish you would write me a line giving me your impressions of how it was carried on. I will not use it in my column!"[21]

Elliott had been called to testify at a subcommittee hearing into alleged hospitality connected with government contracts.[22] "I expect that by now the newspapers and radio have made it clear to you that Senator Ferguson's investigation hasn't turned out as planned," Doris wrote Eleanor. "Ferguson hasn't got the brains and integrity to plan a proper investigation or the ability to make it stick. Elliott had no trouble with it. He made a good showing, always polite and plenty articulate. I think he rather caught them by surprise; they had probably believed all they read about him. . . . I hope you are getting a rest. Please do ask me about anything, any time. When I can do anything for you, it is a privilege."[23]

Dismal for Democrats, the mid-term elections of 1946 also brought to a new low the number of women in political office with any real power. There were three Democratic and four Republican women in the House, no women in the Senate or Cabinet, no women governors. Marion Martin, hired eleven years earlier at "the nadir of Republican misfortunes," was fired by the Republican Central Committee for comments in an interview that disparaged "tea-pourers and orchid-wearers." The Maine state legislator, according to Doris, had come on board amid concern that the party was "long on ladies who gracefully wafted sables, real pearls and corsages to the front row of Landon meetings." A commotion in her behalf was narrowly averted at a National Committee meeting in Kansas City, but the dismissal stirred the voice of Maine's Republican Representative Margaret Chase Smith. "Her efforts to get a better deal for women in politics represent probably Margaret Smith's first crusade," Doris wrote. Representative Smith could speak from experience. During her fourth term she was denied an assignment on the Appropriations Committee, and placed on Armed Services behind six men she outranked, including one freshman. Now she addressed women audiences with candor: "There has been too much polite 'head in the sand' avoidance and denial of the fact that men basically have opposed women taking their rightful place in the public office. . . . We, the women, must do something about it—the men have clearly demonstrated that they won't voluntarily give us a greater voice."[24]

Improbable though it might seem, considering Doris' strong identification as a liberal, and Representative Smith's affiliation as a Republican, the two had become friends. "Many thanks for the Nation's Business story," Smith had written from her home in Skowhegan in 1946. "My election is over, the fifth for me, and I am trying to catch up from it all after which expect to return to Washington. Maybe you, May, I and others can get together and talk it over. I'll call you and hope you will have the time." She penned at the bottom of her letter: "Wish I could have you as my campaign manager sometime."[25]

Their mutual friend May Craig had been writing, in some way, in Washington since she was twelve years old. Small, with blue eyes, she wore her hair in a bun, dressed in blue and chose flowered hats to leave an impression at the White House and on Capitol Hill. The effect was disarming as she aimed devastating "issue-oriented" questions. She was said to have a mind "as tough as a very old down-East lobster," although actually she was a Southerner by birth. Born Elisabeth May Adams in Coosaw Mines, South Carolina, in 1888, she was adopted following her mother's death by owners of the phosphate mines which employed her father. Often alone, she read books in the family's library. When the family moved to Washington, Elisabeth May wrote articles and poems for school newspapers. Rebelling against her parents' plans for a finishing school, she began a dual career in writing and nursing, enrolling in the George Washington University Nursing School. The break with her parents was complete when in 1909 she married Donald A. Craig, journalist and columnist in the Washington bureau of the *New York Herald*. The couple had a son in 1910 and a daughter in 1915. Elisabeth May hired a housekeeper, pursued a writing career and immersed herself in women's and children's issues. She marched in the homemakers' section of the suffragist parade at Woodrow Wilson's inauguration.

Donald Craig, who became Washington bureau chief of the *Herald*, was severely injured in an automobile accident in 1923. Elisabeth May began helping him with his work, including his column, "On the Inside in Washington," for the Gannett Publishing Company's chain of newspapers in Maine. When Donald died in 1936 she began writing her column, "Inside in Washington," for four Maine newspapers. She shortened her name to May Craig at the time she added a radio broadcast for two stations in Maine. Throughout the years, May and Doris were often together on the front lines, protesting discrimination against women journalists in Washington. May annually attempted to attend the all-male dinner of the White House Correspondents' Association.[26]

Thus any slight against May became an affront to Doris, as it did in August 1947 when May was excluded from returning aboard the battleship Missouri from the Inter-American Defense Conference in Brazil. As the only woman in the press contingent scheduled to fly with the Trumans to Rio, she had foresightedly written officials weeks earlier, joined by her friend, Representative Smith, member of the Armed Services Committee.

Shortly before departure, White House Press Secretary Charles Ross informed May that there was no room for her to return with the Trumans and twenty-five male journalists. In writing of the affair, Doris cited the military frame of mind faced by women war correspondents, and denounced the Navy as "by far the most discriminatory." The President was breaking no precedent in taking his wife and daughter aboard a battleship. In fact, Herbert Hoover also had used one. She added:

> The Missouri is a cozy craft one-sixth of a mile long. It carries a wartime complement of 2,700 men and a peacetime crew of 2,000. The Trumans will occupy the admiral's handsome suite. There are 88 other staterooms normally occupied by 100 officers. Four of these have private bath.[27]

In spite of efforts of her friends, May was flown home. With the "funny little hats" (a Ben Bradlee comment) that became her trademark as a television panelist on "Meet the Press," May represented what was considered an inferiority in fashion among women in Washington, compared with those in San Francisco, Dallas or Kansas City. "Despite all the entertaining there are no famed shops here," Doris had written. "Women go in for white shoes, flowered dresses, fluttery pink and blue."[28] Mrs. Craig would not change (one observer later pointed to Barbara Bush as continuing the Washington fashion preference), but in the summer of 1947 others had become sensitive to the indictment that they lacked style. Doris reported:

> The stigma is about to be challenged by a dauntless one hundred who have each paid a substantial annual retainer to an experienced stylist to advise them how to dress for their high-powered politico-social life. She will also do their shopping for them. . . . The group includes at least one cabinet wife and numerous names known and influential in politics.
>
> The stylist who expects to refurbish so important a segment of the capital scene is described as gifted and very firm. One customer bearing an honored name saw her clothes closet emptied of all but one dress which she was told she must do with until she reduced.[29]

Both in weather and accommodations the Taft entourage was

getting a break over the dozen reporters who had accompanied Thomas A. Dewey on a "vacation trip" to test the waters in the summer of 1947. With the governor using regular trains, reporters had to scramble for sleeping berths. Robert A. Taft, powerhouse of Republican legislation in the Senate, had arranged for three sleeping cars to bring reporters to California to cover appearances in the early fall. Doris, covering appearances in Los Angeles, Santa Cruz and San Francisco, wondered at the candidate's penchant for putting both feet in his mouth simultaneously: "Is Taft merely tactless? Do headlines, though accurate, do him an injustice as the pitiless cameras always did Mrs. Roosevelt?"[30] In both parties the prospect of a dark horse was compelling. Back in Washington in October, Doris reported that while a campaign to make Eisenhower the Republican candidate had not really started, a campaign to keep it from starting was well under way: "Taft and Dewey will not need much imagination to recall when they go to Philadelphia next June that eight years before they had expected to battle it out in that spot only to see the prize get away." The foes were building a backfire with the battle cry "Remember Willkie!"[31] Questions also surrounded the plans of MacArthur, yet to return for a hero's welcome. Many guessed that it would be in early spring, in time for the Wisconsin primary. In his home state this could mean "jet propulsion into the presidential picture."[32]

At what time Truman decided to run for re-election is uncertain, according to David McCullough. Acknowledging his own low ratings after the mid-term election, he had been willing to step aside if Eisenhower, the most popular man in America, would head the Democratic ticket. According to one source he also had offered to be Eisenhower's running mate if that would suit the General. But by 1947 his inquiries had yielded no sign of interest, and Democratic spirits were rebounding with evidences of Truman's popularity. His State of the Union message in January, 1948, as Doris described it, hoisted "the bright pink flag of Roosevelt liberalism over the Democratic campaign of 1948." It was a clear signal that he would base his fight for re-election on the traditional alliance of labor, independents, minorities and Democrats. Recalcitrant Henry Wallace had rendered an inestimable favor, she said, by accepting the helm of the Progressive Citizens of America, drawing Communists to a third party and removing from the Truman candidacy "a really serious taint—one that many blame for the '46 debacle."

Other journalists, studying Doris' "art," could analyze the writing, but it was more difficult to fathom the sources. In a time when the term deep throat was unknown, she had not one, but many. The approach was reminiscent of *The New York Daily News* of the twenties when reporters had their remarkable contacts with police and judges. Thus, on September 13, 1947, Doris provided details of a secret meeting of Republican leaders, concerned with a split over the Marshall Plan and the cost of a party vendetta in the coming election. "This is the real story behind the secret conference of twenty G.O.P senators Monday night," she related. "Thus diehards and middle-grounders rang the doorbell of Senator Reed who offered his spacious, centrally located apartment for Monday's occasion." Because Senator Reed was Clyde Reed of Kansas, Doris may well have had an insider's help. It was possible that she was present. She named each of the twenty attending. "Wherry took the chair and a verbal cyclone rustled the curtains," she reported. "The Senators spoke in language not only banned from Senate debate but for which no Senator would care to take responsibility in the cold print of the Congressional record."[33]

With assorted aspirants, open and covert, Republicans seemed drawn in all directions. Stassen denied that he had made a deal with Taft to stop Dewey.[34] The New York governor, casting himself as the front-runner, was taking a silent approach and withholding a program. In April, Wisconsin's primary brought victory for Stassen, ending the boomlet for MacArthur who had been supported by the *Milwaukee Sentinel* and the *Chicago Tribune*. The latter was being published by varitype because of a Typographical Union strike, and was giving him a substantial share of its scarce white paper, though it had "not gone overboard like Hearst," Doris said. "The appearance of anti-MacArthur veterans clubs revealed the controversial nature of the General's candidacy; they had adopted the slogan "Don't let MacArthur occupy America."[35]

Briefly, the bandwagon rolled for the "young 6-foot-3 interloper from Minnesota." Stassen had been elected to three terms as Governor of Minnesota, resigning early in the third to serve in the Navy during the war, and had been a delegate to the San Francisco conference which founded the United Nations. Doris found Ohio "flirting giddily" with Stassen, the moderate who offered a chance to vote against the author of the Taft-Hartley Act. "He is confident and clear; disarmingly ready to handle any topic," she noted. "He is unquestionably internationalist; domestically, a moderate progressive. Actually he says little that could startle any Republican to the left of Colonel McCormick in these matters." She described Stassen as attractive to women, a "young Lochinvar out of the West."[36]

In Philadelphia in June, Republicans nominated Dewey on the third ballot after Stassen refused to release his delegates to Taft. Delegates were confident they were heading toward the finish line—"there was never anything but a feeling of victory in the air," David McCullough observed.[37] Clare Boothe Luce drew cheers when she appeared and declared Truman a "gone goose," and later in Omaha generated a flurry of headlines when she suggested that Eleanor Roosevelt would be Truman's running mate. Doris characterized the statement as "entirely unrealistic . . . possible only to one who, like Mrs. Luce, is not in Mrs. Roosevelt's confidence." The former First Lady, she related, had just refused urgings by Mrs. India Edwards, head of the Democratic women's division, to make at least one appearance at the coming convention. Although Mrs. Roosevelt rarely refused party chores, she had done so now because of "present turbulent developments." Three of her four sons, in fact, were active in the effort to dump Truman—Elliott and Franklin Jr. openly pro-Eisenhower, and James sparking the effort to substitute Eisenhower or Justice William Douglas. Wrote Doris: "At a secret White House meeting Wednesday to canvass the vice presidency, attended by Mr. Truman, his staff, Leslie Biffle, FSA administrator Ewing, Interior Undersecretary Chapman and National Chairman McGrath, Mrs. Roosevelt's name was not mentioned."

Another view was presented by Joseph P. Lash who said that

several correspondents cautioned Eleanor that Republicans wanted her on the Democratic ticket in order to raise the issue of Yalta, and with it a hint of Communist appeasement.[38] Eleanor, in fact, enjoyed friendly personal relations with Truman; she thought he had refrained from the wisecracks of some of his circle with considerable dignity. Following FDR's death, Bess Truman had intervened decisively when told that a Truman assistant was rushing Eleanor's stenographers to leave the White House. Truman agreed with his wife and insisted upon sending a stenographer to Hyde Park to help Mrs. Roosevelt with her accretion of mail. "As for Mrs. Luce," Doris wrote, "she is not friendly with Mrs. Roosevelt and has frequently made her the victim of one of the sharpest tongues in politics."[39]

Eleanor wrote Doris:

> Dear Doris:
> Edith Helm sent us your column about my "nomination" by Mrs. Luce. I think it is fine and you stated my position very clearly.
> I do not think we have yet reached a point where the electorate is ready for a woman Vice President who might possibly become President.
> Many thanks for all you say about me.[40]

As Republicans convened in Philadelphia, the Berlin crisis erupted on June 24. Four days later Truman responded to the Russian blockade with the order of a massive airlift. The dangerous situation in Germany was a backdrop for the opening of the Democratic convention, in the same hall in Philadelphia, on July 12. With Eisenhower and Douglas rejecting overtures, the Truman bandwagon now rolled on "with hardly a jolt," said The Associated Press. Truman made an overnight trip to Philadelphia to accept the nomination on the first ballot.

The epic rail campaign of the 1948 election had been under way, with brief time-outs, since June 3. Truman launched the second phase of the whistle-stop (a phrase coined during the campaign) on

September 6. Crowds began calling, "Pour it on, Harry . . . Give 'em hell, Harry." He had organized the Berlin Airlift and called Congress into special session to deal with his initiatives. Reporters in the Capital had options of traveling with the President, covering Congress or taking a special Air Force flight to Germany to observe the Airlift.

Doris left on September 11 for Furstenfeldbruck Air Base near Munich, and on the 12th accompanied a shipment of coal into Berlin. She toured the city the next day, and on the next flew back to the American zone for a conference with Lieutenant General Curtis Le May. On the 15th she began the twenty-seven-hour flight back to the United States, continuing to Denver to join the Dewey campaign train.[41]

Ninety-two reporters were aboard the "Dewey Victory Special" when it left Albany—ninety eight, when it reached California—nearly twice the number traveling with the President. They were accommodated "with a skill and efficiency unknown on the Truman train," according to McCullough. Reporters on it had to scramble for food and their own lodging, in case of an overnight stop, and to climb down off the train and run to the rear if there were a platform speech. In contrast, the Dewey train was "operation precision."[42]

Paul F. Ewing of *The Oregonian*, talking with Doris upon her arrival in Portland, wrote: "If a chic little columnist who smiles habitually and effortlessly can be pardoned the expression, it's a heck of a fate that deposited her aboard the Thomas E. Dewey campaign train. No one aboard the train ever makes a mistake, Miss Fleeson pointed out. The first one who does will be a hero to the accompanying press representatives, who might even forget newspaper ethics and go so far as to buy said politician a drink." It was much more fun on Roosevelt's train, she told Ewing, because FDR couldn't remember names and was admittedly inefficient; and the Willkie special had been a shambles "multiplied by six."[43]

Doris wrote of Frances Dewey: "She is invariably poised, gentle and smiling. She is extremely pretty and carefully costumed. Her slip never shows and when she received a reporter who was a personal acquaintance she kept her hat on. . . . She has yet to open her mouth in public or to discuss any question beyond her personal role as the wife of the candidate."[44]

Newsweek magazine had begun a poll of fifty political writers, and on October 11 published the result—unanimous prediction of a Dewey victory. The list included Marquis Childs, Roscoe Drummond, Frank Kent, Arthur Krock, Ernest K. Lindley, Raymond Moley, John O'Donnell and Mark Sullivan. The magazine had contacted a single woman—Esther Van Wagoner Tufty who wrote for newspapers in Michigan and New Jersey.[45] Truman reportedly dismissed the poll, telling Clark Clifford, "I know every one of these 50 fellows. There isn't one of them has enough sense to pound sand in a rat hole."[46]

Doris sensed Truman's confidence as she covered his appearances in Boston and New York in the final days of the campaign. "It appears to intimates that he now cherishes real hopes for victory," she reported. "They think this was not the case three months ago. The President gets a great deal of comfort out of recalling his last election to the Senate, in 1940. He had emerged victor from a tough 2-cornered primary but nobody, as he puts it, gave him a dog's chance to return to Washington. But he said then that he would go home and play the string out, he was the nominee and that was his duty. He won then; he thinks it can happen again."[47]

On election night, National Democratic Chairman J. Howard McGrath presided at a suite in the Hotel Biltmore in New York City. The head of the Secret Service and metropolitan policemen were at the Roosevelt Hotel, Republican headquarters, expecting a celebration. There had been rare unanimity in the press on election eve. *The New York Times, The Wall Street Journal, Time* and *Newsweek* declared Dewey the winner; Alistair Cooke, Walter Lippmann, Drew Pearson and Joseph and Stewart Alsop were in similar agreement.

As the long night wore on at the Biltmore, Doris mingled with party leaders, who one-by-one made their token appearances and departed. It was not until the early morning hours that the drama began to unfold, revealing the startling error of the forecasters, and not until 10:15 that Dewey conceded. Doris, still with the remnant band, was one of those who spoke personally with the President when he phoned from Independence. The great moment in history ("It shook the bones of all the smarties," Mencken said) was the subject of a memorable column. Doris wrote:

New York—Mr. Average Man was elected Tuesday by the average men and women of America as President of the United States.

The results were announced to a rank-and-file gathering here of Democratic workers on Wednesday morning in a scene unprecedented in American political annals.

National Chairman J. Howard McGrath sat quietly at his desk in a suite on the first floor of the Hotel Biltmore with Mrs. India Edwards, chairman of the women's division, at his elbow. Party notables, elder statesmen, political bosses, the men of note who have amassed fortunes and become household names of 16 years of Democratic rule, were absent.

They had believed with the poll-takers, the correspondents and political leaders everywhere that Harry S. Truman's cause was hopeless. They had not frequented the Biltmore headquarters during the crucial weeks of the campaign, they had not contributed funds, even those who made a politeness appearance during the late hours Tuesday, had gone home, already in their mouths the platitudes about the game little fellow who put up a great fight, which was, of course, hopeless.

By two o'clock in the morning a small group remained, almost exclusively the headquarters staff and a few personal friends of McGrath. Of all the fabulous New Deal, the only "big names" staying to play the string out were souvenirs of the Little Cabinet, Lawrence Wood Robert Jr., ex-assistant secretary of the treasury, and Louis Johnson of West Virginia, an ex-assistant secretary of war. No cabinet member, no diplomat, no angel eager for one reason or another to identify himself with a victor, no socialite, no Hollywood star, no ambitious brain truster—none of these ornaments of four Roosevelt victories showed.

There had never been a day since the campaign started when you could see three people in the headquarters corridors at one time. Nobody knew it better than the campaign workers; an almost cozy calm enveloped them as the early hurly-burly died away and they were left alone to take whatever news the final returns might bring.

There has probably never been a club so exclusive as the one which drew close to the young Rhode Island senator with the pleasant smile and the relaxed manner who bent an ear to the radio, made an agreeable comment on the snatches of press-association copy, chatted comfortably with leaders reporting by telephone from here, there and everywhere. Mrs. McGrath backstopped him with an equally pleasant smile and reposeful manner. Young David McGrath guarded the door with a New York city fireman; the head of the secret service and the relays of policemen were over at the Roosevelt, waiting upon, they figured, the president-elect.

It turned out of course that the club wasn't so exclusive as they thought; a majority of Americans seem to belong to it.

About 4 a.m. the tally sheet that Jimmy Sauter was so carefully keeping for McGrath showed 233 electoral votes for the president, 169 for Governor Dewey, 38 for Governor Thurmond. He pushed it over to McGrath. The chairman ringed California, Colorado, Illinois, Idaho, Nevada, Ohio, Washington, Wyoming. "We're still fighting," he said calmly. They bent their heads over the certainties, the doubtful states, discussing what was really safe.

By 7:30, New York was gone forever but the Truman tally showed 245 and Ohio was apparently crucial.

"How in hell did he do it, Howard?" asked a wondering voice.

"Labor, farmers, housewives, the poor campaign Dewey made, the appeal of Truman's courage," McGrath answered succinctly.

The magnitude of President Truman's singlehanded accomplishment was by that time clear. It awed the little circle. Chip Robert rushed a note over to McGrath as the radio blared the news that Democrats would control the senate, the house. It read: "And he did it without the States Righters, the Wallace party, without New York, Pennsylvania, California." McGrath smiled. The tension lessened. Whatever the final result this was a historic occasion. The Democrats have a way of sticking to their own; most of the staff had been there through the good years; they were still happy to be there.

Very quietly, the small chat, the busy pencils, the radio bulletins, the news flashes, ate the hours as the cool Manhattan dawn crept through the windows. Coffee was served; someone passed out tablets guaranteed to keep you awake until the final answer came. There were no late-comers; the news was apparently still untrue to the world at large.

At 9:40 a.m. McGrath lifted the receiver and thanked the secretary of state of Ohio for calling him. While a tense secretary made notes he repeated: "9,360 precincts out of 9,710 show Truman 1,403,000, Dewey 1,390,000. And the precincts to come are from Democratic districts: Thank you for calling me, Mr. Kelly."

Without raising his voice, he said: "That's Ohio. We're going to be all right. We've got 270, maybe more."

The chairman turned back to his tally sheet. The small talk went on. Press Director Jack Redding suggested maybe he ought to draft a statement. "Take your time," McGrath said with a wintry smile. "Mr. Dewey will take his before he concedes."

But the press and radio began swiftly to amass the final proof. Chip Robert disappeared for a few minutes and then the waiters began to wheel in a table full of goblets, cases of champagne. At the exact moment that the corks began to pop, the telephone rang.

"Thanks, Clark," McGrath said. "No, I don't deserve what you say but I appreciate it. Where is the boss? Okay, I'll call him."

But before McGrath could himself call, the familiar cornbelt baritone echoed over the wire from Kansas City. McGrath's voice rose as the room hushed.

"Nobody ever deserved to win like you did, Mr. President," he said. "The President!" echoed the crowd. And in swift contagion, glasses of champagne and cheers were raised.

"Your staff is drinking to you, Mr. President," cried McGrath, "from the bottom of our hearts we drink to you!"

"And to the chairman!" cried many voices, and new cheers echoed over the wire to the President.

"Here's India," said McGrath, putting his arm affectionately around Mrs. Edwards. "She wants to congratulate you."

Mrs. Edwards is a former newspaperwoman who deserted a lifetime of security as woman's editor of The Chicago Tribune to enlist under the Roosevelt banner after her only son had been killed in the war. She knows exactly what she is fighting for and she has made quail many a strong man who sometimes forgot it.

But tears choked her as she tried to tell the President: "The best man won, the best man won! Congratulations and kiss Mrs. Truman and Margaret for me."

"Sissy," McGrath taunted her and the president's answering roar of laughter echoed across the desk.

As he put down the receiver, McGrath raised his

glass again and embraced the room in a gesture of paternal affection. "To each and every one of you," he said clearly. "Without your individual contribution, it couldn't have been done."

Everybody knew who did it, though—they had just drunk to him in an uprush of fidelity and admiration few men enjoy in their lifetime.[48]

20

OUR DORIS

The evening was for the younger set, a dance in Sterling's Masonic Hall to honor the visit of seventeen-year-old Doris O'Donnell of St. Catherine's School in Richmond, Virginia. She was a beautiful debutante, honored at a coming-out party planned by aunts Gertrude Fleeson of Lyons and Eva Lynn Fleeson of Sterling. One hundred twenty-five teens from Lyons and Sterling High were invited to the event of June 30, 1949.

Doris, a June graduate of St. Catherine's, accepted for enrollment in the fall at Vassar, was honored at a luncheon in the Victorian home of Aunt Ida Tebbe.[1] She and her mother were touring the Midwest—"a trip to my native state for my child," Doris had written Eleanor Roosevelt. She was attending a Democratic farm state meeting and the Governors Conference in Colorado. "I am getting a kick from the fact that my sisters-in-law are giving a dance for her at the Masonic Temple in Sterling," Doris wrote Eleanor. "That's where my father wore his white plumes as a Knight Templar and yours truly waited table at the oyster suppers given by the Congregational Ladies Aid Society. . . . My story is that Mark Childs can give his daughter's debut at the Carlton. My daughter is coming out at the Masonic Temple in Sterling where her family really belongs!"[2] In truth, Doris derided her hometown from an Easterner's viewpoint, searching the weekly *Bulletin* for examples of provincialism with which to entertain Mencken.

Doris Jr. actually made her debut the next year at a dance at the 1925 F Street club in Washington.[3] In this she was more cooperative than

Eleanor's daughter Anna had been twenty-five years earlier when, by her account, her mother made her go through tennis week at Newport. Anna had not wanted to attend Miss Chapin's school and she hated the Newport ritual. "She didn't help me a bit," she wrote of her mother.[4] Bob Fleeson, one of the young Fleesons transplanted from Kansas to Eastern schools, has little nostalgia for the debutante events. "Every girl who went to Brearley's had one," he recalls. "I went to a bunch of these when I was at Yale. They were desperate for escorts. They were the most absurd things I ever went to."

Neither mother, apparently, recognized the contradiction. Eleanor and Doris, so liberated and egalitarian in the public's mind, favored anachronistic Eastern Seaboard customs for their daughters. In correspondence, dwelling on the world's problems, they might turn to a discussion of their maternal roles. Eleanor was solicitous of little Doris; she had an empathy for the lonely child, as demonstrated in her care of Diana Hopkins, in her maternal response to student Joseph Lash, and in her relationship with trooper-bodyguard Earl Miller. But viewed by detractors, this was posturing in the extreme, and ironically her harshest critics were her own children, according to historian Peter Collier. Her sons saw "Eleanor's search for protégés as an attempt on her part to make up for the botched motherhood that had had such disastrous consequences for them."[5]

Doris had openly solicited Eleanor's influence in little Doris' application to Vassar. Eleanor invited both to spend the night of March 25, 1949, in New York[6] as they traveled to Poughkeepsie for an appointment at the school.[7]

Following the visit, Doris wrote: "Did I ask you please to write a kind word for us to Vassar? Of course Doris' record will be the most powerful factor but we know that having your good opinion is a powerful recommendation too."[8] Doris knew when to be pragmatic, and the request could hardly have acknowledged "power" more openly. Once in her column she observed that "Washington is a place where results only are applauded."[9] Helen Fleeson recalled an incident that illustrated that way of life. Helen, after graduating from college and working for the hospital administrator in her hometown in Kansas, had decided to apply for the Peace Corps. She also had decided not to give her prominent aunt's name as a reference. When Doris learned of the fact she upbraided Helen for being "so Kansan."

Eleanor promptly sent a letter to Vassar: "I have known Doris and her mother for 16 years and feel sure if she is accepted she will be a completely satisfactory student."[10]

In contrast to breezy jottings to Mencken, Doris' letters to Eleanor were more circumspect, reflecting the arcane and Victorian style of Eleanor's own correspondence. Did the messages mean what they might today? Seemingly nothing has been more frustrating to Roosevelt scholars than passages of intimacy and affection in the letters. In August of 1949 Doris had reported her daughter's acceptance by Vassar and had accepted Eleanor's invitation to come to Hyde Park on the weekend Doris Jr. would begin school. She wrote on August 7: "Doris and I deeply appreciate your invitation to her. . . . I would like to see you during the next week. Would Tuesday be allright? I would not spend the night but would make it at your convenience during the day. I just want to see you, that's all."[11]

In her column datelined Hyde Park, Eleanor wrote:

> Doris Fleeson, Washington columnist, spent the day on her way from Nantucket back to Washington. I am always happy to see her because one expects journalists and war correspondents to lose some of their enthusiasm and convictions. Doris always feels strongly and bolsters my feeling that it is worth fighting for the things one believes in. This is something all of us at times get a little weary of doing.[12]

Eighty-year-old Bernard Baruch, a mutual friend of Doris and Eleanor, was one of "a most surprising assortment of friends" who proposed to Eleanor when she was widowed, according to biographer Cook. He had defended her against cruel remarks since the first days of the New Deal, and was often her escort. Beyond Eleanor, Baruch's "strong need for feminine companionship" (his official biographer's phrase)[13] created perpetual rumors. Doris and Inez Robb were among women Baruch befriended. "You are a gallant girl and I love you very much—Inez is tops also," he wrote Doris.[14]

Bernard Baruch was "the only man who came to dinner." As guest-of-honor in Doris' home in 1950, he is surrounded by co-hostesses Inez Robb and Doris (at left and right on the floor) and (clockwise) as identified in the Washington *Evening Star*, Mrs. Charles Pepper, wife of the Florida Senator; Mrs. May Craig, Maine newspapers; Miss Elizabeth Novarro of New York; Mrs. Blake O'Connor, Washington; Mrs. Irene Ibbitson, Toronto artist; Mrs. Brien McMahon, wife of the Connecticut Senator, Senator Margaret Chase Smith, Republican of Maine; and Christine Sadler Coe, *McCall's* magazine. (University Archives, Spencer Research Library, University of Kansas Libraries)

As a tribute to the elder statesman, they planned a dinner at which he would be the only man present. Guests in evening gowns and Baruch in white tie gathered in Doris' P Street home on January 27, 1950.

Listed in *The Washington Star* account were Mrs. Claude Pepper, wife of the Florida Senator; Mrs. May Craig, Maine newspapers; Miss Elizabeth Novarro, New York; Mrs. Blake O'Connor, Washington; Mrs. Irene Ibbitson, Toronto artist; Mrs. Brien McMahon, wife of the Connecticut Senator; Senator Margaret Chase Smith, Republican, of Maine; and Christine Sadler Coe, *McCall's* Magazine. Inez Robb toasted Baruch: "As wise as he is good. . . . tall, handsome and completely solvent."[15] From his apartment at 4 East 66th Street, Baruch wrote the next day to express his thanks, signing the letter "Affly Bernie."[16]

"I am sure Mr. BMB enjoyed his party," wrote Eleanor.[17] Baruch also proposed a reciprocal engagement: "I have in mind when the flowers are in bloom at Hobcaw to charter a plane to bring the girls at your dinner party if they would come some Friday afternoon say 3 oclock from W. and take them back on Sunday late or Monday early."[18]

In March some of the same women attended a dinner at the Carlton Hotel as guests of Dan Kimball, the fun-loving Under Secretary of the Navy with whom Doris had become acquainted. The event took place a few days before the annual male-only gathering of the White House Correspondents' Association. Kimball hosted forty women journalists at a First Annual Dinner of the Foundation for the Elimination of Preferential Classifications, coincidentally on his fifty-fourth birthday anniversary. Liz Carpenter, one of the guests, remembered that the women brought neckties as gifts. *The Washington Post* pictured the host as he blew out candles of a cake, flanked by Ruth Montgomery of *The New York Daily News* and May Craig.[19]

Earlier, as the guests arrived, May and Doris had waited in the hotel lobby for Alice A. Dunnigan, lone black woman in the WHCA, for there was still segregation in downtown hotels and they were uneasy until the journalist was seated.[20]

Bob Fleeson remembers Washington of that time as "almost a provincial capital." A student at Kent, away from his home in Kansas, he spent three-week spring breaks at the house on P Street. "For me, going to see Doris was always a vacation," he recalls. "Doris just assumed that you were grown up and could take care of yourself. She was always busy, but once in awhile I would meet her for lunch—once with Margaret Chase Smith. She always had passes to the Senate and House, or for special tours of the Justice Department. You could get on a streetcar at Washington Station and go right to her house."

The house, to Bob, seemed quite small. "She would come home most afternoons about 4:00," he remembers. "From 4 until 5:30 she wrote. At 6:00 a Western Union man rang the doorbell. Once that was done she was free."

Doris usually entertained at the F Street Club, but Bob remembers an occasion on which Alben Barkley was a guest on P Street. When the Vice President left the house, a red MG was parked at the curb. "I think I'll take that one," he said, getting in under the wheel, before eventually departing in his chauffeured limousine.

As had his brother Dick, Bob helped out at Tex O'Connor's antique and decorating shop, and was useful in other ways, as he recalls: "I can remember my senior year at Kent I'd come down for spring vacation. Doris was graduating at Vassar. Doris got some friend's Cadillac—it was a great, huge ark of a car. I'd never driven before in the East. It's something my own parents would never have let me do." The seventeen-year-old drove to Poughkeepsie, loaded the car with Little Doris' belongings, and returned to the capital.

On April 11 Truman dramatically dismissed General MacArthur from his Far East post. He had been silent for weeks as the General flouted his policies and humiliated him—a restraint so novel that columns were filled with speculation. Journalists felt that the key was MacArthur's secondary role as Supreme Commander of the Allied Forces. In this Russia had a vote in choosing his successor. Doris wrote on April 12:

> Mr. Truman became convinced that Gen. MacArthur had to go after the March incident of the MacArthur truce offer to the Chinese Reds which jumped the gun on the President and belittled Presidential authority in plain view of our allies. The President then had some hope of riding along with him, no matter how trying he became, until the

Japanese peace treaty was signed and the occupation could be ended. While this hope was disintegrating the General's letter to Minority Leader Martin was published. It indorsed a suggestion directly contrary to the President's policy, that Chiang's troops be brought into the war.

It was the end. . . .[21]

Had MacArthur forced his recall by studied defiance of the administration? The White House saw the general as prone to a martyr complex and believed so, Doris observed. Fortuitously the general's farewell speech at the Capitol coincided with the annual convention of the American Society of Newspaper Editors. "It so happened that the nation's editors got a revealing glimpse of Douglas MacArthur, the septuagenarian who hoards his strength for major appearances and lets others adjust their routines to his," Doris related. The general was to have dropped in on the editors following his speech. Truman had cancelled his own engagement with the editors to avoid a conflict. "But the general found the long afternoon nap of his Tokyo schedule an imperative so compelling, the editors had to sit and wait for him until well beyond the dinner hour."[22]

In an overview of the job being done by fifteen hundred Washington correspondents, *Time* magazine in 1951 cited as the most telling criticism the charge that many "newsmen" were hiding behind a cloak of objectivity, merely reporting the who, what, when and where. "They leave the much harder and more important job of telling the 'why' to a small, hard core within the corps," said the *Time* article, which included comments from a few of the journalists themselves. "There's too little reporting, too much thumb-sucking in this town," it quoted Doris, identifying her as "the capital's top woman reporter." In a sidebar, *Time* profiled thirteen leading members of the Washington corps. Listed were Arthur Krock, James "Scotty" Reston, Paul Leach (*Chicago Daily News*), Joseph and Stewart Alsop, Raymond "Pete" Brandt (*St. Louis Post-Dispatch*), Bert Andrews (*New York Herald Tribune*), Walter Lippmann, Paul Ward and Mark Watson (*Baltimore Sun*), Edward T.

Folliard (*Washington Post*), Drew Pearson and Doris Fleeson.

Of Doris *Time* wrote:

> Columnist Doris Fleeson, fortyish, witty and lively, learned the columning trade while teamed up with ex-husband John O'Donnell of the New York Daily News, now goes it alone in 72 papers. Her "interpretive articles," as she calls them, make informative reading, thanks to her well-used pipelines to congressional offices and the Democratic National Committee. She attends no off-the-record conferences, yet frequently knows what the Administration is up to before many of its brasshats."[23]

Accompanied by Eleanor Roosevelt, Doris received a distinguished service award from the Auxiliary of the Veterans of Foreign Wars on August 29 during the national encampment in New York City. With plans for an imminent departure for Europe, she stayed that evening in Eleanor's spare room in the Park Sheraton Hotel.[24] She and new Secretary of the Navy Kimball had resolved a difficult matter.

Kimball, like Doris' brother Howard, was a Midwestern youth who had become an aviator in World War I. Having dropped out of high school in St. Louis in his second year to work at an electric automobile garage, he enlisted in the Army Air Force in 1917, serving in a squadron in which he and Jimmy Doolittle were commissioned second lieutenants on the same day. After the war Kimball became a salesman for General Tire and Rubber Company in California and signed up with the International Correspondence School for a course in electrical engineering. Within a few years he was General Tire's sales manager for eleven Western states. He came to Washington in November 1941 as the company's vice president. "Everybody knew by that time we were going to get into the war," he later observed.

Kimball saw an opportunity for the company to pioneer in the manufacture of rockets and guided missiles. The result was Aerojet Engineering Corporation, a subsidiary of General Tire founded at Azusa,

California, a few weeks after Pearl Harbor. It began to develop JATO—the jet-assisted takeoff rockets that helped bombers become airborne off short runways.

In and out of Washington during the war, Kimball became a colorful figure known for his fun-loving nature and his ability to get along with people. John L. Sullivan, Assistant Treasury Secretary and later Under Secretary of the Navy, persuaded him to enter government service in 1949. He was appointed Assistant Secretary of the Navy for Air in March 1949, and became Under Secretary two months later. Colleagues were impressed with his ability to handle a sizable workload. With his six-foot-three, 212-pound frame, and his trademark Hawaiian sport shirts, he had high visibility on the Washington scene. He was often on Burning Tree golf course or cruising on the presidential yacht. He enjoyed taking over the controls of a government plane when he traveled on official business. Truman liked Kimball for his earthy language and direct approach.[25]

Doris first met Kimball as a news source. By the time he was named Secretary of the Navy in August 1951, they were linked romantically as a not-too-secret couple. Raymond P. Brandt, writing of the new Secretary, divulged:

> While Kimball thought his job in Washington was temporary, Mrs. Kimball, to whom he was married in 1925, kept their home in Los Angeles. She has moved to Washington. The Kimballs have no children. She was Dorothy Ames of Chicago.

Doris and Dan almost met at the Hotel Excelsior in Naples in early September while he was on an official trip, but apparently had second thoughts. Dan wrote:

> Darling
> Here I am all anxious to write a letter & this is the best paper I can find (a telegramma).

Arrived last night at 6 after a nice trip . . & proceeded as usual to get a little tight with the fleet Carney Gardner et al. . . . . the hotel is lovely overlooking the bay & the beautiful fleet which is in the harbor.

I find now that I made a big mistake. You should have been with me.

More news when I have some to report.

Always,

Love

Dan[26]

Arrangements had been made for Naval Air Transportation for Doris from Paris to Naples on September 1 to interview Admiral Carney. The date, however, was changed to September 5,[27] after which she remained in Europe for other news contacts. Dan had received a letter from Wiesbaden when he wrote from the Pentagon on September 9 on the Secretary's letterhead:

Darling

Arrived here last night from Cin & was much too lonesome. Tried to phone you and you are not in Rome. . . .

Wash is dull—you're not here. . . .

Almost as much as you I have missed your columns on the coast.[28]

The rise of McCarthyism troubled Doris, and it is thought that she coined the term itself in her column of June 15, 1951, expressing dismay at the Senator's sixty thousand-word indictment of General George Marshall, which she called "a new manifestation of McCarthyism." She had earlier deplored use of FBI loyalty checks as a weapon: "Such checks are made on thousands of people here, routinely. They include all manner of hearsay evidence inadmissible in a court of law."[29]

In October 1951, columnist Joseph Alsop made an unusual appearance before the Senate internal security subcommittee chaired by Patrick McCarran. Louis Budenz, a former Communist editor, had testified that former Vice President Henry Wallace's 1944 mission to China "carried out a Communist objective toward which Mr. Wallace was guided by John Carter Vincent, who was a member of the Communist party." Vincent, a career officer of the State Department and a China expert, had accompanied Wallace on the China mission. Alsop came before the panel with "masses of documentation" to show that Wallace's main recommendation called for the replacement of the "pro-Red General Stilwell with the anti-Red General Wedemeyer." This was done and constituted, he said, "the heaviest blow that could have been struck at the Reds at that time." Vincent not only concurred in the Wallace recommendation but urged it on him, he testified. Alsop had been in China in 1944 as staff aide to General Claire Chennault.

For injecting himself into the painful controversy during the "present public temper," Alsop could reap little profit from headlines, Doris observed. "The whole newspaper tradition dictates anonymity for its own. The Alsop background is conservative, it includes the Republican Roosevelts. Allsop's compelling motive, of course, was the service of truth. . . . Alsop and his counsel, Ganson Purcell, have shown at the expense of their own time, money and energy, how an objective test can be made of the serious charges now hurled about so nonchalantly."[30]

Alsop wrote on October 22:

> How can I possibly thank you adequately for your column on the McCarran hearing? It touched me very deeply, and I shall always remember it with utmost pride and gratitude.[31]

Truman had been answering "no comment" to the subject of McCarthy at press conferences, though obviously enraged. At this point, his friends, the "cronies" on which Doris had directed her criticism, were under scrutiny in the investigation of the Reconstruction Finance Corporation. When in October Truman said of the solicitors for funds for a Truman library that they were dear friends, but that sometimes friends were overzealous, "the press restrained itself with some difficulty from an amen," according to Doris.[32] She had remarked before of his loyalty to friends who diminished his stature. The scandal symbolized by deep freezes and mink coats had become full-blown by December when Doris quoted the philosopher Hobbes describing hell as "the truth seen too late," and suggested that Truman, "one of the most history-minded of United States Presidents," was in a position to appreciate the definition. "Mr. Truman has felt that in laying the groundwork for a peaceful world, he was securing his place in history. He was calmly confident that it would be a great deal higher than his contemporaries admit; indeed that in Valhalla he would not need to bow to his brilliant predecessor," she wrote in her column of December 12.[33]

The Truman temper was rising at the press conference at which the President addressed his critics the next day. No, he was not going to fire Frank McKinney, chairman of the Democratic National Committee, who had come under fire for profiting in a stock transaction. He discussed the Korean truce talks, then put the subject off the record in the presence of reporters for Tass and the Communist *Daily Worker*. He had just said that his administration always had taken drastic action against wrongdoers in the government, when he paused and looked at Doris. What, he asked, was she looking at him like that for? Maybe, he declared, she had "one of those sob stories of hers" in mind, and he didn't think any sob stories were needed.

The Associated Press gave the incident a ride,[34] prompting the Portland *Oregonian* to protest, under a headline "Nasty Cut at Our Doris." For a president to single out a correspondent for a personal attack was so unusual that *The Oregonian* could recall only one other example—Roosevelt's sending an Iron Cross to John O'Donnell "in a fit of pique."

"But we positively do protest the pettish action of the president in singling out our Doris—the columnist, Miss Fleeson—as a victim of his peevishness," The *Oregonian* declared. "As those who follow her column in this newspaper know, Doris Fleeson is a top reporter. She works close to the news, avoids retreat into the think tank, and writes with clarity and economy. . . . One thing she is not is a sob sister. . . ."[35]

Doris jokingly said that she was wearing a new hat and that Truman must not have liked her hat. The hat incident could only enhance her reputation for holding her own with men. One day Frank Waldrop, editor of the *Washington Times Herald*, fell into a trap as panelists on the Georgetown University Radio Forum discussed a speech Eisenhower had given before bankers in St. Louis. "The way you describe it," Waldrop told Doris, "I would be a little at a loss to say yes, but I did not read the speech because I did not pay much attention to what he was saying." Waldrop received a sobering observation from Doris: "It is on page one of your newspaper." Frank Blair had a lively time moderating the dialogue, a combination of lecture by Dr. James Leahigh, Georgetown's chairman of political science, and fast-paced commentary by journalists. From Eisenhower the discussion turned to the question of whether Truman would run. "I am not in the President's confidence," Doris said. "He doesn't even like my hats."[36]

Dressed to meet a Duchess: Doris with Wallis Warfield Windsor. (University Archives, Spencer Research Library, University of Kansas Libraries)

Events of the previous few days had eliminated much uncertainty about Eisenhower's intention. In a letter dated January 1 he had told Truman he would not run. Five days later Henry Cabot Lodge announced the formation of the Eisenhower-for-President campaign. The next day Eisenhower disclosed that he would be prepared to accept the Republican nomination. He had been president of Columbia University from 1948 until 1950, and then Supreme Commander for the North Atlantic Treaty Organization. Still, *The Wall Street Journal* insisted that Eisenhower, based on its correspondent's inquiries in Paris, would prefer to return to his Pennsylvania farm. It was a tenet of Doris' conviction, after years of political coverage, that the presidency "goes to men who prize it." The Eisenhower situation presented a unique example of one who might not have such a burning desire. "If Ike and Mamie Eisenhower prefer to return to their farm at Gettysburg next door to George and Mary Allen and play canasta, they should be allowed to do so," she wrote.[37]

The next move was Truman's. Democrats suggested that Adlai Stevenson, governor of Illinois, would attend the Jefferson-Jackson Day dinner "ready to catch the crumbs which may fall from President Truman's table."[38] On March 30, as they paraded to the dais, Truman told Vice President Barkley, Speaker Rayburn, National Chairman McKinney and National Vice Chairman India Edwards that he would make an important announcement at the end of his speech. All expected him to say that he would be a candidate for re-election. "So surprised were they when he didn't, they sat frozen almost into immobility for a few seconds," Doris reported. He had, in one stroke, robbed the opposition of its principal emotional impetus, the anti-Truman drive. Stevenson would wait until after the Illinois primary to declare himself, and he might wait too long. Being an intellectual, he would see all sides too clearly and weigh all possibilities too carefully, Doris believed.[39]

The Washington Star splashed an eight-column banner across the top of Page One: "General Eisenhower Submits Resignation." The story, under Doris' byline, reported that the resignation "is at the White House." Capital newsmen had been "nibbling at the story," *Time* magazine noted, but none had said "straight out that it was on the President's desk. The

Star's confidence in Doris Fleeson's sources was not misplaced. Next day the White House confirmed the news."[40]

Stevenson, rather than temporizing as Doris had predicted, announced in April that he would not be a candidate. In this intriguing year a new stallion might be brought from the darkest corner of the stable, in Doris' phrase, perhaps "a truly ebony steed." A sense of urgency was apparent among Eisenhower backers, anxious for the General to return home to finally square off with Senator Robert Taft. But there was a thought that pre-convention enthusiasm might have insulated him from the harsh realities of politics. "It may be a blow to the General who has been told so much and so often about the great public demand for him to learn that he actually is in a bitter neck-and-neck struggle for the nomination," Doris observed.[41] Truman, on the other hand, was having a wonderful time. In his own party, politicians who would have "gladly ditched him" in 1948 could find no acceptable candidate. The split in the Republican party was music to his ears.[42]

The Eisenhowers returned on June 1, stepping down briskly from their plane, Mamie conveying the sense of a relaxed and joyful home comer. The General was plainly a man with a lot on his mind, Doris wrote.[43] The next day she boarded a special train en route to Abilene, Kansas, for the cornerstone laying at the Eisenhower Foundation, where Eisenhower would begin his drive for the presidency. Correspondents generally felt they had come a long distance for "pallid fare," in the candidate's opening speech June 4. Doris pronounced it consisting chiefly of generalities. "Nor is the general an inspired orator," she wrote, "though a deep sincerity permeates his every platitude."[44]

Both parties had conventions scheduled in Chicago. A political drama loomed for Republicans as they convened July 8 amid a Taft-Eisenhower contest for Southern delegates, with Eisenhower backers driving for a rules change. Eisenhower's victory, after "a violent advertisement of party differences," represented a political shift as vivid as that Doris had covered twenty years earlier, awaiting the arrival of Franklin Roosevelt on a hot Chicago airfield. Its smoothest operation, in her view, was the promotion of Nixon by Dewey forces touting his "readily recognizable" assets. "Republicans also believe Senator Nixon will attract women voters in somewhat the same way Senator Kefauver obviously has," she observed. "Governor Dewey was able to testify of his own knowledge that various New York women influential in his party admire the Californian and say women generally will vote for him." But detractors were said to distrust Nixon as an expedient politician. "He is, they think, too clever," Doris wrote.[45]

The focus now turned to the Democrats. "It now looks as though Gov. Adlai Stevenson will be dragged protesting to the presidential altar by the Democrat Party. His shrieks are growing fainter. His suitor more importunate," Doris reported.[46] As for the old guard: "The best suites of the Chicago hotels are filled with these gentlemen. There has, however, been a noticeable lack of the bounce that characterizes Democratic conventions. This is because the numerous parties are taking on the aspect of wakes."[47]

It was the closest approach to a draft in modern times. Stevenson was a virtual unknown facing a national hero, but that had been his calculated risk in shedding Truman's mantle. Doris sensed Eisenhower's bond with the electorate as she traveled aboard his eighteen-car special, the biggest in history, that September. "The crowds are still immense, bigger than any since the halcyon days of Franklin Roosevelt," she related. "They are family crowds, many young people, fathers and mothers holding up their children to see the great man. It touches the general and his voice gets a little husky as he says 'Thank you. . . . this is really inspirational. . . . from you I gather strength to make this fight.'"[48]

If reporters were confounded by Truman (information had to be dug out of the White House with a bulldozer, they said), they were similarly perplexed by Eisenhower. The thirty-seven traveling aboard his special train rarely saw him; he never relaxed with them. They charged that he had dealt too long with military news and its protective cover of security. Doris complained that Eisenhower had not held a press conference for weeks, but increasingly substituted off-the-record visits with reporters. "This practice, in which all the advantage rests with the holder of the conference, has obvious dangers," she wrote. "Washington correspondents avoid it; many will not attend off-the-record conferences unless the circumstances are very unusual."[49]

In Los Angeles, having disembarked from the Eisenhower Special, Doris heard of an off-the-record train session at which she had not been present. Those who attended were sitting on the story, encumbered by their acquiescence. She, however, was under no such agreement, and her sources were impeccable (the journalists who had been there). In a column headlined "The Case of the Non Military Secret," she described the event as it unfolded: "Gen. Eisenhower sauntered into the press car of his train last Sunday, accepted a beer, replied in answer to questions that he was not then inclined to discuss his personal finances in public, suddenly put the entire visit off the record and retired to his private car."[50] Eisenhower had been pressed to make a financial statement since Stevenson's disclosure of his income tax returns. Soon his strategists said that it would be forthcoming.

Two "impulsive, bull-headed" men—Truman and Taft—were entering the campaign, and nominees could only hope that the crowds would not "unduly excite" the President and Senator, Doris wrote. "Meanwhile Democrats and Republicans alike will count that day gained whose cold descending sun sees not their own troops wounding their own party."[51] The quotation paraphrased was: "Count that day lost whose low descending sun, Views from thy hand no worthy action done" from Stanford's Art of Reading. Doris' readers with a literary bent could plan on going to Bartlett's now and then, especially with Truman's predicaments. As tax scandals had evoked the "truth seen too late," the spectacle of cronies called forth Richard III: "But thou too careless patient, That thou are submittest thy anointed body, To the care of these that made thee ill. . . ." Dick Fleeson recalled hearing that as a child Doris had memorized quotations with her sister Elizabeth, practicing as they washed and dried dishes, one beginning a passage and the other finishing it.

Truman reportedly had become disillusioned with Eisenhower while battling for his military budget in the spring. As Taft rallied forces for a deep cut, Truman awaited word from Eisenhower. The message from NATO headquarters was tepid and, Truman believed, politically motivated.[52] The President, now on his own whistle-stop for Stevenson, was drawing cries of "poor taste." "It is high drama when a President of the United States taunts a famed general to whom he once entrusted the greatest armies ever built," Doris observed. She was at that time traveling aboard the train in Montana.

In a parting shot at another national hero, Truman infuriated MacArthur with the allegation that politically inspired attacks on Korean policy were the cause of forty-seven thousand military desertions. The President gave the story exclusively to Doris as he prepared to leave the White House, and in fact read it before publication, noting on the copy: "Miss Fleeson: I've made some interpolations and suggestions—not to act as an editor but to make the facts clear. I hope you will accept the suggestions. In my opinion it is an excellent report. H.S.T."[53] The Associated Press saw the matter as a new peak in the feud between the Chief Executive and the General, provoking a blistering response from MacArthur, including the adjectives puerile, venomous and savage.[54]

"Could we lunch together on Thursday, January 8th?" wrote Eleanor Roosevelt. "I am going down just for a few hours to say good-bye to the President."[55] Cabinet members and others planned a private tribute for Truman on Inauguration Day, January 20. The day began with an awkward moment—a "shocking moment"—recounted in Truman biographies. The snub was public as the President-elect drove up to the front door of the White House. The staff waited to see if he would enter. Only when the Trumans emerged did Eisenhower get out of the car. After the ceremonies the Trumans, their entourage and two press station wagons departed for Georgetown. As Doris described the scene:

> At Seventh street, the little cavalcade turned north. Encountering a red light, Citizen Harry Truman stopped obediently. The almost empty side streets brought him quickly to the Revolutionary Georgetown home of his Secretary of State, Dean Acheson.
>
> Men and women, housewives and children, crowded

around the steps. They cheered as the Trumans entered the Acheson residence. . . .

The President came out and spoke to them. . . . "You know," he said, "I am just Mr. Truman, a citizen from Missouri." "No, no, no," the crowd called.

The crowd melted, exchanging news about the President's departure. They—and many more—were at Union Station a few hours later to wave him good-by. Refreshed from a nap at the apartment of his secretary, Matt Connelly, the President was gay and smiling. With Mrs. Truman and Margaret, he repeated his goodbys, shook hands with close friends.

He was still smiling, still waving, as the train pulled out of Union Station.[56]

Robert G. Nixon of International News Service was among those accompanying the Trumans to Independence. In an oral history interview for the Truman Library eighteen years later, he recalled:

It was emotional. I remember seeing Doris Fleeson, who was a lady columnist. She wasn't going out to Kansas City, so she was able to go back to the car in which Mr. Truman had his accommodations, and bid him good-by. She came out, streaming tears, weeping and crying."[57]

21

⚛ ⚛

FLOWER OF EVIL

According to his chosen biographer, nothing annoyed Bernard Baruch more than to be used as "bait" to lure others to a party. Once at a dinner in New York, he and friend Fleur Cowles found they had been invited on that pretext. After coffee, Baruch announced, "Fleur is going to take me home." In the elevator she chided him about getting old. "I want to go to the Stork Club," he replied. They did, and remained for three hours.[1]

If not at his Fifth Avenue apartment, the elder statesman in later years was likely to be at Saratoga Springs, or at Hobcaw Barony, his antebellum plantation. The estate was on the coast of his native South Carolina, where his Sephardic family had settled. It was from Hobcaw that Baruch wrote a letter to which biographer Margaret Coit referred in considering her subject's views on "feminine companionship." The letter thanked Doris for her gift of a volume on "women," adding an interesting personal view:

> Xmas 1952
> My dear Doris,
>   It has been my practice to try to have Xmas during the off season. Yet I find myself a bit ashamed when I receive such evidence of affection as your sending me the little volume on "women"—a subject that has intrigued me nearly eighty years but one to which I can find no solution as yet. Except this . . .

they are wonderful, alluring and ever different but so difficult to get and hold. A most beautiful and charming one told me once that the reason we had remained such constant friends was that I never tried to make love to her. It is seldom that I find friends amongst women—only friends—for I am so weak where beauty charm and figure are combined—I love you and could make love to you (if permitted) but our relations are very precious and understanding and they will remain so thru all the years. . . .

In order that there can (be) no breach of promise suit till you chuck all those 987 other suitors this is to say that nothing herein contained means other than that I love and admire you.

Affly

Bernie[2]

With its distinction as home of the world's finest school of journalism, founded in 1908, the University of Missouri established the Distinguished Service to Journalism award in 1930. Dean Earl English invited Doris to accept the award for 1953. "It is an invariable rule that this medal must be awarded in person," he wrote. Doris traveled to Columbia on May 1 to receive the honor and to address seven hundred fifty guests at the Journalism Banquet.[3]

She returned to Missouri on June 1, delivering the commencement address celebrating the centennial of Culver-Stockton College, which conferred an honorary degree. Harry Truman, in reply to her letter asking if she might call on him in Independence, wrote, "Of course, I'll be glad to see you if you will come by this way on your way back from Canton. Things are working out in a way that almost makes a prophet out of Stephenson and me. I'll talk to you about it when you come out."[4]

Doris found Truman in his office in the Federal Reserve Bank in Kansas City, Missouri, amid row upon row of filing cabinets, getting ready to write "the truth" about his life. The office did not seem to be a writer's sanctum; Truman did not appear to be going into seclusion, with his name on the door and his telephone number available from information. "Promptly at noon, too, he sets off down the hill, swinging his cane, for lunch with friends at the Muehlebach Grill," Doris wrote.[5]

Why did not Eisenhower and the Republicans speak out against Joseph McCarthy? The question became a theme of the Fleeson column in 1953. Doris reported an ugly incident at the Gridiron show (although it was still an all male event, she had pipelines), when McCarthy greeted Thomas E. Dewey with the "heavy-handed" suggestion that the Governor ought to come to Washington and be counsel for the McCarthy committee. "Mr. Dewey tartly replied that he was not coming to Washington until investigating committees stopped smearing innocent people so it would be possible to work here," she wrote. "Thoughtful Republicans in the White House and in Congress are shaking their heads. They don't like any part of it."[6]

McCarthy may have erred fatally, she proposed, when he underestimated Senator John R. McClellan, ranking Democrat on the committee. "If McCarthy had deliberately set out to pick on the colleague most allergic to bullying, he could not have done better than McClellan,"[7] she declared.

Eisenhower's speech to the American Society of Newspaper Editors had been several weeks in the making. With the death of Stalin, Eisenhower saw opportunity for a striking new move by the United States, and he called on the new Soviet leadership "to help turn the tide of history." It was Eisenhower at his best, Doris observed, although noting that much credit was due the White House speechwriters who had delivered the President's instincts from his involved prose. Similarly, she felt, he was displaying great courage and patience in the Korean peace negotiations.[8] Why, then, did he not speak out against McCarthy, after the Senator had impugned his nominee for Ambassador to the Soviet Union, Charles E. Bohlen? Eisenhower was on the brink of attacking the Senator when he delivered a "magnificent defense" of Bolen, Doris related. Those studying Eisenhower as a public figure had concluded that he felt the commander's role required conciliation. Eisenhower was known to have been critical of Truman's scrappiness. In contrast to Eisenhower, Doris noted, "Mr. Truman never backed away from a quarrel, he sometimes seemed to invite them and he always gave the impression of enjoying them. He could not see any one's bluff without calling him."[9]

Doris provided a light moment at the White House press conference of November 4, 1953, when she briskly raised the issue of the absence of women at White House dinners:

> Q. Mr. President, Doris Fleeson, Bell Syndicate. You have given about seven dinners at the White House for one hundred fifteen people, that have been described as dinners for the leaders of America. None of those one hundred fifteen guests has been a woman. How do you square that with your anti-discrimination policy?
>
> The President: I will tell you, Miss Fleeson, I tried to get two or three for dinner, and they have told me that I have to be very careful, because the women couldn't decide who should come. Now that's exactly what happened.
>
> Doris: Did women tell you that, or did men tell you that?
>
> The President: Yes, Exactly. Women. I wouldn't take a man's advice in such a thing.
>
> Doris: Were they women leaders of the Republican Party then?
>
> The President: Well, I don't think I will identify them.[10]

The exchange ended as laughter erupted in the male-dominated press corps, but it would not be the last of Doris' prodding on the subject. "A fact-hungry reporter usually emerges from an Eisenhower press conference feeling that he has been swimming under water for half an hour," she said.

A hometown does not always welcome a native, especially one who has gone on to fame, and a visit from Doris could leave relatives in a state of shock. "Doris was furious with her brothers that they were all Republicans, especially when Harry Truman ran against Dewey," Helen Fleeson recalled. "In 1952 or 1953 when she was against Eisenhower,

Howard did not want Doris' column in *The Wichita Eagle*." Family members recall incidents in which both Doris' sister-in-law Eva Lynn Fleeson of Sterling and her brother Dick Fleeson of Lyons felt that her behavior was outrageous.

One such incident occurred during a visit in November, 1953, when her brother and sister-in-law, Dick and Gertrude Fleeson, invited friends to a reception at their farm near Lyons. The reaction of the local residents was mixed. More than one thought Doris overbearing, according to Sterling editor Max Moxley. The high point came when a guest, Dorothy Dulles, left abruptly. Those inside could only watch as her car sped out of the drive—especially the friend who had come in her car. Mrs. Dulles, whose late husband was a first cousin of John Foster Dulles, apparently had had all she could take of Doris' criticism of the Secretary.[11]

At the peak of her career in 1952 Doris was cited by *Time* magazine as "the top news hen in Washington. (University Archives, Spencer Research Library, University of Kansas Libraries)

Doris arranged for presentation of Chi Omega sorority's National Achievement Award to Margaret Chase Smith, finding Eisenhower agreeable to presiding at a ceremony in the White House. There was a complication, however, in the attendance of Eleanor Roosevelt, previous winner. Eleanor wrote from Val-Kill Cottage, Hyde Park:

> I am horrified that you haven't my new telephone numbers and address. They are Hyde Park 2300 and in New York, TEmpleton 8-0330. The address of my new apartment in the city is 211 East 62nd Street, New York 21.
>
> My real reason for not coming down was not as much Margaret Smith for I realized she would probably not object but as it was held in the White House I felt it was not quite right to appear there when the President had never invited me to the White House. I had been told he had a special feeling of animosity against me because he thought that I had said Mrs. Eisenhower drank! Needless to say I did nothing of the kind but in Paris rumors were rife to this effect and I once asked Mrs. Mesta later in New York whether there was any truth in this rumor, knowing she is a great friend and had stayed there with them more than once. Under these circumstances I thought it wiser not to embarrass the President by appearing until he first invited me to the White House.[12]

Doris left the Bell Syndicate for United Features in 1954 as a replacement for liberal columnist Marquis Childs. There had been other honors following the recognition in Missouri: a distinguished alumni citation from the University of Kansas, and an invitation to deliver the main address for "newspaper week" at the University of Colorado. On April 17, 1954, she received the Raymond Clapper award for "exceptionally meritorious work during 1953."[13] The award was named for her fellow Kansan who had begun his career as a printer's devil, rising through the ranks from a reporting job on *The Kansas City Star* to manager of United Press in Washington. The popular Clapper was killed in a plane crash while covering the war in the Pacific in 1944.[14] Doris received $500 as the first woman honored by the award, still conferred annually, now with a prize of $10,000.

In the ferment of McCarthyism, Dean Acheson told editors meeting in Washington that he and his associates were victims of "this mad and vicious conspiracy," while members of the press were unwilling participants. Doris contended, however, that McCarthy was in part a creation of the press, that the first charges which brought him to the front pages were the product of dog days when legitimate news was scarce. Since erupting on the scene in 1950 he had manipulated the front pages, "almost at will, creating the conflicts which the news feeds upon."[15] Now Army Secretary Stevens was to be "keel-hauled" before television cameras for protesting that Army officers should not be abused and degraded in McCarthy's secret sessions.[16] Doris reported: "Secretary Stevens, fresh from a sheltered life in his family's textile business, was led like a lamb to the slaughter into a capitol hideaway for lunch with McCarthy. Vice President Nixon stood by in an adjacent office, presumably to stanch any telltale gore before it could trickle out on the waiting reporters."[17] A press conference on the Stevens case drew a record-breaking number of correspondents anticipating a climax, but it didn't arrive. "The President in mild tones read a statement so general that reporters hunting leads and headlines threw the first page away," Doris said.[18]

Televised live for one hundred eighty-seven hours, the Army-McCarthy hearings brought a dramatic confrontation on June 9 when Army counsel Joseph N. Welch assailed the Senator for a verbal attack on Frederick G. Fisher, a member of his law firm. Doris' column of June 10 drew widespread response. She wrote:

> The flower of evil which is McCarthyism bloomed in the Senate caucus room late Wednesday, rank and noxious, a fitting funeral blossom for the death of a republic.
> An angry man cut it down and plunged it deep into the

clear, cool waters of the New England conscience.[19]

Typical of the letters Doris received was a note from Georgetown resident Peggy Talbott:

> Dear Doris
>   I invariably read your articles with eager appreciation for you are the most lucid, brief, crystal clear writer in my humble opinion I know of. Today you surpassed even yourself. What you said was like a diamond writing on glass. I thank you for being so supremely articulate in so few words and for expressing what so many of us feel regarding this creature McCarthy's latest and most revolting action.

The letter was signed with a postscript: "Dont please answer this, just keep on writing!"[20] Voting unanimously, the Watkins committee recommended censure, effectively immobilizing McCarthy in the final weeks of the mid-term Congressional campaign. Yet Nixon carried the Communist issue into areas of the West and Midwest against Democratic Senate candidates, branding them "members of the left wing, ADA branch, of their party." Why, Doris wondered, did Eisenhower not act upon his recent statements that such charges should not be an issue in the campaign? Nixon was showing himself an intensely practical politician, "an unterrified partisan and a gambler of events and of his own future."[21]

In the past Doris had alluded to Republican Party women in mink stoles and orchids, wafting their way to the front of Landon meetings. But Eisenhower's dinner parties at the White House provoked a new sympathy. Press Secretary James Hagerty found himself fending off the criticism of women party leaders stirred by Doris' words. A column cited Eisenhower's dinner for various political associates, heralded as his first step toward reshaping the party into a progressive moderate force in 1956:

The President's failure to include any women in this important takeoff is not quite the kind of Christmas present Republican women feel they merit. The GOP has at present an excellent group of women leaders who made a substantial contribution toward General Eisenhower's victory.

They have still to be included in any of the President's long list of small dinners for his friends and associates.[22]

Hagerty soon heard from Bertha Diggs Warner, party worker in Brooklyn. "This same question of the top level recognition of women in Party affairs has worried me for some time," she wrote.[23] But Hagerty was dismissive: "It does not seem to me that recognition of top women in Party affairs is dependent on whether or not they are invited to a 'stag' dinner at the White House. . . . It was good to hear from you, Bertha. Keep up the good work."[24]

Renovation of the White House had given Truman the chance to shift the Presidential press conference from the intimacy of the oval office to the old State War and Navy Building across the street. Obviously, the larger space was needed, and in January 1955 Eisenhower presided at the first televised conference. He felt that the experiment went off well, and authorized Press Secretary Hagerty to release an edited version to public stations. Journalists were somewhat less enthusiastic, Doris observed: "It will be largely up to the reporters to furnish the excitement by their questions. Some of them are already grumbling that they are not actors, especially when they are not paid for acting."[25]

The month had been a confrontational one in the Washington press corps, since Clare Boothe Luce had caused an uncomfortable moment during a luncheon of the Women's National Press Club. Mrs. Luce, new Ambassador to Italy, had said as she looked over the mixed audience that she noticed that newspaperwomen didn't discriminate. The comment pleased Doris, May Craig and others who had never let up their protest of the National Press Club and its all-male policy. It had four thousand members, about nine hundred of whom were working journalists, and many of the rest lobbyists (lawyers). While they were privileged to attend luncheons addressed by world leaders, working women journalists were relegated to a balcony. (Pulitzer Prize-winning author Nan Robertson used the policy as a symbol of discrimination in her 1992 book *The Girls in the Balcony*.) Doris and her friends now were especially interested in the case of Louis Lautier, correspondent for the National Negro Press Association and the *Atlanta World*, seeking NPC membership. His application had survived a 6-4 vote of the board, but rules required a fifteen-day posting of his name, and "shot and shell are falling," Doris reported. She observed: "Newspaperwomen have long pointed out that lobbyists can hear the club's guests make their major pronouncements and reply to questions while newspaperwomen are sternly refused admittance, even when they promise not to eat but just to listen."[26]

Family members today are uncertain of the details of an accident in which Doris suffered injuries in April 1955. "I was terribly sorry to see you laid up and realized on looking at you what a lot you must have suffered," wrote Eleanor Roosevelt.[27] Doris mentioned the injuries when she wrote Harry Truman on May 25: "I am sorry I didn't see more of you on your visit last month but my sprained arms were really hurting We are looking forward to seeing the Trumans on TV Friday night."[28] Doris had not known Bess well when, early in the presidential years, she obtained an interview at the summer White House in Independence. The First Lady rarely granted such requests, but although answering Doris rather formally, she ended the note with "Best of luck to you on your article." The kindly thought revealed something of the woman whose image, especially in photographs, seemed to cast her as stiff and humorless. She became formal in public and froze in front of a camera, according to friends. Notes from Bess to Doris in the years following their return to Independence vividly contradicted the image. In her flowing hand Bess might refer to a mutual acquaintance: "Hear our gold plated friend is going Derbying. That gal certainly doesn't stay put for long." A frequent expression was "thanks loads and loads." On one occasion she wrote: "You surely were an angel to bring me that delicious Rose Marie but I must say in the same breath, you had no regard for the span of my waist line! (And it's getting spannier all the time.)"[29]

At noon on June 15 Eisenhower led the White House staff to cars to start Operation Alert. "The President is taking the new drill seriously and levity regarding it is not encouraged," Doris related. However, the men had learned of some of the program's deficiencies that morning from their wives. "Apparently it had not dawned on these ladies until they actually saw their husbands pack a suitcase for a three-day stay that no such plans had been made for them or their children. Their wives' farewell embraces were described by some of the men as rather lacking in warmth." Her column was headlined, "Men First; Women, Children Last."[30]

Doris wrote Truman: "Operation (not very) Alert is so silly as to be a reflection on your sex. I cannot believe women would be so unrealistic. What I omitted from my column was that the wives complained most about the fact that the secretaries (feminine) were taken along. "Just like the war!" they said, pointing the finger at Ike. My cynical nature suggests again that this was one reason Ike went home to Gettysburg to dinner both nights!"[31]

When Eisenhower suffered a heart attack in September, 1955, the press immediately concluded that he would not seek a second term. He had been vacationing in Denver, with a light schedule of work in an office at Lowry Air Force Base. On that day he went on to the Cherry Hills Golf Course where he played a morning round of eighteen holes and an afternoon round of nine. According to an account in Robert E. Gilbert's 1992 study of presidential illness, The Mortal Presidency, Eisenhower had been exuberant until he received word of a call from Secretary of State John Foster Dulles, which he felt was unnecessary. Succeeding interruptions soon triggered his well-known Type A temper. He complained of indigestion before leaving the golf course for his mother-in-law's home where he and Mamie were staying. In the early-morning hours Mamie called the President's personal physician, Dr. Howard Snyder, to the Doud residence. The first information to the press came after 7:00 when an aide announced that Eisenhower had indigestion. . . . that it "wasn't serious." He was transferred to the hospital at noon, being allowed to walk to his limousine after being carried down the stairs of the Doud home. At 2:40 reporters were told that Eisenhower had suffered a "mild coronary thrombosis." In fact, according to Gilbert's study of information now available, a cardiac specialist had diagnosed a "massive infarct" early in the morning. By 10:20 p.m. the word "mild" had been dropped in the description of the President's condition, and later, reporters were told that the attack had been moderate.[32] Doris wrote of the accidental nature of politics, as she had on July 4 when Lyndon Johnson, "in custody" at the Naval Medical Center, faced losing the momentum of his presidential bid.[33] Overnight, she observed, Eisenhower's heart attack had changed the 1956 political picture: "It is not expected that doctors will advise a man who will be 65 next month to undertake another grueling Presidential campaign and possibly four more years in the world's most responsible job."[34]

If Gilbert's interpretation is correct, there is evidence to suggest that the heart attack was not Eisenhower's first, but his third, and that a pattern of deception extended back to a "mystery illness" in 1949, when he was president of Columbia University. A medical history compiled by Dr. Thomas Mattingly, who was Eisenhower's cardiologist during his White House Years, now is available for review at the Eisenhower Library in Abilene. Mattingly concluded that the 1949 illness had been a mild heart attack and that Snyder had deliberately "misdiagnosed" it to avoid damaging a future political career. Again, in 1953, it said, Eisenhower was stricken as he labored on his speech on world peace for the American Society of Newspaper Editors. During his address he became pale, began to perspire heavily, to hold the podium with both hands, and finally to skip sentences. The White House blamed food poisoning, but in Mattingly's opinion the episode was an "impending" or a "mild" heart attack, hidden from the press.[35]

As Eisenhower convalesced at Gettysburg, he saw reporters and photographers on "prepared occasions," Doris informed readers. Senate Leader William Knowland was "cut off at the pockets" when he sought an indication of the President's political plans. Reporters at the

Gettysburg White House were summoned to a press conference and told by Dr. Snyder that if he were in the President's shoes he would wait until February to decide. "This obviously is not a medical opinion in the accepted sense. It is a political opinion volunteered to the press by a medical man," Doris observed.[36]

On June 7 Eisenhower attended the White House news photographers dinner. Dr. Snyder, called to the White House later in the evening, found him in great pain. The public knew little of Eisenhower's history of abdominal discomfort, but according to Gilbert it began shortly after his son's death in 1920 and he suffered from it greatly. Suppressed from Eisenhower and the public had been the disclosure of a "burned-out terminal ileitis," in a physical examination the previous month. When Snyder learned that Eisenhower had eaten a Waldorf salad he suspected that pieces of undigested celery were lodged in his constricted intestine. Procrastinating, doctors delayed surgery until the early-morning hours of June 9. They found a celery "plug" and symptoms of Crohn's disease, which gradually narrows the intestine and produces a bulge that must be removed.

They performed an ileotransverse colostomy; the diseased section of intestine was bypassed and left in the President's abdomen. There was considerably less information for the press than had been the case with the heart attack, when Eisenhower ordered full disclosure from Fitzsimons Army Hospital.[37] In recent months the President also had been candid in publicly acknowledging the health factor in his candidacy. The troubling spin ("propaganda of a high order," in Doris' phrase) came from those surrounding him, first from the Republican political leadership. "The President's doctors have gone even further," she declared. "They indicate now as before that somehow, in some way not clear to laymen, the President is better than he was. The fact that the American people have not altogether swallowed this assumption is proved by the flood of 'heart disease is good for you' jokes that are going around the country."[38]

She referred to Dr. David Allman, candidate for president of the American Medical Association, who had told reporters in Chicago that "when President Eisenhower recovers he will be in better physical condition than any of his opponents, Republican or Democrat, have been at any time in their lives."

"Dr. Allman never attended any of these men," she wrote. "As the Milwaukee Journal points out, such silly stuff tends to degrade the medical profession."[39] Dr. Burrill Crohn, according to Alistair Cooke, had "tried to tread a tightrope between professional disinterestedness and loyalty as a citizen." He had said on NBC's March of Medicine that the President had had a relatively mild attack, but that more than one-third of victims who are operated on suffer a recurrence of the disease.[40]

For a source, Doris went to the Armed Forces Medical Library in Washington, where she found an article by Dr. Crohn and Henry D. Janowitz, published the previous November in the *Journal of the American Medical Association*. In it they expressed a conclusion that there was "no specific therapy for regional enteritis and all available measures are strictly supportive." In patients treated surgically they found the rate of recurrence increasing, and the use of more surgery ineffective. Dr. Frederick F. Boyce of Tulane University had written the most recent text that January, observing that there "are few diseases which should leave the physician with a greater sense of humility."[41] In the insurance underwriters' bible, Risk Appraisal by Dr. Harry W. Dingman, was the information that life insurance was "possibly acceptable on 10-year endowment plan rated for 300 percent mortality. Disability coverage, positively no." On the other hand, Doris noted, "it is a truism that doctors disagree and patients often confound the body of research. It also has been a long time since Winston Churchill could pass a medical examination."[42]

As her columns exposing McCarthyism had drawn praise, the series advocating a public right to information in presidential illness was widely denounced as partisan, supplying ammunition to the Democratic party. Her admiration of Adlai Stevenson, Democratic front-runner, certainly had been visible in the past. Among the harshest critics was her brother Howard, counsel for *The Wichita Eagle*, who, according to Helen Fleeson, hotly advocated dropping her column.[43]

No public comment by Doris appeared following the death of

her great friend Henry Mencken. It was ironic that Mencken, for whom all things Kansan were a target of ridicule, died on January 29, Kansas Day, 1956. He is said to have requested that no obituary tributes be paid to him. Of course, he already had told Doris in somewhat contradictory instructions that he wanted to be "planted" in Sterling (Kansas) and that Brother Porter be given the contract to stuff him for the National Museum.

Bess Truman and Margaret wondered why they had not seen Doris at the reception. On April 21, 1956, fifty relatives and close friends witnessed the Margaret Truman-Clifton Daniel vows in the small Episcopal church in Independence where Harry and Bess were married in 1919. One hundred fifty were guests for the reception in the Truman home. When Bess learned the truth, she exploded. She wrote in a letter to Doris: "Margaret and I have both wondered about it and really missed you. I purposely waited until about the 18th to mail your invitation to the Muehlebach and wrote very plainly 'Hold until arrival on April 20th.' Some hotel service in our town!! It's too late to raise h____ now. However, the first time I see Barney Allis he is going to be told some facts."[44] In any case, the wedding was covered in relentless detail. Betty Beale wrote two galleys for readers of *The Washington Star*, including the information that "Mrs. Daniel wore a light blue lace and silk dress and matching small hat of horsehair braid. . . . The former First Lady wore a gray silk dress printed with white leaves shot with gold."[45]

Typical of those implying a partisan move in Doris' writing was Alistair Cooke, then U.S. correspondent for the *Manchester Guardian*. He portrayed her as "one of the few Washington correspondents who is an outright Democrat," and suggested that she had "barbed" her report on the President's health by quoting only texts in the Armed Forces Medical Library.[46] Detractors, however, had slight effect on her mainstream following, an estimated eight million families reached by one hundred papers that carried her column.[47]

Doris proudly followed her daughter's career in New York City. After graduation from Vassar, Doris Jr. worked for Edward Steichen on the Family of Man exhibit at the Museum of Modern Art, then for ABC and NBC. On February 8, 1957, she married Richard Anthony, Detroit correspondent for *Life* magazine, in a ceremony in the Church of All Souls in New York City. The New York society writer noted:

> The families of both the bride and bridegroom are writers. The bride's mother is a political columnist for the United Features Syndicate; her father is Washington columnist for The New York Daily News, and an uncle, James P. O'Donnell, is an associate editor in Europe of the Saturday Evening Post.
>
> Mr. Edward Anthony is an author ("Bring 'Em Back Alive," with Frank Buck, etc.), editor and publisher. He is a former publisher of the Woman's Home Companion and Collier's. Mrs. Anthony has been a writer on musical topics. Honorary Membership in the Order of the British Empire was conferred on her for her work with the Royal Air Force in World War II.[48]

Within a nine-day period in the spring of 1957 heart attacks claimed two of Doris' brothers. Richard, who was fifty-eight, was stricken while mowing the lawn for his mother-in-law in Lyons. Howard of Wichita, sixty-one, died after returning from a business trip to Washington. Along with his law practice, his activities included directorships on the family newspaper, on banks and radio stations, and involvement in various phases of the city's development. In the city that became the air capital, he had been one of the leaders in establishing the first Wichita Municipal Airport.[49]

"My you have had two terrible blows in the last two weeks," Alf Landon wrote. "I had a nice visit with Howard the day before he was leaving for Washington. I thought he looked better than any time in the last few years. We always visited about you in our talks. He valued highly your opinion on politicians and events, and I valued greatly my visits with him. For twenty five years he was as close a friend as I had."[50]

It was a television icon of the Fifties. Friday evenings meant Edward R. Murrow's "Person to Person," an intimate visit in the home of the nation's greats and near-greats. To be chosen conferred instant celebrity, and who could refuse, even though an invitation might come at the worst possible time. Doris received a call on Monday, May 12, 1958, asking if she would be Murrow's guest on the 23rd. On her schedule that day were drafting a speech to be delivered Saturday in Cleveland, editing a speech for publication, working on a magazine article and on a script for the Women's National Press Club stunt dinner. On Thursday she hosted a cocktail party for twenty-three guests at the dinner, including Mrs. Ronald (Marietta) Tree of New York, who also was her houseguest. The television crew had by that time arrived to begin installations. On Friday and Saturday Doris was in Cleveland, and on Sunday she went to Grosse Point, Michigan, to visit Doris Jr., with the hope of persuading her to return with her. Back in Washington she made spot appearances promoting the show and celebrated her birthday on the 20th at a dinner for twenty-four in the 1925 F Street Club. She and Doris Jr. supervised preparations in the house and the bricked area at the rear patterned after a Charleston camellia garden. Finally, as "zero hour" approached, Doris Jr. took all the vases in the house to be filled with flowers, and her black French poodle to be clipped (the veterinarian advised giving the poodle a couple of Miltowns). The program went without a slip as Doris and Doris Jr. spoke with Murrow and led viewers through the home and garden.[51]

"We are just <u>delighted</u> about you and Mr. K. (but not a bit surprised)!" wrote Bess Truman. "Of course I am eager to know where you will live. I can't imagine Washington without you. . . . Harry and I send our affectionate wishes for a vast amount of happiness to two <u>real</u> people."[52]

Margaret wrote: "How exciting about the first of August! One or the other or both of us will be there. I have a slight baby sitting problem, but will work it out or else!"[53]

From Eleanor Roosevelt: "I am delighted to hear about your wedding and I plan to be with you on August 1st at 4:00 o'clock. What do you want as a wedding gift? I would like to give you something you really need and would enjoy. . . . Thank you for telling me your news which makes me very glad."[54]

(Eleanor's gift was a dozen china plates in ivory, blue and gold.) *Time* magazine reported in the "People" column:

> In the Truman Administration, a trusty news source for hard-working, Fair-Dealing Columnist Doris Fleeson, fiftyish, was Navy Secretary Dan A. Kimball. At long last on the asking side of a question, California Businessman (Aerojet-General Corp.) Kimball, 62, earned the right answer, last week provided News hen Fleeson, ex-wife of the New York *Daily News*'s Washington Columnist John O'Donnell, with a hometown item: she and Dan, whose first marriage was dissolved last year, will be married next month at the home of Manhattan friends.[55]

Dan, returning to California at the close of the Truman administration, had resumed his role as dynamic leader of Aerojet-General Corporation, and now was at the forefront of the missile age, employing a workforce of ten thousand at a sprawling complex at Nimbus near Sacramento. The missile boom had occurred within a two-year period, taking the corporation from an employment of six hundred four in 1955. Now it was at work on $200 million in military contracts; Aerojet and the government had invested $80 million in military facilities and planned to spend another $20 million in the coming year. Aerojet was working on six hundred thousand solid propellant rocket engines, from small ones for pilot seat ejection to the largest, such as the Polaris. The company also was working on the liquid fuel engine for the Air Force missile Titan, on Polaris, the Navy solid-fuel missile to be fired from submerged submarines, and the second-stage rocket for Vanguard, the Navy's so-far unsuccessful earth satellite. There was a booster for Bomarc, the atomic-tipped missile to intercept bombers, and also the Sparrow, Bullpup, Aerobee, Dyna-soar and Minuteman. Kimball, with no high school diploma, had gathered three hundred scientists with master's and doctoral degrees to make Aerojet Nimbus the "General Motors of U.S. Rocketry."[56]

Doris and Dan Kimball, former Secretary of the Navy, at their wedding in 1958. (University Archives, Spencer Research Library, University of Kansas Libraries)

The wedding was in the apartment of Mr. and Mrs. J. Addison (Add and Inez) Robb, with vows exchanged before a fireplace and the beautiful copper tray Inez had been given by the Pasha of Safi in Casablanca in 1943 when she was a war correspondent. Tall vases of pink carnations and gladioli decorated the room. Doris' dress was of blue chiffon (the bridegroom's favorite color), with lace bodice and draped skirt with velvet ribbon inserts; with it she wore a matching blue pillbox hat, blue satin shoes and peacock green hose, according to the wedding accounts in several newspapers. Her wedding ring was a double band of alternating diamonds and sapphires.

A fashion parade ensued. Eleanor Roosevelt arrived, wearing a dress of black crepe with black lace bodice, and a tangerine beret. Bernard Baruch came from Saratoga with his nurse companion Elizabeth Novarro. Clifton and Margaret Truman Daniel were a stylish couple, she in a royal blue and black print satin dress and royal blue satin turban, and he in a gray shadow plaid suit with pleated shirt and black and silver bow tie. May Craig, in a print dress, pearls and a hat piled with roses, remained a devotee of Washington fashion, while designer Sally Victor wore a Nettie Rosenstein green printed chiffon with harem skirt, with green feathers in her hair. Others among the guests were Elizabeth Jordan, Mrs. Fiorello LaGuardia, Admiral and Mrs. Sidney Souers and Mr. and Mrs. Blake O'Connor.

A lace-covered buffet table featured the wedding cake, pale pink roses and candelabra. After toasts, Eleanor Roosevelt left (she had a large group of guests "champing at the bit to leave for the Roosevelt home in Hyde Park") The Daniels departed for their home in Sands Point, Long Island, talking of their first-born, now beginning to walk and, in his mother's words, becoming a Dennis the Menace.[57]

The couple left for a honeymoon in Quebec, planning to return to homes in Washington and Sacramento.[58]

22

WOMEN THE REALISTS

Teddy Roosevelt wanted to be the bride at the wedding and the corpse at the funeral—a description credited to his daughter Alice—but he was a piker compared to Lyndon Johnson, Doris suggested.[1] She considered the Senator temperamental and vain, a demon organizer whose operations were always diverting to watch.

Doris said that Lady Bird deserved a pedestal as "an effective thermostat for the blast furnace that is Lyndon Johnson."[2] In turn, Johnson characterized Doris and Liz Carpenter, the journalist who became Lady Bird's staff director, as the kind of women who would charge hell with a bucket of water."[3] It was an old Texas expression, Mrs. Carpenter reminisced, recalling that LBJ used it often about her.[4]

For Doris to socialize with LBJ seemed tantamount to adversarial divorce attorneys leaving a conference scene for an afternoon of golf. Doris often lectured that reporters should maintain a detachment with politicians and presidents; she declared in a speech at the University of Minnesota in 1957 that "the pampering by the press of politicians, no matter how exalted their status, is a crime so heinous it should be forbidden by law."[5] Her own mingling with national leaders was not mentioned, and the credible words in Minneapolis may have fallen more questionably in Washington, scene of her active social life.

To LBJ, the ranch was more than a retreat, according to biographer Robert A. Caro. He relates in *Master of the Senate* that Johnson was eager to entertain journalists, with the objective of creating an image. . . . "that the ranch helped him to relax and reflect that he was a different man down there from the frenzied, driven Lyndon Johnson whom they knew in Washington."[6]

When Lyndon and Lady Bird invited the newly wed Kimballs to the ranch for September 27, 1958, he wrote: "I would think that if you were flying commercial, the best thing to do would be for you to come down to Austin and I would have someone meet you there. . . . I can't provide golf, although Lady Bird plays bridge and there is some good fishing. But maybe we can forget both war and frivolity for a while."[7]

Upon their arrival the Kimballs were soon touring the ranch, with Johnson at the wheel. Doris, writing upon their return, portrayed their host as looking ahead to the 1959 Congress, "bumping over his broad acres in an antique, high-riding open car, giving each fat LBJ cow his searing attention, and occasionally popping a plump dove with his .22. . . . As the Senator from Texas all but rehearses his moderation arguments on his cows, he looks browned and healthy, and he is as nearly relaxed as it is possible for him to be." Johnson was at work on his lands, she said, but with half his mind, the other half "plainly busy with 1959 and beyond—including that presidential nominating convention in 1960."[8]

Two years earlier, Doris had written of an event in Washington—on the worst day of winter, with icy streets and biting winds—that had caught journalists by surprise. At his most recent press conference Eisenhower still had withheld endorsement of Nixon as his running mate in 1956. As Doris described it, Nixon was being given a birthday party by old, close House associates at the National Press Club. It was a large party to which hosts normally figure that only two thirds will attend. But everybody came. Sherman Adams led a complement of White House staffers, and "ornaments" of the Burning Tree Golf Club and "prima donnas" of the press were on hand. "The doors were even opened for a selection of the better known women correspondents whom the Press Club normally permit to enter only the balcony," Doris reported. In somewhat rambling comments Nixon disclosed that it was the tenth anniversary of his first public speech, both a description of his own meteoric rise and the opportunities existing in United States politics, "The party itself," she wrote, "was typical of such gatherings with lashings of food and drink. . . . There was that indescribable tension which appears when the participants all know that here is a chapter— minor perhaps but a chapter—in the perennial struggle for the greatest power any one man of the Western world can wield."[9]

By June 1959, although he had been the party workhorse since 1952, Nixon pressed uncertainly toward the 1960 Presidential nomination. The cultivation of journalists at small dinner parties in his home had become one of his strategies. He was said to feel keenly conscious of his lack of experience in foreign affairs, but efforts to enhance his image in this respect had been especially frustrating. In 1957 he had postponed a trip to Europe because the State Department could not arrange the important and extensive tour he had in mind. The goal was to promote his image as an authority on foreign affairs and to appeal to ethnic and minority groups in pivotal states. It was a large order for the State Department, and there was limited time to fill it, Doris noted. "To start with, both the Vice President and Mrs. Nixon are now known to those who serve them as having a whim of iron on top of which they are perfectionists. They want what they want when they want it and they have a passion for detail."[10]

Nixon had encountered violence on his visits to Venezuela and Peru. Now, in 1959, plans were almost complete for a trip across the Soviet Union, with a complement of more than sixty reporters. At a late stage the White House announced that Dr. Milton Eisenhower, brother of the President and president of Johns Hopkins University, would accompany him. The move intrigued Washington. "The question arises as to whether his inclusion is fact-finding or political or both," Doris observed.[11] The trip was memorable for its "kitchen debate" between Nixon and Khrushchev in the model home of an American exhibit in Moscow. Doris pronounced the quality of the dialogue, "read in cold type," as "far below the casual exchanges of a dull day in the United States senate."[12]

She had first acknowledged Kennedy's bid in 1957, reporting the young senator's expensive and extensive campaign to become the first

Catholic President or Vice President.[13] In late 1958 Hubert Humphrey, member of the Senate Foreign Relations Committee, distinguished himself with a journey in Europe and an eight-hour conference with Khrushchev. Eleanor Roosevelt, impressed with his performance, endorsed his bid for the Democratic nomination, saying that he came closest to having "the spark of greatness" needed in the White House.[14] But as the momentum increased, it became evident that Kennedy was the pace-setter, chartering planes and seeking commitments among potential delegates. "He is also answering a great many questions, not all of which people are asking," Doris noted. "Kennedy's friends report they have cautioned him on such points and that he replies fatalistically that it is now or never."[15] However, in April 1959, Doris believed that the prized Democratic nomination "could land in one of many laps, including some just beginning to be discussed."[16]

With an apartment in California and Doris' home in Georgetown, she and Dan were frequent commuters. Agnes Murphy, columnist of "At Home With..." in the *New York Post*, gave this account of a visit with Doris on March 27, 1959:

> Miss Fleeson, just back from the hairdresser, and clad in a bright blue wool skirt and matching sweater and shoes, with a white-and-the-same-blue striped cotton shirtwaist, was sitting in her book-lined living room before lunchtime on a Friday.
>
> "Friday's my free day—I don't do another column until Sunday," she said. "And Dan's home, that's why we're having flowers arranged all around. I always have flowers when he's here for the weekend. "And," she finished, "I think I'll have a cocktail before lunch. A whisky sour would be about right, I think."
>
> Miss Fleeson herself took over the mixing of the sour, while her secretary, who is part of the daytime household since the columnist's office is upstairs, offered sherry and tomato juice.

Then we went in to lunch in the yellow-and-white Regency dining room. It is a room that looks far larger than it really is, because the mistress of the house had selected an especially scaled-down table and sideboard, about two-thirds standard size and made by an expert New York cabinet maker.

Lunch was cheese soufflé, fresh asparagus in butter sauce, China tea and broiled grapefruit.[17]

On a perfect September day Nikita Khrushchev arrived late at Andrews Field, his cream-colored transport having encountered Atlantic headwinds. Eisenhower was waiting. That touch of inefficiency was appreciated by Americans aware that a Soviet lunar rocket had landed a pennant on the moon on schedule. "Finally the familiar figure stepped out—dumpy, toothy and bareheaded, a full head shorter than his host," Doris wrote.[18] The fireworks to come were not anticipated at that encouraging point.

Doris accompanied the Russians on a cross-country tour, which was highlighted by the Hollywood can-can incident. By Hollywood standards, the popular musical "Can-Can" had seemed a representative entertainment offering. The Soviet leader declared the film as a lavish display of "female backsides," no answer to the Russian ballet, and a confirmation of his low opinion of Western culture.[19] By the time the entourage returned to Washington for talks at Camp David, Doris had assessed Khrushchev as not a gentleman. She wrote: "He has no use for taste, good or bad, and he has no sporting blood. This aspect is reinforced by a razor-keen instinct for the jugular and the quick wit to take advantage of every fault of his opponent. He has both humor and the theatrical instinct. Charm is a word more commonly associated with women, but when men of obvious virility possess it, such as Khrushchev, it is hard for men or women to keep up their guard."[20]

The kitchen debate and the Khrushchev visit elevated Nixon's standing; much of the public credited him for a change in the Cold War climate. Polls within a month after the visit showed Republican officials certain he would win the nomination. This was met with disbelief by

Democratic leaders, equally convinced that Nelson Rockefeller would be the nominee.[21] As the final stretch began in January, the Democratic field included Kennedy, Humphrey, Johnson and Senator Stuart Symington, with Adlai Stevenson in the wings. "It has even been suggested by some ardent Stevensonians that their hero should be busy on the international scene somewhere—or anywhere—while the convention is meeting so that if and when he is drafted, he could fly dramatically to Los Angeles as thousands cheered," Doris wrote.[22] She considered the Democrats lacking a star of sufficient political magnitude to meet Nixon on equal terms.

In May 1960, eight months after his visit, Khrushchev interjected himself into the American presidential contest with the U-2 incident, the downing of an American spy plane and the capture of pilot Francis Gary Powers by the Soviet Union. Doris termed Eisenhower's denial "presidential ignorance inflated to a pious virtue and fairy tales about bad weather and oxygen troubles fed to the public."

"The crashing climax came with the decision made by Secretary Herter to tell the truth not because it is the truth, but because we were caught red-handed," she wrote. The imminent summit in Paris loomed uncertainly, as the Soviet leader exploited his advantage. Exploding in hostility to Eisenhower, he implied that he would prefer to deal with the next President. To Doris, such interference in an American presidential election was a potential threat not only "to the hapless beneficiary who might receive Khrushchev's clumsy blessing, but it could, if unchecked, poison the whole campaign dialogue." The Soviet leader, she proposed, had now made it absolutely impossible for the nominee of either party to take anything but a firm line toward the Kremlin.[23]

Nixon and Lodge, Kennedy and Johnson had emerged from the conventions. Adlai Stevenson was scheduled for "skull practice" during a weekend with Kennedy in Hyannis Port. On schedule were unprecedented television debates which Doris felt might furnish a spark yet lacking in the campaign: "While both men are temperamentally cool, they are intensely competitive, and any idea that they really like each other is nonsense. Both have had enough experience to know that the one thing they dare not do to their network audience, which some experts say could reach 200 million, is to bore it."[24]

Both candidates were seen as offering unusual youth and relatively little executive experience, thus making the debate issues less important than the chance to convey an impression of maturity. Along with the youth factor was the glamor of their wives. Doris was convinced that the American public wanted to tear every First Lady to bits. When Jacqueline Kennedy became a campaign issue, she was incensed, and equally displeased with Democratic and Republican campaign managers. The Democrats, she had learned, had dispatched a team consisting of Lady Bird Johnson, a Kennedy sister and sister-in-law to Texas to explain that the candidate's wife was not with them because she was expecting a baby. Who had thought up the idea that the party should take the defensive regarding Mrs. Kennedy, Doris demanded. She wrote in her column on September 2, 1960:

> Since when is glamour a bad word in the United States? Smart Republicans, knowing the answer had to be that it wasn't, huddled with their Madison avenue friends and moved in fast.
>
> Without even a bow in the direction of the magazines which incessantly photograph Mrs. Kennedy or a nod to the fashion industry, Hollywood and television, stern reports began to be circulated that glamour in the White House distaff side was out. The American voter, it was said on no authority, does not want youth, beauty and chic there, even when redeemed by a notable husband and an enchanting child.
>
> This offensive upon a great natural asset of the opposition party is legal and normal. Democrats would do the same if they were smart enough, which is doubtful, since they have fallen for it at the hands of their rivals. . . .
>
> The silly issue is now in the open and seems to center upon Mrs. Kennedy's hair-do, which is full-blown in the current style . . .

It was a blow to the authors of the anti-Jackie-for-first-lady campaign when it was announced that she was having a baby. Not even a minority party backed by *Time* magazine can oppose motherhood, but the sly suggestion has been made that it was planned that way to keep that supposedly lethal glamour out of circulation . . .

Comparisons are odious, but it might be pointed out that Mrs. Nixon is not precisely dowdy—as her couturiere, Mrs. Elizabeth Arden, would be the first to say.[25]

A handwritten letter from Jacqueline Kennedy, in her inimitable style, expressed thanks:

Dear Doris—

Jack told me about your article so I searched the Hyannis news stores yesterday, and found it in the *New York Post*. I cannot tell you how touched and grateful I am that you should write such a thing—

You are so many altitudes above "Women's Page" subjects—so for you to write about it means more than you can imagine.

I have been confused and upset about all this business—not because I care what they might say about me—but because it gives me such pain to think I might be any hindrance to Jack.

My longed-for baby really didn't choose a very good time to come—no matter what the Republicans say!—as I could be flattening my hair and working harder than Mrs. Nixon.

So in my present state of mind can't you see how happy it made me to read your story -

My very best to you and Dan.

Affectionately

Jackie[26]

Doris hailed Kennedy's moving inaugural address calling for austerity, but noted that none had appeared in the inaugural festivities. The only resemblance to Valley Forge was dreadful slush around the Armory, she reported.

The first One Hundred Days were underway. The advent of televised press conferences in the Eisenhower administration and recently the unprecedented television debates gave pause to consider the effect on journalism. Expressing a view typical of veteran journalists, Doris charged that television was not training reporters as newspapers did, but relying too much on "fruity voices and a portentous air." "I will go a little further," she told an audience. "I will add that all too many reporters today have become ladies and gentlemen. . . . Instead of coming out of the universities, they should come off the street or out of the hellbox."[27] (Hellbox referred to a little cart found in pressrooms in the days of letterpress printing. Printers, tearing down page forms, tossed lead slugs into the cart, which was wheeled to the melting pot. The slugs were melted in an inferno of molten metal to be reused in the linotype machines.)

During an appearance on Edward R. Murrow's "Small World," Doris and panelists Marya Mannes and Marguerite Higgins targeted newsmagazines and group journalism in which a single story might be written by ten people. Mannes, poet, critic and essayist, labeled the style a composite like a processed food. Higgins, Pulitzer Prize winning correspondent, condemned losing the flavor and losing the individual. An excerpt from the dialogue:

> Fleeson: I always wondered what all these researchers did on *Time* and *Newsweek*. Let's just don't run out and say now who we're talking about.
>
> Mannes: Don't ask too closely, Doris.
>
> Fleeson: No, in all seriousness, I think they tend—I used to think when they used to pick all their news out of the newspapers, that this was wrong. I have about come to the conclusion they ought to go back to that technique, that

because of the elaboration, they tend to get lost in the words. And in some point of view or idea they're trying to convey, and then they take the human beings, whom they're quoting, and the situations with which they deal, and they take their sharp scissors and cut them to fit that. This is no good. This will never be any good.

The panelists carried on with an animated discussion of discrimination against women, and Murrow closed with, "Thank all three of you very much indeed. This has been a very stimulating and illuminating conversation. I think we ought to have the three of you here once each week with the fourth participant being an outstanding politician. I think he'd have a very rough time."[28]

By the time he retired as New York *Daily News* bureau chief in Washington in September 1961, John O'Donnell had represented a spectrum of American political thought. He had strongly supported the New Deal when he opened the bureau in 1933 at the beginning of the Roosevelt administration. The break with Roosevelt, dramatized by the Iron Cross incident, was a turn to isolationism and increasingly pointed criticism of FDR. Truman was heir to the attack, as O'Donnell opposed the Marshall Plan and U.S. intervention in the Korean war. He hailed the Republican victory in 1952, but almost as a repeat of the years following 1942, he broke with the Eisenhower administration when it denounced McCarthyism in 1954. His third marriage, to Betty Potter, an employee in the Washington bureau, had ended in divorce. During his months of sick leave before he officially retired, *Daily News* colleagues assembled a scrapbook of his colorful career. He died December 17, 1961, in the Georgetown University Hospital at the age of sixty-five.[29]

Eleven days later the death of Edith Bolliing Wilson recalled the era she had symbolized for decades, living in her home at 2340 S Street in the capital. Doris had first seen the President's widow in 1932 at the Democratic convention in Chicago, where she was prominent as a party figurehead.

After selling the house on P Street, Doris and Dan moved to a new townhouse at 2120 S Street. In a handwritten letter dated April 7, 1961, Edith Wilson had written Doris: "My dear Mrs. Kimball: Your gracious note and the flowers have come. And I can't tell you how much I appreciate them. Of course I have been one of your readers for years but did not know S Street had the distinction of being your home." She explained that her sister who lived with her was desperately ill and that she was making no engagements.[30]

For the New Frontier, the "hour of euphoria"[31] was nearly over. Planning for the invasion of Cuba by a force of exiles had been ongoing and secret at the White House from the earliest days. It was generally known among Washington journalists, however, that something was approaching a climax.

When news of the disastrous Bay of Pigs broke, Doris reached Cord Meyer, the head of CIA international operations, who at that moment was dealing with a plumbing leak in Georgetown. Meyer refused comment and referred her to Richard Bissell, CIA deputy director for operations, who, along with Director Allen Dulles, had originated the invasion plan.[32]

The operation had begun on April 17, and by April 20 the extent of the debacle and the futility of concealing U.S. involvement was known. Doris went to the Statler Hilton to cover the President's speech to the American Society of Newspaper Editors.

Kennedy, who had agonized and then decided against an American rescue, faced criticism in the form of rallies at home and abroad and an angry message from Soviet leader Khrushchev. According to Arthur Schlesinger, Jr., his prepared text was replaced by one written through the early morning hours by Ted Sorenson and reviewed by a gathering of aids at breakfast. Fearing an outcry for violent action against Castro, they sought to reassure the world of U.S. restraint, but warn against Communist infiltration in the Western Hemisphere.

"It was a brave and prescient speech," Doris wrote, "ranking with the deathless phrases of Winston Churchill in England's mortal crisis."

But while colleagues loudly exposed the U.S. role, Doris accepted

Kennedy's version, referring to "Cubans who took perhaps a too-long chance to quickly overturn the Soviet-backed Castro regime and have apparently failed."

To detractors, the column was predictable and the praise for Kennedy excessive, as Doris characterized his stand as almost a new Monroe Doctrine. "It does not cast us wholly in the role of protector," she observed. "It says to our good neighbors that they are grown up now and can recognize the facts of Communist subversion; it invites them to become a full partner in defense of freedom."[33]

Within four days, however, she acknowledged charges that the invasion was badly timed, the product "more of emotion than wisdom." She considered the possibility that a closer liaison of Cuba and Communist nations could bring pressure in the United States to do something about the Castro regime.

The invasion had come exactly one year after a decision in the Eisenhower administration to train Cuban exiles, making the action something of an inheritance and lessening Republican criticism. But Kennedy summoned Richard Nixon, who as Vice President had advocated an aggressive policy toward Castro.

Doris believed the effort to avert a partisan attack a waste of time: "He has less chance of persuading the main body of Republicans in Congress to lay off his Cuban errors than Fidel Castro has of being named the father of the year."[34]

As news photos showed Kennedy and Eisenhower gravely strolling a path at Camp David, Eisenhower impressed Doris as a true statesman and "every inch a 5-star general" for endorsing the purposes of the Kennedy foreign policy. Eisenhower had candidly disclosed his administration's participation in the early planning, and had vigorously warned against any immediate public airing of the fiasco.[35]

Cuba remained the Achilles' heel, and by fall 1962 Doris observed a fresh outbreak of belligerence toward Castro. "Senators are all but telling President Kennedy to furnish the troops and they will furnish the war," she wrote. "With his accustomed candor, Senator Barry Goldwater has sounded the tocsin for the attack."

The decision by Cuba and the Soviet Union to install nuclear missiles in Cuba had come in July, with shipments beginning that month. A U-2 flight at the end of August showed evidence of surface-to-air anti-aircraft (SAM) sites under construction.

"So far it is the conservatives in both parties who constitute the Goldwater political shock troops," Doris wrote. She portrayed Kennedy as on the defensive because of the Bay of Pigs, as the exodus of Cuban refugees mounted and Russians were heading for Havana.[36]

On October 14 a U-2 flight produced photos of a launch pad, buildings for ballistic missiles and a missile on the ground. Under cover of a scheduled amphibious exercise, the administration readied forty thousand Marines. One hundred thousand Army troops were massed in Florida and fourteen thousand reservists were recalled to fly transport planes. Kennedy's dramatic speech to the nation on Monday evening, October 22, declared the Soviet action "a deliberately provocative and unjustified change in the status quo which cannot be accepted by this country, if our courage and commitments are ever to be trusted again by either friend or foe."

He announced a naval quarantine (advisors had rejected the word blockade) and warned of full retaliation against the Soviet Union should any missile be launched from Cuba.[37]

The story was developing too rapidly and seriously to stir partisan "I-told-you-so's" in Congress, Doris found. That was not the case in California as she arrived to cover West Coast politics. Richard Nixon, running for Governor, had inserted himself into the Cuban crisis with a half-hour radio address in which he called on citizens to support the President. Doris wrote:

> You could almost hear Richard M. Nixon's sigh of satisfaction come through the television screen as he shifted his campaign emphasis from California to Cuba, to Russia and the rest of the world.
>
> For while politicians of both parties in every state were debating what effect President John F. Kennedy's quarantine

would have on November 6, it was apparent that the Republican nominee for Governor had made his decision. . . .

His half-hour television presentation of his views of the Cuban situation, coming four days after the President's action, was the result of careful planning and of consultation with party leaders, from former President Dwight D. Eisenhower down.

The partisanship was there for all to see, but was frosted over with pledges of support for the President. . . .

In all his claims about world experience, there was implicit the contention that he, and other Republicans, know how to recognize the Communist peril at home and abroad far better than do any Democrats. . . .[38]

Khrushchev's capitulation came two days later, on October 28, with word that work would stop at the sites, missiles would be returned to the Soviet Union and negotiations would begin at the United Nations.[39]

Although Eisenhower would later return to a partisan attack of the administration—as elder statesman Truman campaigned "luridly" against Republicans—his saving act sped Kennedy's recovery. In less than a year the President enjoyed overwhelming public support. Streams of polls showed his popularity rising "to incredible heights," Doris reported.[40]

Doris and Adlai Stevenson were among the few non-family members who saw Eleanor Roosevelt in the last days of her fatal illness. Doris visited her in the hospital. Stevenson made a final call to her Manhattan apartment on the night of her death, November 7, 1962, to pay his respects, arriving shortly before the body was removed.

Although Eleanor had been active in Democratic politics for fifty years and instrumental in shaping the Democratic state ticket, she was too ill to vote on November 6. She had entered Columbia Presbyterian Medical Center on September 26 to be treated for anemia and lung congestion. When her condition failed to improve, she was discharged October 28 to return to her apartment.

Her death at the age of seventy-eight shared headlines with the landslide Democratic victory in mid-term elections.[41]

Doris wrote in a moving tribute:

> Mrs. Roosevelt's secret was her total commitment to the power of love. All of us are admonished to this end but few acquire the ability to practice it outside of a relatively narrow circle. Even those who try find it fatally easy to become bored or disenchanted with fallible humanity and, particularly as they grow older, practice various forms of withdrawal from life.
>
> Not Mrs. Roosevelt. To the end, she loved and participated to the fullest extent of her unusual powers. . . .
>
> Yet like the shepherd in Virgil who became acquainted with love and found him a native of the rocks, Mrs. Roosevelt had to seek amid the rocks to become the person now universally mourned. With great candor she has told that part, too, of her story, and it is relevant only as it helps toward appreciation of her.[42]

Within the past fifteen days the administration had faced down the Cuban missile crisis, and the Democratic party had received a strong vote of confidence in the statehouses and both houses of Congress. Richard Nixon, losing in California, had lost his composure before television cameras with the now-famous comment: "You won't have Nixon to kick around any longer because this, gentlemen, is my last press conference."[43]

Doris considered Kennedy's address to Congress on January 15 the hardest-hitting State of the Union message in ten years, "a campaign blueprint for 1964."[44] By spring, tensions had eased to the point that Kennedy could deliver a comical parody of the missile crisis at the Gridiron Club dinner. In his light-hearted speech he spoke of criticism he had been receiving from columnist Arthur Krock. "The Vice President complained to me that Doris Fleeson was still criticizing him," Kennedy said. "I told him I'd rather be Fleesonized (a then-popular dry-cleaning method) than Krocked."[45]

In a moment of levity, Doris jokes with President John F. Kennedy in Washington.

In addition to needling Johnson, Doris kept the administration in her sights. She alleged that the recruiting of new talent, so pronounced in the early days, had come almost to halt. "A test of the present drift looms in the Pentagon where there is plainly a crisis of morale," she observed. "Whatever the rights and wrongs of the TFX contract, managed news and the sudden switch of the Chief of Naval Operations, Secretary McNamara has not established himself as a reliable friend of his own people, and they resent it."[46]

As interest turned to the 1964 presidential field, *The Washington Star* claimed that Nixon and Eisenhower planned to support Governor

George Romney of Michigan because they considered Nelson Rockefeller's remarriage a political liability. Nixon had just moved to the East Coast in what Doris termed "a spiritual retreat from California and an advance into the greenback pastures of New York." Joining the Wall Street law firm of Mudge, Stern, Baldwin and Todd, he had purchased a twelve-room co-op at 810 Fifth Avenue, the same building in which Governor Rockefeller, his new wife, and the former Mrs. Rockefeller resided.[47]

Doris, preparing to cover the President's trip to Europe in June, reflected that presidential travels in the jet age were a hard job for even the most conscientious reporters. Except for a few pool reporters, she said, the majority rarely could get closer to the President himself than the crowds. Between transportation and deadline problems, there was little time to talk to native experts and sources.[48]

When the entourage reached Berlin, the city from which Doris had reported the beginning of the European ground war and the visit of Sumner Welles, the number of accredited news representatives had reached a thousand. "For one press conference, most of them will not get closer to him than the East Germans behind their tragic wall," she reported. The wall would be the high spot, as well as the greatest test of statesmanship, in that Kennedy needed to offer hope without making unattainable promises.[49]

"The President still is in the first half of his third year in office. Political observers agree that, barring some unusual crisis or Act of God, he will be re-elected," Doris had written on May 21.[50]

She and Dan were traveling in Australia when they heard the bulletins, and hastened to return to the capital. They arrived in time to see the crowds, lined for three miles to pass before the President's bier. Doris, in her first reaction, harshly indicted the American citizenry:

> It is impossible not to believe that such people can run a democracy, make good choices and do what needs to be done. Yet they had failed their President and their country by indifference or lack of judgment permitting a rage of hate

to flourish. . . Even when not of it, too many have lived side by side with it, without protesting. Somehow it has been unfashionable to join battle with the haters, their publications and their contributors. . . .

Now they have had their blood sacrifices in one of their hate capitals.[51]

Lyndon Johnson had come to Washington in the first year of Roosevelt's second term. Now, just as the nation had accepted a transition to a younger generation, it turned to the complex LBJ whose ties stretched back much further. Doris again reviewed the Johnson temperament. "He bears down and not always with a light touch," she observed. "He keeps books on his helpers and hinderers." As she knew first-hand, he was sensitive to criticism. She said that it sometimes seemed that what he wanted above all was to be loved, which she termed occasionally irksome, occasionally "rather touching in so confident and successful a man."[52]

As spring returned after the tragic winter, the rose garden commissioned by Jacqueline Kennedy was Johnson's "special lovesome plot," Doris told readers. It was a setting for every kind of presidential occasion, and clearly "doing much for the repose of his restless spirit."[53]

A potential trouble spot was the summer civil rights campaign in Mississippi being organized by the Student Nonviolent Coordinating Committee. "White citizens councils and the Mississippi legislature have mounted a counter offensive, and an ugly confrontation lies ahead," Doris predicted.[54] She felt that at the rude Republican confrontation in San Francisco, marked by the booing of Rockefeller and shutout of dissenters, the party had practically drawn a picture for Democrats, with Hubert Humphrey as the beneficiary.[55]

She covered Humphrey's vice-presidential nomination in August in Atlantic City. "Immense warmth, political sense, brains and a teacher's instinct for sharing what he knows have formed the public personage welcomed by Democrats to their national ticket," Doris wrote. "By now they know their Hubert very well, warts and all."[56]

In the Goldwater candidacy, she declared, were revivalist overtones of new conservatives lacking a sense of proportion and humor. These were the "discontented haves" facing not greater freedom of choice, but less. "They have fled to the cities and find them uncomfortable, occasionally even dangerous," she observed. "In truth the American frontier today consists of its great cities."[57]

She said that, traveling aboard the Goldwater campaign train through the Midwest, she could not reconcile the charming couple with the angry rhetoric. They were attractive to look at, delightful to talk to. Mrs. Goldwater was simply dressed and perfectly groomed. The Senator was all "square-shouldered elegance," relaxed and serious, until he suddenly delivered a barrage of accusations. "This is the language," Doris wrote. "It is rough, slashing, bold, bitter. But the incredible fact is that in delivering it he rarely changes inflection, keeps his hands firmly flat on the lectern, and is fully as restrained as if he were reading the first lesson in the Episcopal church to which he belongs."[58]

The Lady Bird Special, described in Liz Carpenter's memoir *Ruffles and Flourishes*, in the chapter "The Last of the Big-Time Whistlestops," traveled through the South featuring fifteen "LBJ hostesses," all Southern by birth and training. In addition there were three masters of ceremony who spoke the Southern idiom: Commerce Secretary Luther Hodges; Representative Hale Boggs of Louisiana, House whip; and former Tennessee Governor Buford Ellington. Doris, one of the journalists aboard, was unstinting in praise of Lady Bird: "While the accent may suggest magnolia blossoms, it would never occur to the cool and prudent business woman now the wife of the President to leave things to chance and charm. Her whistle-stop speeches are carefully organized and splendidly brief. . . . She is polite about it but she asks for votes and mentions the thorny issues."[59]

Liz Carpenter, Staff Director and Press Secretary to Lady Bird, had organized the event from the beginning, first making a quick run through four Southern states with an advance man and the Secret Service. They had tried to anticipate everything that could go wrong, but still there were emergencies. For reporters, especially, the trip was grueling—a fact dramatized when Doris collapsed en route. Nonetheless LBJ's two indomitable women found humor in the scene, as Liz Carpenter wrote in her book:

> At Charlotte, North Carolina, we had another medical crisis. Veteran newswoman Doris Fleeson suffered a mild stroke. My husband, bless him, volunteered to accompany her back to Washington by plane. As we said goodbye at the train platform, where Doris was lying on a stretcher waiting for the ambulance to the airport, I tried to think of something cheerful to say.
>
> "You're the only woman in the world, Doris, whom I could trust flat on her back with my husband," I said.
>
> She lifted up her head from the stretcher, glared at me and shouted defiantly, "Dammit! I'll never be that sick."

Resuming her column in the final days before the election, Doris noted a phenomenal reaction to the Goldwater candidacy in her native Kansas, where the *Iola Register* and *Parsons Sun*, long associated with Republican politics, had, in contradiction to the image often perpetrated in the East, rejected neo-conservatism and endorsed the Democratic ticket.[60]

For the Official Inaugural Program, Doris wrote a special article, "Two Presidents for One,"[61] which drew Lady Bird's warm acknowledgment: "Now that the tumult and shouting have died down, I have had my first opportunity to sit down and read in full the Inaugural Program that contains your very generous story about me. It will be the proudest part of my personal archives. Thank you for taking the time to 'take a long look' even though I fear your vision is blurred by your affection. . . ."[62]

Doris had produced a daily column for twenty years. Now sixty-four years old, and dividing her time between homes in Washington and Palm Springs, she was in the capital when her niece, Helen Fleeson, arrived from Lyons, Kansas to begin indoctrination for the Peace Corps.

Helen found herself taken under Doris' wing in unexpected ways. For the first time she felt that she merited her aunt's approval—that Doris thought she was doing something with her life. It was exciting to visit the house on S Street, with crystal chandeliers in every room and champagne in the refrigerator. A sofa table in the living room held books three and four deep, and Doris was apt to pick one out for a visitor to read and offer an opinion. Helen, who was preparing to go to Nigeria, might be given a book related to the Peace Corps or Africa, and she was flattered with the assignment. But on another occasion Doris abruptly took her purse, emptied it, discarded tissues and gum wrappers and rearranged the contents. "She was a neat freak," Helen said.

On Sundays she often found Mary McGrory, close friend and colleague, visiting Doris. The two had much in common, although they were strikingly dissimilar physically, Helen remembered, with McGrory towering over Doris. After years of obscurity as a secretary and book reviewer, McGrory had covered some of the McCarthy hearings and had shown new talent which launched her career as a political writer on *The Washington Star*.[63] When the journalists were together, Helen could expect a review of the week's events, with colorful barrages against male public figures. The visits always ended with Doris insisting that she call a cab, and McGrory insisting that she could take the bus.[64]

Doris cited McGrory following Adlai Stevenson's death in July 1965, and McGrory's view of Stevenson as the only person she knew who regarded a political speech as an art form. "Those of us who had deadlines to meet still vibrate to the memory of watching Stevenson, pencil in hand, agonizing over his script even when the television cameras were inexorably focusing on him," Doris wrote.[65]

As the war escalated in Vietnam, she saw the nation saddled with the liabilities of a policeman, without the compensating assets of a shopkeeper. It must puzzle Asians, she suggested. "They are accustomed to the practice of self-interest by the West, not to morality plays."[66] Republicans challenged Johnson to name one act of militarism he had charged to Barry Goldwater in 1964 that he had not now done. "It is no wonder that the situation has developed a rumor that the President will not run again in 1968," she wrote on February 17, 1966. And she felt that in events of the previous month the "silent prison" of the vice presidency had never been more poignantly displayed. As Humphrey prepared for a mission to the Far East, the White House announced that he would be replaced in Vietnam by Jack Valenti ("like appointing a Carthaginian to guard Caesar's wife," Doris declared). A final snub occurred when the administration sent Averell Harriman from Cairo to Tokyo to explain U.S. policy, days after Humphrey had completed high-level talks there. Doris believed he had gone from being merely ignored to being misused, and even publicly abused.[67] She told an audience at the University of Colorado: "We are seeing sharply today . . . how the vice president is cribbed, cabined and confined within the narrow cage of his Constitutional office. It would have seemed impossible not long ago that people would ask: 'Whatever happened to Hubert?' His lively presence seemed as pervasive as smog."[68] Most of all, she said, it was depressing to watch Humphrey, father of the Arms Control and Disarmament Agency and the Peace Corps idea, being nailed politically to a cross of war in Saigon.[69]

Doris Jr. greets President Lyndon B. Johnson. (University Archives, Spencer Research Library, University of Kansas Libraries)

Doris, in failing health, discontinued her column in 1967, her voice silent on the violent events of 1968. Doris O'Donnell, single again, had returned from a career in foreign service as an assistant press chief in the U.S. Information Service in Rome[70] and a cultural affairs officer at the embassy in Morocco. In 1968 she energetically joined the presidential campaign of Senator Eugene J. McCarthy,[71] and the house on S Street was at times a nerve center. Doris prepared large trays of sandwiches several times a week to send to campaign headquarters.[72]

The Lyons Daily News reported on February 14, 1969: "Famous Native Ill." Doris was hospitalized in Tucson after suffering a stroke while visiting in the home of Inez Robb.[73] She returned to Washington, but was confined to a wheel chair. "There were not many visitors, but the Jesuits up the street would visit her," recalled nephew Harry Fleeson, referring to Georgetown University.[74]

Their deaths occurred thirty-six hours apart. Dan Kimball died on July 30, 1970, at the age of seventy-four, four days after being hospitalized for internal bleeding. On August 1, the twelfth anniversary of their marriage, Doris died of a massive stroke in their home in Georgetown.

Some three hundred friends attended the service on Monday morning at the Navy Chapel on Nebraska Avenue.[75] Eugene McCarthy paid tribute to Dan as an industrialist with deep social obligations, whose last effort had been to establish a technical university in Morocco. Doris, he said, "considered her calling in journalism to tell this world what was wrong with it and who was wrong and to suggest in terms that no one could misunderstand what she thought ought to be done."[76]

"The king is dead, long live the king," Doris had quoted at the time of Franklin Roosevelt's death, as leadership passed to Harry Truman. Seven days after President Kennedy's assassination she spoke of an exciting year ahead in which new faces would try to capture the nation's imagination.[77] Time moves on. Women are the realists, she said.

Max Moxley, retired editor of the Sterling Bulletin, wanted to preserve Doris' memory, and as a guide to commencement visitors at Sterling College he told of the famous native. By the 1980s few recognized the name. One day he heard that the Fleeson family home on Main Street was being torn down. Moxley, an old news type, grabbed his camera and ran to capture a final image.

The golden age of newspapers is over, and even Mencken's *Baltimore Sun* is now a casualty. But though its brilliant commentary is a relic of the time, such "art," as Mencken called it, is imperishable and, in Doris' case, incomparable.

Columnist Lars-Erik Nelson of *The New York Daily News* wrote:

> Every so often I pull down from the shelves a volume of yellowing Daily News clippings from 1937 and read these words by reporters John O'Donnell and Doris Fleeson:
>
> "Washington, Jan 20 Head bared to an angry sky, his face lashed by the chill fury of a wind-whipped rain, Franklin Delano Roosevelt took the oath of office for his second term as President and pledged his administration to continue the fight against need and poverty, which still are the lot of millions."
>
> . . . . No, we don't write that well anymore, and our leaders don't think that grandly.

NOTES

ACRONYMS USED IN CITATIONS:

NYDN: *The New York Daily News*
ER: Eleanor Roosevelt
FDR: Franklin Delano Roosevelt
NYPL: New York Public Library
KU: University of Kansas
Columns cited with headlines but without datelines are found in the form of clippings in the Doris Fleeson Papers, University Archives, Spencer Research Library, University of Kansas Libraries.

CHAPTER 1

1. Article datelined New York, Jan. 14.—(AP), *The Lyons Daily News*, January 14, 1928.
2. *The New York Daily News*, January 13, 1928. Microfilm files at New York Public Library.
3. The New York Daily News, January 6, 1928.
4. Wilda M. Smith and Eleanor A. Bogart, *The Wars of Peggy Hull*, (El Paso: Texas Western Press, 1991), pp. 203,204.
5. This Fabulous Century (1920-1930), (New York: *Time-Life Books*, 1969), p. 184.
6. Ibid.
7. Ibid., p. 201.
8. "Society Girl Student Lost in Mystery,: *The New York Daily News*, January 15, 1928.
9   "Clews to Lost Girl Fail," The New York Daily News, January 17, 1928.
10. Ibid.
11. *Bring Me A Unicorn*, Diaries and Letters of Anne MorroW Lindbergh, 1922-1928, (New York: Harcourt Brace Jovanovich, Inc., 1971, 1972), p. 81, n 22.
12. Ibid., p. 104.
13. "Parents See Smith Girl's Fate Sealed," *The New York Daily News*, January 19, 1928.
14. "Ransom Letter Laid to Crank," Ibid., January 21, 1928.
15. "College Under Fire," Ibid., January 25, 1928.
16. Bring Me A Unicorn, p. 104.

17. Kay Mills, *A Place In The News*, (New York: Dodd, Mead & Company, 1988), pp. 24, 25.
18. Finis Farr, *Margaret Mitchell of Atlanta*, (New York: William Morrow & Company, 1965), pp. 59-62.
19. John William Tebbel, *An American Dynasty*, (New York: Doubleday & Company, Inc., 1947), pp. 310, 311.
20. A Place In The News, p. 27.
21. Address by Eric Sevareid to American Booksellers Association, May 29, 1956, Doris Fleeson Papers, Spencer Research Library, the University of Kansas, Lawrence, Kansas.
22. H.L. Mencken to Doris Fleeson, handwritten on stationery imprinted "The Johns Hopkins Hospital," undated, Fleeson Papers, KU.
23. Jack Popham to Doris Fleeson, May 13, 1954, Fleeson Papers, KU.
24. "Reporting the Space Age," address by Doris Fleeson to Boston Press Club, April 21, 1958, Fleeson Papers, KU.
25. Doris Fleeson, "Far Right Wing Loses," Column, March 18, 1954, clipping from *The Washington Star*, Fleeson Papers, KU.
26. Barbara Belford, *Brilliant Bylines*, (New York: Columbia University Press, 1987), p. 258.

CHAPTER 2

1. Robert Lewis Taylor, *Vessel of Wrath*, (New York: The New American Library, 1966), pp. 74, 81-84, 113-119, 126, 128, 131, 134, 137, 150, 152-154, 163, 169.
2. The *Sterling Bulletin*, January 25, 1901.
3. Ibid.
4. Ibid.
5. Ibid., August 6, 1970: May 24, 1901.
6. Conversation with Helen Fleeson (granddaughter of Helen Tebbe Fleeson), November 27, 1991.
7. Sterling, Kansas, 1887 prospectus of The Sterling Land & Investment Company (reprinted 1984), p. 25. Conversation with Max Moxley, May 32, 1991.
8. Information on Tebbe family, Doris Fleeson Papers, KU.
9. Helen Fleeson obituary, the *Sterling Bulletin*.
10. Conversation with Helen Fleeson, April 29, 1993.
11. Conversations with Thelma Pence Tichenor, September 11, 1991; July 20, 1993; conversation with Bernadine Steierl, June 10, 1993.
12. Conversation with Helen Fleeson, November 27, 1991.
13. Conversation with Helen Jacobs Crooks, January 24, 1992.
14. Doris Fleeson, "And Lately?", *The Kansas Teacher*, September 1963, Fleeson Papers, KU.
15. Letter from U.S. District Judge Martin Pence, July 26, 1993.
16. William Benson Dunmire obituary, the *Sterling Bulletin*, October 17, 1946.
17. "Death Claims Two Citizens," the *Sterling Bulletin*, January 25, 1917. "The Round Up" (1916 Cooper College yearbook).
18. *Cooper Courier*, October 18, November 19, 1918.

19. "Won A Medal For Bravery," the *Sterling Bulletin*, October 31, 1918.
20. *Cooper Courier*, February 11, 1919.
21. Ibid., April 22, 1919. Conversation with Helen Jacobs Crooks, January 24, 1992.
22. Letter from Doris Fleeson to Elizabeth Fleeson, May 21, 1919, Fleeson Papers, KU.

CHAPTER 3

1. Clifford S. Griffin, *The University of Kansas*, (Lawrence: The University Press of Kansas, 1974) p. 446, 447.
2. Richard Sheridan, "John Ise, 1885-1969, Economist, Conservationist, Prophet of the Energy Crisis," *Kansas History*, Topeka, Volume 5, No. 2 (Summer), p. 83. Footnote 1: Jonn Ise, "K.U. Says Farewell to the Ise Age," *Alumni Magazine*, Lawrence, v. 53, no 7 (March 1955), p. 6, editor's introduction.
3. Conversation with Dick Fleeson, February 27, 1992.
4. Letter from Doris to Elizabeth Fleeson, October 19, 1919, Fleeson Papers, KU.
5. Duke Shoop, "Young Woman, Go East," the *Kansas City Star*, January 29, 1937.
6. Griffin, The University of Kansas, p. 447.
7. Sheridan, John Ise, *Kansas History*, pp. 83-85.
8. Ibid., p. 98.
9. Ibid., p. 83.
10. Ibid., p. 85.
11. Conversation with Dick Fleeson, February 27, 1992; "Journalism in the Space Age," address by Doris Fleeson to the Matrix Table, Philadelphia, Pennsylvania, April 29, 1963, p. 7, Fleeson Papers, KU.
12. John Ise, *The American Way*, (Lawrence: Faculty of the Department of Economics and School of Business, University of Kansas, 1955) Forward by Doris Fleeson, pp. v, vi.
13. Letter from Doris to Elizabeth Fleeson, Fleeson Papers, KU, December 28, 1920.
14. *Brilliant Bylines*, cited, p. 261; *Notable American Women*, 1980, biography of Doris Fleeson by Mary McGrory, p. 240.
15. Sinclair Lewis, *Main Street*, (New York: Grosset & Dunlap, Copyright 1920 by Harcourt, Brace and Company, 31st printing November 1922.
16. Robert Smith Bader, *Hayseeds, Moralizers, & Methodists*, (Lawrence: The University Press of Kansas, 1988) pp. 46-48, 51, 52, 55.
17. H.L. Mencken to Doris Fleeson, January 10, 1938, and letter dated "November 7th," Fleeson Papers, KU.
18. "Dry Leaders Spread Note of Optimism," *The Evanston News-Index*, May 15, 1926.
19. "Young Woman, Go East," cited.

CHAPTER 4

1. "Fleeson-Murdock Nuptials celebrated Monday Evening," *The Wichita Eagle*, November 22, 1927. (Clipping, Fleeson Papers, KU.)
2. *History of Kansas Newspapers*, (Topeka: Kansas State Historical Society, 1916), p. 38.
3. Rolla A. Clymer, "A Golden Era of Kansas Journalism," Address of The President of the Kansas State Historical Society, October 15, 1957, *The Kansas Historical Quarterly*, Spring 1958, p. 101.

4. Victor Murdock, *It May Chance of Wheat*, (Kansas City, Missouri: The Lowell Press, 1965), inside dustjacket.
5. "Three Newspaperwomen Tell Their Bosses a Thing or Two," clipping of article on April 22, 1939, on American Society of Newspaper Editors convention, Fleeson Papers, KU.
6. Clymer, "A Golden Era of Kansas Journalism," p. 99.
7. Catherine Sayler, "Hot-Lead Editors—A Fiery Breed," paper presented at South Central Journalism Historians' Conference, April 19-20, 1980, p. 13.
8. Robert Smith Bader, *Hayseeds, Moralizers, & Methodists*, (University Press of Kansas, 1988), p. 56.
9. "Fleeson-Murdock Nuptials Celebrated Monday Evening," *The Wichita Eagle*, November 22, 1927.
10. "The Jane to Betty Notes," *The Wichita Eagle*, November 23, 1927.
11. "Howard T. Fleeson Now A Partner In Wichita Law Firm," *The Wichita Eagle*, clipping, Fleeson Papers, KU.

CHAPTER 5

1. John William Tebbel, *An American Dynasty*, (Garden City, New York: Doubleday & Company Inc., 1947), p. 254.
2. Silas Bent, *Ballyhoo*, (New York: Horace Liveright, 1927), pp. 197, 198.
3. Duke Shoop, "*Young Woman, Go East*," clipping from *The Kansas City Star*, marked 1937, Fleeson Papers, KU.
4. Doris Fleeson to Henry Mencken, April 1, 1943, May 16, 1943, Henry Louis Mencken Letters, New York Public Library.
5. An American Dynasty, cited, p. 16
6. Ibid., p. 56.
7. Ibid., pp. 279-287.
8. Ibid., pp. 101-103.
9. *Ballyhoo*, cited, p. 186.
10. *An American Dynasty*, cited, pp. 253-255, 258.
11. *Ballyhoo, cited*, p. 189,190.
12. Ibid., p. 198.
13. Ayn Rand, *The Fountainhead*, (Indianapolis New York: The Bobbs-Merrill Company, Inc., 1943), p. 419.
14. *An American Dynasty*, cited, pp. 278,292.
15. Ibid., pp. 293,294.
16. Ibid., p. 296.

CHAPTER 6

1. "Film: A Bridled 'Paper'; an Unbridled 'Ref'," *The Wall Street Journal*, p. A14, March 17, 1994.
2. Articles by Beth J. Harpaz, October 27, 1992, and by Larry Neumeister, January 8, 1993, The Associated Press.
3. Gene Fowler, *Beau James*, (New York: The Viking Press, 1949), pp. 63, 64, 106.

4. Letter from Forrest Davis to Doris Fleeson (undated), Fleeson Papers, KU.
5. Terrence Rafferty, "Getting The Story," *The New Yorker*, March 28, 1994, p. 105.
6. Articles in *The New York Daily News* from July 31 to August 15, 1929.
7. Tebbel, *An American Dynasty*, cited, p. 261.
8. "Pajama Pioneers Crash Movie Fans' Sympathies," *The New York Daily News*, August 15, 1929.
9. Fowler, *Beau James*, cited, pp. 81, 92.
10. Alistair Cooke, *Alistair Cooke's America*, (New York: Alfred A. Knopf, 1973), p. 326.
11. Gloria Kamen, *Fiorello*, (New York: Atheneum, 1981), pp. 5-33.
12. Fowler, *Beau James*, cited, pp. 246-255.
13. Doris Fleeson, "Mourned by Liberals," column September 23, 1947.

CHAPTER 7

1. Forrest Davis to Doris Fleeson, March 22, 1928, Fleeson Papers, KU.
2. Barbara Belford, *Brilliant Bylines*, cited, p. 261.
3. Duke Shoop, "Young Woman, Go East," cited; "John O'Donnell, Columnist, Dead," *The New York Times*, December 18, 1961.
4. Scrapbook for John O'Donnell, "All of Us," compiled by *New York Daily News* colleagues, "a brief picture story of your career with the News hopes and prayers for your recovery," Fleeson Papers, KU.
5. Ibid.
6. Columnist Helen Escary, in introducing Doris at a meeting, made the reference to John. Scrapbook clipping, Fleeson Papers, KU.
7. Betty Houchin Winfield, *FDR and the News Media*, (Urbana and Chicago: University of Illinois Press, 1990), pp. 67, 68.
8. John Tebbel, *An American Dynasty*, cited, pp. 262-265.
9. FDR and the News Media, cited, p. 68.
10. Eric Sevareid, *Not So Wild A Dream*, (New York: Atheneum, 1976), pp. 220, 221; "John O'Donnell, Columnist, Dead," *The New York Times*, December 18, 1961.
11. H.L. Mencken to Doris Fleeson, December 19, 1942, Fleeson Papers, KU.
12. *An American Dynasty*, cited, p. 265.
13. George McWilliams, "Political Columnist Forgets Femininity In Writing Career," *The Denver Post*, March 21, 1958.
14. Conversation with Helen Fleeson, April 29, 1993.
15. Wedding announcement, Fleeson Papers, KU.
16. Conversation with Helen Fleeson, April 29, 1993; "John O'Donnell, Columnist Dead," *The New York Times*, December 18, 1961.
17. Conversation with Robert Fleeson, June 29, 1992.
18. "Miss Fleeson Becomes A Bride," clipping from the *Sterling Bulletin*, undated, Fleeson Papers, KU.

CHAPTER 8

1. Gene Fowler, *Beau James*, cited, p. 190.
2. Ibid., p. 141.

3. Itid., p. 136.

4. Ibid., p. 153.

5. Ibid., p. 91.

6. Ibid., 214.

7. Duke Shoop, "Young Woman, Go East," cited.

8. *Beau James*, cited, p. 258.

9. Ibid., pp. 263,264.

10. "Roosevelt Tells Tammany Leaders to Talk to Jury," *The New York Daily News*, September 29, 1930.

11. *Beau James*, p. 278.

12. Ishbel Ross, *Ladies of the Press*, (New York and London, Harper & Brothers,1936) p. 351.

13. Samuel Seabury to Doris Fleeson, March 7, 1939, Fleeson Papers, KU.

14. Ladies of the Press, p. 351; Beau James, p. 287.

15. *Beau James*, p. 293.

16. Ibid., pp. 21, 11, 50, 51, 59, 65.

17. Ibid., p. 276.

18. "Roosevelt Signs Probe Bill," *The New York Daily News*, March 16, 1932.

19. "Bronx Permit Spoils Bared by Provers," *The New York Daily News*, March 16, 1932.

20. *Ladies of the Press*, cited, pp. 351, 352.

21. *Brilliant Bylines*, cited, p. 261.

22. "Seabury Urges Abolition of Magistrates' Courts," *The New York Daily News*, March 28, 1932.

23. Doris Fleeson, "Mayor Got $246,692 Cash," *The New York Daily News*, May 26, 1932.

24. *Beau James*, cited, p. 303.

25. "Mayor Got $246,692 Cash," cited.

26. *Beau James*, cited, p. 317.

27. John Tebbel, *An American Dynasty*, cited, p. 259.

28. "Republicans Face Split Over Repeal As Keynotes Fade," NYDN, June 15, 1932.

29. "Cops Halt Reds Seeking To Storm G.O.P Stadium," NYDN, June 15, 1932.

30. Doris Fleeson, "Dolly Gann Begs Drys Not To Bottle Curtis," NYDN, June 16, 1932.

31. Fleeson, "Lady Wets 'Arent' Mad' But Start Home Early," NYDN, June 17, 1932.

32. "Roosevelt Opposition Stiffens; Foes Block Stampede Effort," NYDN, June 27, 1932.

33. Fleeson, "Tammany Chiefs Gather For Caucus," NYDN, June 27, 1932.

34. Carl Bode, *Mencken*, (Carbondale and Edwardsville: Southern Illinois University Press—London and Amsterdam: Feffer & Simmons, Inc., 1969), pp. 313-316.

35. Fleeson, "Glad Wet Tidings Hailed by Women With Jubilee Tea," NYDN, June 30, 1932.

36. Fleeson, "Woman Candidate For Vice President Arizona's Choice," NYDN, June 28, 1932.

37. Fleeson, "Women Lorgnette Stadium Doings In Latest Style," NYDN, June 30, 1932.

38. Fleeson, "Bridesmaid Pleads Roosevelt's Cause," NYDN, July 1, 1932.

39. *Beau James*, cited, p. 316.

40. Fleeson, "Huge Crowd Awaits Governor At Airport," NYDN, July 3, 1932.

41. "Roosevelt Goes to Ohio For 1st Campaign Speech," NYDN, August 20, 1932.

42. *Ladies of the Press*, cited, p. 352.

43. Doris Fleeson, "10,000 In Uproar As Walker Tells Albany: 'I'll Fight!'," NYDN, August 11, 1932.
44. "Walker Wins First Round," NYDN, August 12, 1932.
45. "Gist of Charges Walker Faces At Hearing," NYDN, August 12, 1932.
46. "Gag Governor On Walker," NYDN, August 13, 1932.
47. "'Frank' Looks Like Fighter to Garner, NYDN, August 15, 1932.
48. "Walker Plea Gets Rebuff By Governor," NYDN, August 20, 1932.
49. "Roosevelt Goes to Ohio for 1st Campaign Speech," NYDN, August 20, 1932.
50. "Roosevelt Closes Hearings and Refuses to Comment," NYDN, September 3, 1932.
51. *200 Years*, (Washington, D.C.: Books by *U.S. News & World Report*, 1973), p. 147.
52. "10 Banks Close In Northwest," NYDN, September 1, 1932.
53. "17-Story Plunge Kills Coal Chief," NYDN, August 19, 1932.

CHAPTER 9

1. Doris Fleeson, "Huge Crowd Awaits Governor At Airport," *The New York Daily News*, July 3, 1932; "Bucking Headwinds Delays Nominee's Ship," Ibid.
2. Eleanor Roosevelt, *The Autobiography of Eleanor Roosevelt*, (New York: Da Capo Press, 1992; originally published: New York: Harper & Brothers, 1961), p. 160.
3. Doris Fleeson, "The Public Wife," address at Ladies Luncheon of the United States Chamber of Commerce, Washington D.C., May 3, 1960, p. 3, Fleeson Papers, University of Kansas.
4. Doris Fleeson, "A Kind Word For Politicians," The George Fullmer Reynolds Lectures, The University of Colorado, February 15, 16, 17, 1966, p. 6, Fleeson Papers, KU.
5. Blanche Wiesen Cook, *Eleanor Roosevelt*, (New York: Viking Penguin, 1992), p. 406.
6. Autobiography (ER), cited, p. 113.
7. Cook, cited, p. 108.
8. Autobiography (ER), cited, p. 61.
9. Cook, cited, p. 245.
10. Autobiography (ER), cited, p. 112.
11. Cook, cited, p. 293.
12. Ibid., pp. 293,296.
13. Ibid., p. 325.
14. Ibid., p. 284.
15. Cook, cited, p. 394.
16. Doris Fleeson, "Beaten Path to Hyde Park," August 1, 1950 column, Fleeson Papers, KU.
17. Joseph P. Lash, *Eleanor and Franklin*, (New York: W.W. Norton & Company, Inc., 1971, p. 263.
18. Ishbel Ross, *Ladies of the Press*, cited, p. 352.
19. Conversation with Dick Fleeson, February 7, 1992.
20. Elliott Roosevelt and James Brough, *A Rendezvous With Destiny*, (New York: G.P. Putnam's Sons, 1975), pp. 62-65.
21. Duke Shoop, "Young Woman Go East," cited, Fleeson Papers, KU.
22. Scrapbook compiled by John O'Donnell's *New York Daily News* colleagues, Fleeson Papers, KU.

23. Charles Fisher, *The Columnists*, (New York: Howell, Soskin, 1944), pp. 7-12.
24. Ibid., p. 199.
25. Ibid., p. 158.
26. Ibid., pp. 273-275.
27. Ned Seaton, article, the Associated Press, October 10, 1992.
28. "Washington: How Reporters Cover the Nation's Capital," *NEWS-WEEK*, January 9, 1937, clipping, Fleeson Papers, KU.
29. Eleanor Roosevelt, autobiography, cited, pp. 171,172.
30. "Columnist Doris Fleeson Dies at 69," *The Washington Post*, August 2, 1970.
31. "Fleeson Boys Have Fine Trip William and Dick Fleeson Spent Pleasant Summer in East, Seeing Many Worth While Things," the *Sterling Bulletin*, September 6, 1934.
32. Conversation with Thelma Pence Tichenor, September 11, 1991.
33. Letter signed F. and A.D., apparently written by Alice Dains, November 8, 1934, Fleeson Papers, KU.
34. Letter from Dr. Mary Halton, no date, Fleeson Papers, KU.
35. Westbrook Pegler, "Fair Enough," column April 6, 1935, clipping, Fleeson Papers, KU.
36. Letter from Doris Fleeson to Elizabeth Jordan, April 10, 1935, Fleeson Papers, KU.

CHAPTER 10

1. "Landon Is Favorite, Borah The 'If' Man," *The New York Daily News*, June 7, 1936.
2. Donald R. McCoy, *Landon of Kansas*, (Lincoln: University of Nebraska Press, 1966), pp. 209, 211.
3. "Gov. Landon the Favorite, Borah Big 'IF' Man on Convention Eve, NYDN, June 7, 1936; John O'Donnell, "Landon Forces Drive For 1st Ballot Victory, NYDN, June 9, 1936.
4. *Landon of Kansas*, cited, p. 231.
5. "Washington: How Reporters Cover the Nation's Capital," *NEWS-WEEK*, January 9, 1937.
6. John O'Donnell and Doris Fleeson, "Vandenberg Dodging Anti-Landon Alliance," NYDN, June 8, 1936.
7. Carl Bode, *Mencken*, cited, pp. 317, 318.
8. Ibid., p. 318.
9. O'Donnell, "Kansas Takes G.O.P. Rule: Landon Nomination Sure," NYDN.
10. Waldo W. Braden, "William E. Borah's Years in Kansas in the 1880s," *The Kansas Historical Quarterly*, Volume XV 1947, pp. 360-366.
11. Ben Jones, *Sam Jones Lawyer*, (Norman: University of Oklahoma Press, 1947), p. 5.
12. John O'Donnell, "Old Guard Abandons Stop-Landon Tactics," NYDN, June 7, 1936.
13. Doris Fleeson, "Borah Blasts Landon Plans for Platform," NYDN, June 9, 1936.
14. Fleeson, "Hoover Hopeful of Draft in Deadlock," NYDN, June 10, 1936.
15. O'Donnell, "Hoover Snatches G.O.P.'s Spotlight," NYDN, June 11, 1936.
16. Arthur Degreeve (United Press), "Angry Borah Hints Last-Minute Bolt In Platform Row," NYDN, June 12, 1936.
17. O'Donnell, "Hoover Snatches G.O.P. Spotlight," cited.
18. Fleeson, "Landon Whip Cracks Over Party Plank," NYDN, June 12, 1936.
19. McCoy, *Landon of Kansas*, cited, pp. 256, 257.

20. O'Donnell, "Knox Named To Run With Landon; Convention Ends," NYDN, June 13, 1936.
21. Elliott Roosevelt and James Brough, *A Rendezvous With Destiny*, cited, p. 134.

CHAPTER 11

1. Western Union Telegram, September 25, 1936, Fleeson Papers, KU.
2. *Landon of Kansas*, cited, p. 284.
3. "The Homespun Troupe," *The Lyons Daily News*, August 28, 1936.
4. *Landon of Kansas*, cited, pp. 303-307.
5. "News Team With President," *Fort Worth Star-Telegram*, scrapbook clipping, no date, Fleeson Papers, KU.
6. J.M. Patterson to Harvey Deuell, November 5, 1937, Fleeson Papers, KU.
7. H.L. Mencken to Doris Fleeson, December 11, 1936, Fleeson Papers, KU.
8. Articles in *The New York Daily News*, December 10-17, 1936.
9. Doris Fleeson, "Missy—To do This," *The Saturday Evening Post*, January 8, 1938.
10. Wilda M. Smith and Eleanor A Bogart, *The Wars of Peggy Hull*, cited, p. 211.
11. John E. Drewry, *The World Book* encyclopedia, B, p. 502.
12. A Rendezvous With Destiny, cited, pp. 46, 47.
13. *Eleanor and Franklin*, cited, pp. 361-363.
14. *A Place In The News*, cited, p. 35, 36.
15. Cook, *Eleanor Roosevelt*, cited, p. 35, 36.
16. *A Rendezvous With Destiny*, cited, pp. 158, 159.
17. *Eleanor and Franklin*, cited, p. 363.
18. Ibid., p. 364; *A Place In The News*, cited, p. 36.
19. Frank Van Riper, "Doris Fleeson Dies; Columnist Famous for Capital Coverage," *The New York Daily News*, August 2, 1970.
20. "Press Women Given Prizes," clipping (no identification, no date), Fleeson Papers, KU; "Achievement Awards Presented by N.Y. Women Writers' Group," *Editor & Publisher*, April 17, 1937.
21. Eleanor Roosevelt to Doris Fleeson (secretary's draft), Eleanor Roosevelt Papers, Franklin Delano Roosevelt Library, Hyde Park, New York.
22. Anne O'Hare McCormick to Doris Fleeson, May 25, 1937, Fleeson Papers, KU.
23. Shoop, "Young Woman, Go East," cited.
24. Murray Illson, "May Craig, Feisty Capital Writer, Dies," *The New York Times*, July 16, 1975, p. 40; *A Place In The News*, cited, p. 94.
25. Fleeson, "Missy To do This," cited.
26. Agreement from The Curtis Publishing Company, December 7, 1937; Marty Sommers to Doris Fleeson, December 23, 1937, Fleeson Papers, KU.
27. "My Day," undated clipping, Fleeson Papers, KU.
28. Clipping from *The Graduate Magazine* (University of Kansas), January 1938, Fleeson Papers, KU.
29. *A Rendezvous With Destiny*, cited, pp. 203, 204.
30. Headline, *The Lyons Daily News*, June 24, 1938.
31. "News Team With President," cited.
32. James L. Wright, "Three Newspaperwomen Tell Their Bosses a Thing or Two," *Buffalo*

Evening News Washington Bureau, April 22, 1939, clipping, Fleeson Papers, KU; "What Women Read and Why Described By Experts," unidentified clipping, April 29, 1939, Fleeson Papers, KU.

33. *A Rendezvous With Destiny*, cited, pp. 230, 231.
34. Malvina Thompson to Doris Fleeson, May 19, 1939, Eleanor Roosevelt Papers, FDR Library, Hyde Park.
35. Doris Fleeson to Malvina Thompson, May 24, 1939, Eleanor Roosevelt Papers, FDR Library.

CHAPTER 12

1. *Brilliant Bylines*, cited, p. 259
2. *An American Dynasty*, cited, p. 263.
3. "Predicts No War," *The Lyons Daily News*, August 3, 1939.
4. "Sail for London," the *Sterling Bulletin*, July 27, 1939.
5. *Brilliant Bylines*, cited, p. 259.
6. Clipping, Fleeson Papers, KU.
7. "Delay Start of European Clash," *The Lyons Daily News*, August 26, 1937.
8. *An American Dynasty*, cited, p. 263.
9. Peter Kurth, *American Cassandra*, (Boston Toronto London: Little, Brown and Company, 1990), p. 201.
10. "The Howard Fleesons Return From European Trip," the *Sterling Bulletin*, September 7, 1939.
11. John O'Donnell, "Britain Grim as Children Flee," *The New York Daily News*, September 2, 1939.
12. The *Sterling Bulletin*, September 7, 1939.
13. The Wars of Peggy Hull, cited, p. 220.
14. Ibid., pp. 205-216.
15. Associated Press photo caption, Fleeson Papers, KU.
16. Peggy Deuell to Doris Fleeson, December 13, 1939, Fleeson Papers, KU.
17. "We Speaks" (photo caption), *The Lyons Daily News*, September 18, 1939.
18. "The Poor Poles," *The Lyons Daily News*, September 19, 1939.
19. *An American Dynasty*, cited, pp. 262-265,297.
20. "U.S. Starts Two Peace Ventures," *The Lyons Daily News*, February 9, 1940.
21. *Current Biography* 1940; *A Rendezvous With Destiny*, cited, pp.57, 58; Geoffrey C. Ward, *A First Class Temperament*, (New York: Harper & Row, Publishers, 1989), p. 473 (n).
22. "Stettinius Named For Welles Post: Crowley shifted," *The New York Times*, September 25, 1943, p. 1; United Press article, *The New York Times*, September 25, 1943, p. 14.
23. *A Rendezvous With Destiny*, cited, pp. 263-264.
24. A First-Class Temperament, cited, p. 473 (n).
25. First Class Passenger List of the Rex, Fleeson Papeers, KU.
26. Articles from *The Lyons Daily News*, "Trouble Covers All of Europe," February 27, 1940; "Welles Invades Land of Hitler," February 29, 1940.
27. *American Cassandra*, cited, p. 201.
28. "Hardboiled Nazi Attitude Aired," LDN, March 2, 1940.

29. "The man who travelled with Mr. Welles told me," cited.

30. Doris Fleeson, "Reich Rations Everything—Except 'Heils'," *The New York Daily News*, March 15, 1940.

31. Doris Fleeson, "Cards, Permits Rule Germans' Every Act," NYDN, March 16, 1940.

32. Doris Fleeson, "Nazi Wives Need Strategy to Run Homes," NYDN, March 17, 1940.

33. Doris Fleeson, "German Girls Work and Like It," NYDN, March 19, 1940.

34. Doris Fleeson, "Nazis Calmly Press Drive To Reincarnate War Dead," NYDN, March 20, 1940.

35. Doris Fleeson, "Reich Jews Suffer More From War," NYDN, March 23, 1940.

36. Articles from LDN, "Welles Trip Is Of Little Avail," March 4, 1940; "Welles Holds A Hope For Peace," March 6, 1940.

37. Doris Fleeson, "War to German Boys Is Work or Fight," NYDN, March 22, 1940.

38. John O'Donnell and Doris Fleeson, "Welles Denies He Got Or Gave Peace Plans," NYDN, March 20, 1940.

39. John O'Donnell and Doris Fleeson, "Hunt Dr. Schacht On Welles Liner," NYDN, March 23, 1940.

40. "Big Ships Start Dangerous Jobs," LDN, March 21, 1940.

41. Clipping of photo from *New York Times-Herald*, March 29, 1940, Fleeson Papers, KU.

42. Fred Pasley and Carl Warren, "Welles Reports to F.D.R. On Europe's War Outlook," NYDN, March 29, 1940.

CHAPTER 13

1. A.L. Shultz, "According to the Republicans," *The Lyons Daily News*, September 19, 1940.

2. "Visits Doris Fleeson Who Is On Willkie Special," the *Sterling Bulletin*, September 19, 1940.

3. Steve Neal, *Dark Horse*, (Garden City, New York: Doubleday & Company, Inc., 1984), p. 143.

4. Shultz column, LDN, September 12, 1940.

5. Ibid.

6. Neal, *Dark Horse*, cited, pp. 150,151.

7. Ibid., pp. 38-41.

8. "Willkie Twenty To One," LDN, September 13, 1940.

9. Ibid., pp. 143, 144.

10. "Willkie Speaks in Plain Terms," LDN, September 12, 1940; "Willkie Favors A Tax Revision," LDN, September 20, 1940.

11. Shultz column, *LDN*, September 26, 1940.

12. Doris Fleeson, "The Public Wife," address at the Ladies Luncheon of the United States Chamber of Commerce, Washington, D.C., May 3, 1960.

13. Neal, *Dark Horse*, cited, pp. 185, 186.

14. Wendell Willkie to Doris Fleeson, November 16, 1940, Fleeson Papers, KU.

15. Kenneth S. Davis, *Experience of War*, (Garden City, New York: Doubleday & Company, 1965), p. 29.

16. David Hinshaw, *A Man From Kansas*, (New York: G.P. Putnam's Sons, 1945), p. 280.

17. "We're On Our Way To War," NYDN, December 20, 1940.

18. Tebbel, *An American Dynasty*, cited, p. 252.
19. John O'Donnell, "Navy Escorting British, Charge," NYDN, April 17, 1941.
20. "Jury Gives $50,000 To John O'Donnell For Pro-Nazi Libel," NYDN, January 29, 1943.
21. Hinshaw, *A Man From Kansas*, cited, pp. 278-286.
22. William Allen White to Doris Fleeson, May 13, 1941, Fleeson Papers, KU.
23. Doris Fleeson, "Lindy Stands Where Father Stood in 1917," NYDN, May 2, 1941.
24. Walter Eli Quigley, "Like Father, Like Son," the *Saturday Evening Post*, June 14, 1941.
25. Doris Fleeson to Marty Sommers, June 11, 1941, Fleeson   Papers, KU.
26. Eleanor Roosevelt to Doris Fleeson, March 24, (1942), Fleeson Papers, KU.
27. Doris Fleeson to Eleanor Roosevelt, April 1, 1942, Fleeson Papers, KU.

CHAPTER 14

1. *An American Dynasty*, cited, p. 261.
2. *Brilliant Bylines*, cited, p. 263.
3. Doris Fleeson to Eleanor Roosevelt, June 2, 1941, Eleanor Roosevelt Papers, Franklin Delano Roosevelt Library, Hyde Park, New York.
4. J.M. Patterson to Doris Fleeson, May 1, 1942, Fleeson Papers, KU.
5. *Brilliant Bylines*, cited, p. 263.
6. Eleanor Roosevelt to Doris Fleeson, June 8, 1942, and June 22, 1942, Fleeson Papers, KU.
7. Doris Fleeson to Henry Mencken, July 7, 1942, H.L. Mencken Papers, New York Public Library.
8. Robert Smith Bader, *Hayseeds, Moralizers and Methodists*, cited, p. 52.
9. H.L. Mencken, *In Defense of Women*, (New York: Time Incorporated, 1963, first published by Alfred A. Knopf, Inc., 1922), p. 3.
10. Charles Angoff, H.L. *Mencken A Portrait from Memory*, (New York: Thomas Yoseloff, Inc., 1956), pp. 170-174.
11. Bode, *Mencken*, cited, p. 151.
12. Fleeson to Mencken, letter marked 1937, H.L. Mencken Papers, New York Public Library; Mencken to Fleeson, December 11, 1936, July 21, 1937, Fleeson Papers, KU.
13. Advertisement, the *Sterling Bulletin*, March 10, 1938.
14. Mencken to Fleeson, letter marked November 7th, Fleeson Papers, KU.
15. Mencken to Fleeson, October 22, 1941, Fleeson Papers, KU.
16. Mencken to Fleeson, letter marked July 8th, Fleeson Papers, KU.
17. The preceding excerpts are taken from letters in the H.L. Mencken Papers, New York Public Library. Copies of letters from Mencken to Fleeson are in the Doris Fleeson Papers, University Archives, Spencer Research Library, University of Kansas Libraries.

CHAPTER 15

1. Memorandum for Grace Tully, signed S.T.E., April 10, 1943, Eleanor Roosevelt Papers, FDR Library.

2. Mencken to Fleeson, dated "May 9th," Fleeson Papers, KU.
3. Fred Hobson. *Mencken A Life*, (Baltimore and London: The Johns Hopkins University Press, 1994), pp. 464, 465.
4. Fleeson to Mencken, May 13, 1943, Henry Louis Mencken Letters, 1920-1955, New York Public Library.
5. Mencken to Fleeson, dated "May 14th," Fleeson Papers, KU.
6. "Awards Given By Newspaper Women's Club," *New York Herald Tribune*, May 14, 1943: clipping in scrapbook, Fleeson Papers, KU.
7. Kay Mills, *A Place in the News*, cited, pp. 41,42.
8. Mencken to Fleeson, "May 14th" cited.
9. "Willkie Fighting for '44—Party or No Party," *The New York Daily News*, December 29, 1942.
10. Malvina Thompson to Doris Fleeson, May 20, 1943, Eleanor Roosevelt Papers, FDR Library.
11. Margaret L. Coit, *Mr. Baruch*, (Boston: Houghton Mifflin Company, 1957), pp. 498, 499.
12. Mencken to Fleeson, dated "May 19th," Fleeson Papers, KU.
13. Fleeson to Mencken, Mencken Letters, NYPL.
14. Conversation with Helen Fleeson, November 27, 1991.
15. Mencken to Fleeson, dated "May 23rd," Fleeson Papers, KU.
16. Malvina Stephenson, "Back as a Big-Timer," clipping of article, apparently from *The Kansas City Star* or *Times*, Fleeson Papers, KU.
17. Article on the Associated Press wire, datelined Key West, Fla., July 15, 1992.
18. Peter Kurth, *American Cassandra*, cited, p. 239
19. Clipping of news item datelined Woodstock, VT., January 2, 1942, Fleeson Papers, KU.
20. *American Cassandra*, cited, p. 373.
21. Doris Fleeson, "650 WACS Defy the Subs," *Woman's Home Companion*, October 1943, pp. 20, 21, 58, 62, 68, 70. Telephone conversation with Wallace R. Best, November, 1993.
22. Eleanor Roosevelt to Doris Fleeson, October 4, 1943, Fleeson Papers, KU.
23. The Autobiography of Eleanor Roosevelt, cited, p. 197.
24. Wendell Willkie to Doris Fleeson, September 20, 1943, Fleeson Papers, KU.
25. Fleeson to Eleanor Roosevelt, Eleanor Roosevelt Papers, FDR Library.
26. Fleeson to Mencken, August 10, 1943, Mencken Letters, NYPL.
27. The Autobiography of Eleanor Roosevelt, cited, pp. 94, 239, 240, 244.
28. ER to Fleeson, October 4, 1943, Fleeson Papers, KU.
29. The Autobiography of Eleanor Roosevelt, cited, pp. 175, 254.
30. Doris Fleeson, "I Keep a Rendezvous with Heroes," *Woman's Home Companion*, November 1943, pp. 4, 143, 144. Telephone conversation with Mrs. William A. Hjulstrom, November 1993.
31. Mencken to Fleeson, August 24, 1943, Fleeson Papers, KU.
32. Fleeson to ER, September 14, 1943, Eleanor Roosevelt Papers, FDR Library.
33. ER to Fleeson, October 28, 1943, Fleeson Papers, KU.
34. Mencken to Fleeson, October 21, 1943, Fleeson Papers, KU.

CHAPTER 16

1. Kenneth S. Davis, *Experience of War*, cited, p. 432.
2. Doris Fleeson, "Within Sound of the Guns," *Woman's Home Companion*, January 1944, pp. 4, 94.
3. Doris Fleeson, "That Feminine Touch," *Woman's Home Companion*, March 1944, pp. 4, 132.
4. Fleeson, Doris Journalist, *Current Biography* 1959, p. 123.
5. Fleeson to Malvina Thompson, February 17, 1944, Eleanor Roosevelt Papers, FDR Library.
6. Virginia Floyd to H.L. Mencken, February 23, 1944, Mencken Letters, NYPL.
7. Conversation with Robert Fleeson, June 29, 1992.
8. Mencken to Fleeson, April 8, 1944, Fleeson Papers, KU.
9. Mencken to Fleeson, April 27, 1944, Fleeson Papers, KU.
10. Fleeson to Mencken, May 10, 1944, Mencken Letters, NYPL.
11. Fleeson to ER, May 1, 1944, Eleanor Roosevelt Papers, FDR Library.
12. ER to Fleeson, May 14, 1944, Fleeson Papers, KU.
13. Fleeson to Mencken, May 10, 1944, Mencken Letters, NYPL.
14. Mencken to Fleeson, May 25, 1944, Fleeson Papers, KU.
15. Fleeson to ER, May 29, 1944, Eleanor Roosevelt Papers, FDR Library.
16. Fleeson to Mencken, June 4, 1944, Mencken Letters, NYPL.
17. Doris Fleeson, "We're On Our Way," *Woman's Home Companion*, August 1944, pp. 4, 100.
18. Doris Fleeson, "Same Old Bombs, Dearie!," *Woman's Home Companion*, September 1944, pp. 4, 120.
19. Fleeson to Mencken, June 19, 1944, Mencken Letters, NYPL.
20. Fleeson to ER, June 21, 1944, Eleanor Roosevelt Papers, FDR Library.
21. Fleeson to Mencken, July 13, 1944, Mencken Letters, NYPL.
22. Nancy Caldwell Sorel, *The Women Who Wrote the War*, (New York: Arcade Publishing, 1999), p. 245.
23. Doris Fleeson, "Into The Heart of France," *Woman's Home Companion*, September 1944, pp. 4, 152.

CHAPTER 17

1. "In Floral Temple, Miss Blair Weds, *The New York Times*, September 21, 1913, Sec. II, p. 15.
2. "William Clark, U.S. Judge, Dies," *The New York Times*, October 11, 1957, p. 27.
3. *The Diary of H.L. Mencken*, edited by Charles E. Fecher, (New York: Vintage Books, 1989), p. 347.
4. "Ex-Judge Clark Weds Miss Tomara in Paris," *The New York Times*, November 1, 1947.
5. "William Clark, U.S. Judge, Dies," cited.
6. Doris Fleeson to Henry Mencken, August 27, 1944, Mencken Letters, NYPL.
7. Fleeson to Mencken, September 28, 1944, Mencken Letters, NYPL.
8. Wendell Willkie to Doris Fleeson, September 20, 1943, Fleeson Papers, KU.
9. Steve Neal, *Dark Horse*, cited, pp. 307-323.

10. Mencken to Fleeson, November 1, 1944, Fleeson Papers, KU.

11. Fleeson to Mencken, November 8, 1944, Mencken Letters, NYPL.

12. Edith Helm to Doris Fleeson, November 24, 1944, Fleeson Papers, KU.

13. Doris Fleeson to Eleanor Roosevelt, December 9, 1944, Eleanor Roosevelt Papers, FDR Library.

14. Eleanor Roosevelt to Doris Fleeson, December 12, 1944, (copy), Eleanor Roosevelt Papers, FDR Library.

15. Doris Fleeson to Eleanor Roosevelt, December 26, 1944, Eleanor Roosevelt Papers, FDR Library.

16. Doris Fleeson to Eleanor Roosevelt, January 1, 1945, Eleanor Roosevelt Papers, FDR Library.

17. "John O'Donnell, Columnist, Dead," *The New York Times*, December 18, 1961.

18. Elliott Roosevelt and James Brough, *A Rendezvous with Destiny*, cited, p. 404.

19. Doris Fleeson to Eleanor Roosevelt, January 9, 1945, Eleanor Roosevelt Papers, FDR Library.

20. Fleeson to Mencken, January 24, 1945, Mencken Letters, NYPL.

21. Mencken to Fleeson, March 15, 1945, Fleeson Papers, KU. (The letter is dated 1944, apparently a typographical error.)

22. Doris Fleeson to Malvina Thompson, February 23, 1945, Eleanor Roosevelt Papers, FDR Library.

23. The Autobiography of Eleanor Roosevelt, cited, p. 283.

24. Eleanor Roosevelt to Doris Fleeson, April 27, 1945, Fleeson Papers, KU.

25. Eleanor Roosevelt to Doris Fleeson, July 6, 1945, Fleeson Papers, KU.

26. Mencken to Fleeson, April 2, 1945, Fleeson Papers, KU.

27. Mencken to Fleeson, July 17, July 21, 1945, Fleeson Papers, KU.

28. Fleeson to Mencken, July 24, 1945, Mencken Letters, NYPL.

29. Eleanor Roosevelt to Doris Fleeson, July 25, 1945, Fleeson Papers, KU.

30. The Autobiography of Eleanor Roosevelt, cited, p. 286.

31. Mencken to Fleeson, July 26, 1945, Fleeson Papers, KU.

32. Fleeson to Mencken, August 4, 1945, Mencken Letters, NYPL.

33. Mencken to Fleeson, August 7, 1945, Fleeson Papers, KU.

34. Fleeson to Mencken, August 19, August 27, Mencken Letters, NYPL.

35. Eleanor Roosevelt to Doris Fleeson, July 25, 1945, Fleeson Papers, KU.

36. Mencken to Fleeson, August 29, 1945, Fleeson Papers, KU.

37. Charles Fisher, *The Columnists*, cited, pp. 16-49.

38. Fleeson to Mencken, September 23, 1945, Mencken Letters, NYPL.

39. Peter Kurth, *American Cassandra*, cited, p. 219.

40. David McCullough, *Truman*, (New York: Simon & Schuster, 1992), p. 468.

41. Doris Fleeson, "Skeptical About The Truman Bite," *The Kansas City Star*, November 3, 1945.

42. Mencken to Fleeson, October 9, 1945, Fleeson Papers, KU.

43. Mary McGrory, biography of Doris Fleeson in *Notable American Women: The Modern Period*, (Cambridge, Mass.: The Belnap Press of Harvard University, 1980), p. 240.

44. Doris Fleeson, "Why Italy Charges Bad Faith by U.S.," November 16, 1945, *The Kansas City Star*.
45. Fleeson to Mencken, October 17, 1945, Mencken Letters, NYPL.
46. Conversation with Robert Fleeson, June 29, 1992.
47. Conversation with Dick Fleeson, October 25, 1994.
48. Fleeson to Mencken, October 20, 1945, Mencken Letters, NYPL.
49. Charles Fisher, *The Columnists*, cited, p. 205.
50. Fleeson to Mencken, November 4, 1945, NYPL.
51. Doris Fleeson, "WAC Aide of Eisenhower Flies to U.S. to Seek Citizenship," the Washington *Evening Star*, November 5, 1945.
52. Mencken to Fleeson, November 6, 1945, Fleeson Papers, KU.
53. Fleeson to Mencken, November 8, 1945, Fleeson Papers, KU.
54. Doris Fleeson, "Bess Truman Brave Hostess," *The Kansas City Star*, November 17, 1945.
55. Doris Fleeson, "Mrs. Roosevelt's Role in U.N.O Team for America," December 19, 1945, *The Kansas City Star*, p. 26.

CHAPTER 18

1. Doris Fleeson, "Clan Spirit of Crusade's Team," June 10, 1955, Scrapbook, Fleeson Papers, KU.
2. Clipping, Fleeson Papers, KU.
3. Martha Sherrill, "Georgetown On My Mind," *Town & Country*, May 1992, pp. 77-82.
4. Margaret Germond, "Old Georgetown House Tour Next Friday and Saturday," *The Washington Star*, March 23, 1947.
5. Susan Mary Alsop, "Katharine Graham's Capital Life," *Architectural Digest*, December 1994, pp. 127-133.
6. "Georgetown On My Mind," cited, p. 80.
7. Constance Casey, "Mixed Blessings," *The Washington Post Magazine*, April 19, 1992, p. 21.
8. Malvina Stephenson, "Back As A Big-Timer," clipping in Fleeson Papers, KU. Dateline: Washington, Jan. 24.
9. Interview with Robert Fleeson, June 29, 1992.
10. Barbara Belford, *Brilliant Bylines*, p. 263.
11. Photographs, Fleeson Papers, KU.
12. "Georgetown, World's Most Powerful Village," clipped article, Fleeson Papers, KU.
13. Fleeson to Mencken, January 8, 1946, Mencken Papers, NYPL.
14. Mencken to Fleeson, January 11, 1946, Fleeson Papers, KU.
15. Mencken to Fleeson, January 16, 1946, Fleeson Papers, KU.
16. McCullough, *Truman*, cited, p. 202.
17. Mencken to Fleeson, February 1, 1946, Fleeson Papers, KU.
18. McCullough, *Truman*, cited, p. 481.
19. "Trip Home A Busy One," clipping, Fleeson Papers, KU. Stephenson, "Back As a Big-Timer," cited.
20. "Doris Fleeson Sees Working Man Claiming Own Labor's Sinewy Grasp Firm," clipping from *The Topeka State Journal*, January 29, 1946, scrapbook of the Native Sons and Daughters of Kansas, Kansas State Historical Society, Topeka.

21. Clipping, scrapbook of the Native Sons and Daughters of Kansas, cited.
22. "The Old Home Editor," *Sterling Bulletin*, February 14, 1946.
23. Doris Fleeson, "Washington Parties are Serious Business, *Nation's Business*, March 1946, Fleeson Papers, KU.
24. Western Union Telegrams, Fleeson Papers, KU.
25. Fleeson to Malvina "Tommy" Thompson, July 15, 1942, Eleanor Roosevelt Papers, FDR Library.
26. Fleeson, "Her Passing Marks End of Era," clipping from the *St. Louis Post-Dispatch*, Fleeson Papers, KU.
27. Joseph P. Lash, *Eleanor and Franklin*, cited, p. 620.
28. "Washington Parties are Serious Business," cited.
29. Fleeson, "Censures Truman Social Calendar," *The Kansas City Star*, February 13, 1946.
30. Fleeson, "President Still Trusts His 'Kitchen Cabinet'," *The Kansas City Star*, January 23, 1946.
31. Fleeson, "No Critic Was Ever Met Halfway," March 19, 1952, Scrapbook, Fleeson Papers, KU.
32. Fleeson, "Frances Perkins Has Last Laugh," *The Kansas City Star*, January 21, 1946.
33. Fleeson, "Mrs. Luce Finds Politics Too Dull," *The Kansas City Star*, February 8, 1946.
34. Fleeson, "Bowles and Mrs. Luce Headed for Senate Race," *The Kansas City Star*, April 18, 1946.
35. Fleeson, "Zhukov as Guest of Eisenhower," *The Kansas City Star*, April 23, 1946.
36. Fleeson to Mencken, April 28, 1946, Mencken Papers, NYPL.
37. Fleeson, "Court Ignores Attack by Bar," *The Kansas City Star*, January 30, 1946.
38. Fleeson, "Stone Fought to Hold Justices," *The Kansas City Star*, April 26, 1946.
39. Fleeson, "Supreme Court Feud, *The Washington Evening Star*, June 11, 1946.
40. McCullough, Truman, cited, p. 507.
41. Ben Reese to Doris Fleeson, June 11, 1946, telegram, Fleeson Papers, KU.

CHAPTER 19

1. McCullough, *Truman*, cited, p. 554; address at University of Texas, broadcast on C-Span.
2. "Doris Fleeson To Talk," clipping of article from *The Kansas City Star*, undated, Lyons Public Library file.
3. "Wallace Speech May Raise Stink," *The Lyons Daily News*, September 13, 1946.
4. McCullough, *Truman*, cited, p. 514.
5. Fleeson, "U.S. Foreign Policy Developing Out in the Open," *The Wichita Eagle*, September 12, 1946.
6. Doris Fleeson to Henry Mencken, November 14, 1946, Mencken Letters, NYPL.
7. Fleeson, "The President Was at His Best," (column), April 17, 1953.
8. Dwight D. Eisenhower to Doris Fleeson, November 14, 1946, Fleeson Papers, KU.
9. Fleeson, "New High Court Plan Might Placate Labor," June 4, 1946, "Truman Message Will Not Be Controversial," December 14, 1946, *The Kansas City Star*.
10. Fleeson, "Share-the-Blame, Plan for Senate," January 14, 1947, *The Kansas City Star*, "Problem Aggravated," February 20, 1947, *The Washington Evening Star*, "Taft Speeches to Praise Congress," July 30, 1947, *The Kansas City Star*.

11. Ben Reese to Roy Roberts, January 9, 1947, Fleeson Papers, KU.
12. Ben Reese to Doris Fleeson, May 27, 1947, Fleeson Papers, KU.
13. B.M. McKelway to Henry M. Snevily (copy), May 23, 1947, Fleeson Papers, KU.
14. Joseph Pulitzer to Doris Fleeson, February 17, 1947, Fleeson Papers, KU.
15. "Doris Fleeson To Talk," clipping of article from *The Kansas City Star*, undated, Lyons Public Library file.
16. Eleanor Roosevelt to Doris Fleeson, June 6, 1947, Fleeson Papers, KU.
18. Fleeson, "A Market Basket Is Tossed to Congress," *The Kansas City Star*, June 25, 1947.
19. Ibid.
20. Fleeson, "Hope of U.S. Taxpayer In European Recovery," *The Kansas City Star*, July 12, 1947.
21. Eleanor Roosevelt to Doris Fleeson, July 30, 1947, Fleeson Papers, KU.
22. "Interesting But Unseemly," clipping from *The New York Times*, dated August 9, "Pass The Peanuts, Please," clipping from *The Washington Daily News*, undated, Eleanor Roosevelt Papers, FDR Library.
23. Doris Fleeson to Eleanor Roosevelt, August 10, 1947, Eleanor Roosevelt Papers, FDR Library.
24. Fleeson, "Better Deal for Women in Politics," clipping from *St. Louis Post-Dispatch*, May 1, 1947, Fleeson Papers, KU.
25. Margaret Chase Smith to Doris Fleeson, September 30, 1946, Fleeson Papers, KU.
26. Jennifer L. Tebbe, biography of May Craig, *Notable American Women*, cited, pp. 171-173; Murray Illson, "May Craig, Feisty Capital Writer, Dies," *The New York Times*, July 16, 1975, p. 40.
27. Fleeson, "They Shy at Women," August 28, 1947, clipping, Fleeson Papers, KU.
28. Fleeson, "Washington Parties are Serious Business," cited.
29. Fleeson, "Capital Society Hires a Stylist," *The Kansas City Star*, August 15, 1947.
30. Fleeson, "Taft's Tour May Outshine Dewey's," August 16, 1947, "Taft Is Tactless On Western Trip," September 15, 1947, *The Kansas City Star*.
31. Fleeson, "Eisenhower Foes Build a Backfire," *The Kansas City Star*, October 7, 1947.
32. Fleeson, "MacArthur Home When He Pleases," *The Kansas City Star*, September 12, 1947.
33. Fleeson, "Senators Seek to Avoid Party Rift," *The Kansas City Star*, January 15, 1948.
34. Fleeson, "No Deal With Taft to Stop Dewey, Stassen Says," *The Kansas City Star*, October 16, 1947.
35. Fleeson, "Wisconsin Vote MacArthur Test," *The Kansas City Star*, March 18, 1948.
36. Fleeson, "Ohio Flirting With Stassen," *The Kansas City Star*, April 24, 1948.
37. McCullough, *Truman*, cited, p. 629.
38. Joseph P. Lash, *Eleanor: The Years Alone*, (New York: W.W. Norton & Company, Inc., 1972), p. 149.
39. Fleeson, "Unrealistic Flurry," clipping, Eleanor Roosevelt Papers, FDR Library.
40. Eleanor Roosevelt to Doris Fleeson, (secretary's draft, marked 1948), Eleanor Roosevelt Papers, FDR Library.
41. Paul F. Ewing, "Columnist Fleeson Yearns For Just One Little Slip," clipping from *The Oregonian*, undated, Fleeson Papers, KU.
42. McCullough, *Truman*, cited, pp. 668, 669.
43. Ewing, "Columnist Fleeson Yearns For Just One Little Slip," cited.

44. Fleeson, "All Too Smooth On Dewey Train," September 30, 1948, *The Kansas City Star*.
45. "Election Forecast: 50 Political Experts Predict a GOP Sweep," *Newsweek*, October 11, 1948.
46. McCullough, Truman, cited, p. 695.
47. Fleeson, "Truman's Hopes Higher At Campaign's Finish," *The Kansas City Star*, October 30, 1948.
48. Fleeson, "The Little Club Around Sen. McGrath Turned Out To Be Not So Exclusive After All," *The Hutchinson News*, November 6, 1948.

CHAPTER 20

1. "Entertain at Dance," "Luncheon Guests," *The Lyons Daily News*, June 29, 1949, p. 3; item in the *Sterling Bulletin*, June 30, 1949.
2. Doris Fleeson to Eleanor Roosevelt, June 4, 1949, Eleanor Roosevelt Papers, FDR Library, Hyde Park.
3. Article on wedding of Doris O'Donnell, the *Sterling Bulletin*, February 14, 1957.
4. Cook, *Eleanor Roosevelt*, cited, p. 300.
5. Peter Collier with David Horowitz, (New York: Simon & Schuster, 1994), p. 360.
6. Fleeson to Eleanor Roosevelt, February 16, 1949, FDR Library, Hyde Park.
7. ER to Fleeson, (secretary's draft, no date), FDR Library, Hyde Park.
8. Fleeson to ER, April 3, 1949, FDR Library, Hyde Park.
9. Margaret L. Coit, *Mr. Baruch*, cited, p. 675.
10. Eleanor Roosevelt to Miss Vera B. Thompson, (secretary's draft), April 11, 1949, FDR Library, Hyde Park.
11. Fleeson to ER, August 7, 1949, FDR Library, Hyde Park.
12. Eleanor Roosevelt, "My Day," clipping, no date, Fleeson Papers, KU.
13. Coit, *Mr. Baruch*, cited, p. 653.
14. Bernard Baruch to Doris Fleeson, February 8, 1957, Fleeson Papers, KU.
15. Copy of toast, Fleeson Papers, KU.
16. Baruch to Fleeson, January 28, 1950, Fleeson Papers, KU.
17. ER to Fleeson, January 30, 1940, FDR Library, Hyde Park.
18. Baruch to Fleeson, dated "Friday," Fleeson Papers, KU.
19. Clippings, Fleeson Papers, KU.
20. Alice A. Dunnigan, "Washington Inside Out," *The Pittsburgh Courier*, March 14, 1959.
21. Fleeson, "Truman Ready for the Big Wind," April 12, 1951, Fleeson Papers, KU.
22. Fleeson, "Editors Preview Trial," April 21, Fleeson Papers, KU.
23. "Covering the Capital," "Core of the Corps," *Time*, July 9, 1951, clippings, Fleeson Papers, KU.
24. "VFW Auxiliary Award Goes to Doris Fleeson," *The Evening Star*, August 30, 1951, clipping, Eleanor Roosevelt Papers, FDR Library; ER to Fleeson, August 16, 1951, Fleeson Papers, KU.
25. Raymond P. Brandt, "Navy's Dan Kimball, A St. Louis Dynamo," *St. Louis Post-Dispatch*, August 5, 1951; "Aerojet at Nimbus——10,000 Work at 'Missile Capital'," *San Francisco Chronicle*, September 24, 1958, p. 10.

26. Kimball to Fleeson, undated, Fleeson Papers, KU.
27. Incoming Dispatch, U.S. Naval Communications, August 29, 1951, Fleeson Papers, KU.
28. Kimball to Fleeson, dated Wed 9/9, Fleeson Papers, KU.
29. Fleeson, "Senate Is Balky On Little Things," *The Kansas City Star*, March 25, 1949.
30. Fleeson, "Alsop Testimony On Budenz Shows Security Group Need," the *Hutchinson News-Herald*, October 22, 1951.
31. Joseph Alsop to Doris Fleeson, October 22, 1951, Fleeson Papers, KU.
32. Fleeson, "'Little Things Count' in Politics," October 12, 1951, Fleeson Papers, KU.
33. Fleeson, "Let Down by People He Trusted," December 12, 1951, Fleeson Papers, KU.
34. "Truman Irked by Her Look," clipping from *The Kansas City Times*, undated, Fleeson Papers, KU.
35. "Nasty Cut at Our Doris," *The Oregonian*, December 15, 1951.
36. Transcript of The Georgetown University Radio Forum, January 6, 1952, Fleeson Papers, KU.
37. Fleeson, "Why Not Speak for Yourself, Ike ?" January 15, 1952.
38. Fleeson, "Six Governors to Be on Hand," March 25, 1952.
39. Fleeson, "Truman Shows Political Wisdom," March 31, 1952.
40. "Lady About Town," *Time*, April 21, 1952.
41. Fleeson, "The General Must Get on the Ball," May 26, 1952.
42. Fleeson, "Truman Really Likes Eisenhower," June 3, 1952.
43. Fleeson, "Eisenhower Interview Crucial," June 2, 1952.
44. Fleeson, "His First Speech No Barn-Burner," June 5, 1952.
45. Fleeson, "Nixon Almost a Frivolous Choice," July 17, 1952.
46. Fleeson, "Stevenson May Be Forced to Run," July 21, 1952.
47. Fleeson, "Washington to Get a New Look," July 24, 1952.
48. Fleeson, "The Inspirational Approach," September 17, 1952.
49. Fleeson, "Candidate Eisenhower Declines," October 10, 1952.
50. Fleeson, "The Case of the Non-Military Secret," *New York Post*, October 10, 1952.
51. Fleeson, "Imperil Those They Seek to Help," September 18, 1952.
52. Fleeson, "Aides Tell Why Truman Turned," October 3, 1952.
53. Copy of typewritten article, Fleeson Papers, KU.
54. "MacArthur Assails President, Blames 'Appeasement Policies; For Any Excessive Desertions," clipping from *The Sunday Star*, January 10, 1953, Fleeson Papers, KU.
55. ER to Fleeson, (draft) December 30, 1952, FDR Library.
56. Fleeson, "Greatest Tribute to Truman," January 21, 1953.
57. Oral History Interview with Robert G. Nixon, Volume I, pp. 974, 975, Harry S. Truman Library, Independence, Missouri.

CHAPTER 21

1. Margaret L. Coit, *Mr. Baruch*, cited, p. 653.
2. Bernard Baruch to Doris Fleeson, "Xmas 1952," Fleeson Papers, KU.
3. Earl English to Doris Fleeson, February 24, 1953, Fleeson Papers, KU; The University of Missouri BULLETIN The Missouri Honor Awards for Distinguished Service in Journalism 1953, Fleeson Papers, KU.

4. Harry Truman to Doris Fleeson, May 20, 1953, Fleeson Papers, KU.
5. Doris Fleeson, "Truman Keeps His Powder Dry," June 3, 1953, Fleeson Papers, KU.
6. Fleeson, "Dewey and McCarthy in Clash," May 15, 1953, Fleeson Papers, KU.
7. Fleeson, "McCarthy and the Southerners," July 16, 1953, Fleeson Papers, KU.
8. Fleeson, "The President Was at His Best," April 17, 1953, Fleeson Papers, KU.
9. Ibid.
10. Transcript of Presidential press conference, November 4, 1953, recorded by U.S. Army Signal Corps, Dwight D. Eisenhower Library, Abilene, Kansas.
11. Fleeson, "Opinions From the Wheat Belt," November 24, 1953, Fleeson Papers, KU; Conversation with Helen Fleeson, April 29, 1953.
12. Eleanor Roosevelt to Doris Fleeson, January 12, 1954, Fleeson Papers, KU.
13. "Star Columnist Doris Fleeson Wins Raymond Clapper Award, *The* (Washington) *Evening Star*, April 18, 1954, clipping, Fleeson Papers, KU.
14. Raymond Clapper, *Watching the World 1944*, (New York, London: Whittlesey House McGray Hill Book Company), biographical information.
15. Doris Fleeson, "The press and individual responsibility," Fleeson Papers, KU.
16. Fleeson, "McCarthy Busy on Two Fronts," February 23, 1954, Fleeson Papers, KU.
17. Fleeson, "McCarthy Holds 5 Aces—Again," February 25, 1954, Fleeson Papers, KU.
18. Fleeson, "Just What Did Eisenhower Say ?" March 4, 1954, Fleeson Papers, KU.
19. Fleeson, "McCarthyism in Full Bloom," June 10, 1954, Fleeson Papers, KU.
20. Peggy Talbott to Doris Fleeson, June 10, 1954, Fleeson Papers, KU.
21. Fleeson, "Nixon Gambles on His Ambition," October 27, 1954.
22. "Ike's Dinners," column by Doris Fleeson, *New York Post* clipping dated 12/54, White House Central Files, General File, Dwight D. Eisenhower Library, Abilene, Kansas.
23. Letter from Bertha Diggs Warner to James Hagerty, December 30, 1954, White House Central Files, General File, Dwight D. Eisenhower Library.
24. Letter from James Hagerty to Bertha Diggs Warner, January 14, 1955, White House Central Files, General File, Dwight D. Eisenhower Library.
25. Fleeson, "Press Conference Goes on TV," January 20, 1955, Fleeson Papers, KU.
26. Fleeson, "Color Line and the Press Club," January 14, 1955.
27. Eleanor Roosevelt to Doris Fleeson, April 25, 1955, Fleeson Papers, KU.
28. Fleeson to Harry S. Truman, May 25, 1955, Fleeson Papers, KU.
29. Notes from Bess Truman to Doris, all undated, Fleeson Papers, KU.
30. Fleeson, "Men First; Women, Children Last," June 16, 1955, Fleeson Papers, KU.
31. Fleeson to Harry S. Truman, June 17, 1955, Fleeson Papers, KU.
32. Robert E. Gilbert, *The Mortal Presidency*, (BasicBooks, A Division of HarperCollinsPublishers, Inc., 1992), pp. 86-89.
33. Fleeson, "Accidental Nature of Politics," July 4, 1955, Fleeson Papers, KU.
34. Fleeson, "Nothing Will Be the Same," September 26, 1955, Fleeson Papers, KU.
35, Gilbert, *The Mortal Presidency*, cited, pp. 81-86.
36. Fleeson, "Who Can Argue With the Doctor ?" December 13, 1955, Fleeson Papers, KU.
37. Gilbert, *The Mortal Presidency*, cited, pp. 80, 99-101.
38. Column for June 11, 1956, typewritten copy, Fleeson Papers, KU.
39. Fleeson, "Question of President's Health," June 14, 1956, Fleeson Papers, KU.
40. Alistair Cooke, "To Run or Not?" *Manchester Guardian*, June 18, 1956, clipping, Fleeson Papers, KU.

41. Fleeson, "Medical Literature on Ileitis," June 18, 1956, Fleeson Papers, KU.
42. Column for June 14, 1956, typewritten copy, Fleeson Papers, KU.
43. Conversation with Helen Fleeson, November 27, 1991.
44. Bess Truman to Doris, undated, Fleeson Papers, KU.
45. Betty Beale, "Margaret Truman Weds In Simple Ceremony,: *The Washington Star*, April 22, 1956.
46. Cooke, "To Run or Not?" cited.
47. George McWilliams, "Political Columnist Forgets Femininity In Writing Career," *The Denver Post*, March 21, 1958.
48. Article in the *Sterling Bulletin*, datelined New York, Feb. 8, February 14, 1957.
49. "Howard Fleeson, Wichita Attorney, Taken By Death," *The* (Wichita) *Evening Eagle*, May 7, 1957, clipping, Fleeson Papers, KU.
50. Alf M. Landon to Doris Fleeson, undated, Fleeson Papers, KU.
51. Isabelle Shelton, "Television Comes To Doris Fleeson," *The Washington Star*, clipping; script for Person to Person, Fleeson Papers, KU.
52. Bess Truman to Doris, undated, Fleeson Papers, KU.
53. Margaret Truman Daniel to Doris, undated, Fleeson Papers, KU.
54. Eleanor Roosevelt to Doris, June 18, 1958, Fleeson Papers, KU.
55. Clipping from "People" column, *Time* magazine, July 14, 1958, Fleeson Papers, KU.
56. Jack Foisie, "Aerojet at Nimbus—-10,000 Work at 'Missile Capital,'," *San Francisco Chronicle*, September 24, 1958, Fleeson Papers, KU.
57. Cathryn McCune, "Chit-Chat," *The Tulsa Tribune*, clipping; "Doris Fleeson A Bride, *The Kansas City Star*, August 1, 1958, clipping; photos, Fleeson Papers, KU.
58. "Doris Fleeson Weds Dan A. Kimball," clipping, Fleeson Papers, KU.

CHAPTER 22

1. Fleeson, "Johnson Readies 4-Day Monologue," November 1, 1966, clipping, Fleeson Papers, KU.
2. Fleeson, "Mrs. Johnson Remains Unflappable," March 22, 1966, Fleeson Papers, KU.
3. Fleeson, "Limited War, Limited Peace," The George Fullmer Reynolds Lectures, The University of Colorado, February 15, 16, 17, 1966, Fleeson Papers, KU.
4. Interview with Liz Carpenter, April 14, 2004.
5. Fleeson, "An Art To Be Practiced," The Guild Memorial Lecture, University of Minnesota, October 24, 1957, Fleeson Papers, KU.
6. Robert A. Caro, *Master of the Senate*, (New York: Alfred A Knopf, 2002), p. 427.
7. Lyndon Johnson to Doris Fleeson, September 17, 1958, Fleeson Papers, KU.
8. Fleeson, "Johnson Ponders Bigger Flocks," October 7, 1958, Fleeson Papers, KU.
9. Fleeson, "Birthday Toasts to Nixon," January 11, 1956, Fleeson Papers, KU.
10. Fleeson, "Nixon's Trip Is Postponed," October 18, 1957, Fleeson Papers, KU.
11. Fleeson, "'Brother Milton' Will Dim Nixon's Mission to Moscow," *New York Post*, June 12, 1958.
12. Fleeson, "Nixon Journey to Poland Has Dangerous Overtones," *New York Post*, July 29, 1959.
13. Fleeson, "Kennedy Looks to the South," July 3, 1957, Fleeson Papers, KU.

14. Fleeson, "Spotlight on Senator Humphrey," December 9, 1958, Fleeson Papers, KU.
15. Fleeson, "Wide-Open 1960 Prospects Spur Democratic Hopefuls," *Minneapolis Tribune*, December 12, 1959.
16. Fleeson, "1960 Presidential Race: Personality Versus Party," *Minneapolis Tribune*, April 14, 1959.
17. Agnes Murphy, "At Home With...Doris Fleeson," *New York Post*, March 29, 1959, clipping Fleeson Papers, KU.
18. Fleeson, "Peace Hopes Were Accented as Ike, Nikita Shook Hands," *Minneapolis Tribune*, September 17, 1959.
19. Fleeson, "Cautious State Department, Hollywood 'Muff' Culture," *Minneapolis Tribune*, September 25, 1959.
20. Fleeson, "Mr. K. Called Cruel, Charming," *Minnespolis Tribune*, September 21, 1959.
21. Fleeson, "Democratic Leaders Think GOP Will Pick Rockefeller, *Minneapolis Tribune*, October 31, 1959.
22. Fleeson, "Adlai Role Worries," *The Kansas City Times*, May 2, 1960.
23. Fleeson, "Double Warning in Democrats' Cable," *The Kansas City Star*, May 20, 1960.
24. Fleeson, "Candidates Seek Spark," *The Kansas City Times*, September 8, 1960.
25. Fleeson, "Jackie Kennedy's Glamor Becomes Political Target," *Minneapolis Tribune*, September 5, 1960.
26. Jacqueline Kennedy to Doris Fleeson, September 3, 1960, Fleeson Papers, KU.
27. Fleeson, "First Clouds Are Appearing on Horizon of the New Frontier," *The Kansas City Times*, January 25, 1961.
28. Typescript of "Small World," broadcast over CBS Television Network, May 15, 1960, Fleeson Papers, KU.
29. "John O'Donnell, Columnist, Dead," *The New York Times*, December 18, 1961.
30. Edith Bolling Wilson to Doris Fleeson, April 7, 1961, Fleeson Papers, KU.
31. Arthur M. Schlesinger, Jr., *A Thousand Days*, (Boston: Houghton Mifflin Company, 1965), p. 239.
32. Ibid., p. 201 (reference to Bissell and Dulles as originators of invasion plan).
33. Doris Fleeson, "A New Foreign Policy for U.S.," *The Washington Evening Star*, April 21, 1961.
34. Fleeson, "The G.O.P and the Cuban Issue," *The Washington Evening Star*, April 27, 1961.
35. Fleeson, "Ike Takes the High Road of True Statesmanship," *The Kansas City Star*, May 3, 1961.
36. Fleeson, "Cuba Gets Into the Campaign," *The Washington Evening Star*, September 7, 1962.
37. Schlesinger, *A Thousand Days*, cited, pp. 667, 668, 669, 670, 677.
38. Fleeson, "Nixon Runs With Cuban Issue," *The Washington Evening Star*, October 30, 1962.
39. Schlesinger, *A Thousand Days*, cited, p. 691.
40. Fleeson, "The Economic Problems Remain," *The Kansas City Times*, April 20, 1962.
41. "Eleanor Roosevelt Is Dead," *The Kansas City Times*, November 8, 1962.
42. Fleeson, "A Woman Ever in Life's Midst," *The Kansas City Star*, November 10, 1962.
43. "Nixon's Farewell Is Blast at Press," *The Kansas City Times*, November 8, 1962.
44. Fleeson, "Kennedy Message Shows New Self-Assurance," *The Kansas City Times*, January 16, 1963.

45. Kenneth P. O"Donnell and David F. Powers, *Johnny, We Hardly Knew Ye*, (Boston: Little Brown and Company, 1970), p. 345; Leonard Baker, *The Johnson Eclipse*, (New York: The Macmillan Company, 1966); *Hugh Sidey, John F. Kennedy, President*, (New York: Atheneum, 1964), p. 391.

46. Fleeson, "Stagnation on the Personnel Front," May 21, 1963, Fleeson Papers, KU.

47. Fleeson, "Nixon's Move to New York," May 9, 1963, Fleeson Papers, KU.

48. Fleeson, "Kennedy Tour Will Be Demanding," April 26, 1963, Fleeson Papers, KU.

49. Fleeson, "Kennedy's Busy German Visit," June 21, 1963, Fleeson Papers, KU.

50. Fleeson, "Stagnation on the Personnel Front," cited.

51. Fleeson, "Those Who Failed Their President, November 26, 1963, Fleeson Papers, KU.

52. Fleeson, "President Facing Urgent Problem," November 29, 1963, Fleeson Papers, KU.

53. Fleeson, "Mrs. Mellon's Rose Garden," Fleeson Papers, KU.

54. Fleeson, "The Real Ordeal of Civil Rights," June 18, 1964, Fleeson Papers, KU.

55. Fleeson, "A Running-Mate for Johnson," July 17, 1964, Fleeson Papers, KU.

56. Fleeson, "Humphrey's Romance With Life," August 28, 1964, Fleeson Papers, KU.

57. Fleeson, "Goldwater and The Stream of American Destiny," typed copy dated August 1, 1964, Fleeson Papers, KU.

58. Fleeson, "Goldwater's Bitter Words," October 2, 1964, Fleeson Papers, KU.

59. Fleeson, "Mrs. Johnson's Persuasion Tour," October 6, 1964, Fleeson Papers, KU.

60. Fleeson, "Humphrey Proving His Worth," October 30, 1964, Fleeson Papers, KU.

61. Fleeson, "Two Presidents for One," January 22, 1965, Fleeson Papers, KU.

62. Lady Bird Johnson to Doris Fleeson, January 21, 1965, Fleeson Papers, KU.

63. Conversation with Helen Fleeson, November 26, 1991.

64. Conversation with Helen Fleeson, April 29, 1993.

65. Fleeson, "A Kind Word For Politicians," The George Fullmer Reynolds Lectures, cited.

66. Fleeson, "Limited War, Limited Peace," The George Fullmer Reynolds Lectures, cited.

67. Fleeson, "Humphrey Beyond Usual Oblivion," January 11, 1966, Fleeson Papers, KU.

68. Fleeson, "Rescuing The Two Party System," The George Fullmer Reynolds Lectures, cited.

69. Fleeson, "Humphrey 'Nailed to Cross of War'," February 17, 1966, Fleeson Papers, KU.

70. Caption on photo, Fleeson Papers, KU.

71. E.W. Kenworthy, "McCarthy Staff Is Growing Professional as Campaign Widens," *The New York Times*, April 25, 1968.

72. Mary McGrory, "Doris Fleeson; an Appreciation," *The Evening Star*, August 2, 1970, Fleeson Papers, KU.

73. "Famous Native Ill," *The Lyons Daily News*, February 14, 1969.

74. Conversation with Harry Fleeson, October 7, 1992.

75. Clipping from *The Evening Star*, August 3, 1970, Fleeson Papers, KU.

76. "Eulogy of Dan Kimball and Doris Fleeson Kimball By Senator Eugene J. McCarthy, Navy Chapel, Washington, D.C., August 3, 1970," typed copy, Fleeson Papers, KU.

77. Fleeson, "President Facing Urgent Problem," November 29, 1963, cited.

BIBLIOGRAPHY

Angoff, Charles, *H.L. Mencken A Portrait from Memory*, (New York: Thomas Yoseloff, Inc., 1956).

Bader, Robert Smith, *Hayseeds, Moralizers and Methodists*, (Lawrence: The University Press of Kansas, 1988).

Baker, Leonard, *The Johnson Eclipse*, (New York: The Macmillan Company, 1966).

Belford, Barbara, *Brilliant Bylines*, (New York: Columbia University Press, 1987).

Bent, Silas, *Ballyhoo*, (New York: Horace Liveright, 1927).

Bode, Carl, *Mencken*, (Carbondale and Edwardsville: Southern Illinois University Press—London and Amsterdam: Feffer & Simmons, Inc., 1969).

Bring Me A Unicorn, Diaries and Letters of Anne Morrow Lindbergh, 1922–1928, (New York: Harcourt Brace Jovanovich, Inc., 1971, 1972).

Caro, Robert A., *Master of the Senate*, (New York: Alfred A. Knopf, 2002).

Clapper, Raymond, *Watching the World 1944*, (New York, London: Whittlese House McGraw Hill Book Company).

Coit, Margaret L., *Mr. Baruch*, (Boston: Houghton Mifflin Company, 1957).

Collier, Peter with David Horowitz, *The Roosevelts An American Saga*, (New York, etc.: Simon & Schuster, 1994).

Cook, Blanche Wiesen, *Eleanor Roosevelt*, (New York: Viking Penguin, 1992).

Cooke, Alistair, *Alistair Cooke's America*, (New York: Alfred A. Knopf, 1973).

Davis, Kenneth S., *Experience of War*, (Garden City, New York; Doubleday & Company, Inc., 1965).

Farr, Finis, *Margaret Mitchell of Atlanta*, (New York: William Morrow & Company, 1965).

Fisher, Charles, *The Columnists*, (New York: Howell, Soskin, 1944).

Fowler, Gene, *Beau James*, (New York: The Viking Press, 1949).

Gilbert, Robert E., *The Mortal Presidency*, (BasicBooks, A Division of HarperCollinsPublishers, Inc., 1992.)

Griffin, Clifford S., *The University of Kansas*, (Lawrence: The University Press of Kansas, 1974).

History of Kansas Newspapers, (Topeka: Kansas State Historical Society, 1916).

Hobson, Fred, *Mencken A Life*, Baltimore and London: The Johns Hopkins University Press, 1994).

Ise, John, *The American Way*, (Lawrence: Faculty of the Department of Economics and School of Business, University of Kansas, 1955).

Jones, Ben, *Sam Jones, Lawyer*, (Norman: University of Oklahoma Press, 1947).

Kamen, Gloria, *Fiorello*, (New York: Athenaeum, 1981).

Kurth, Peter, *American Cassandra*, (Boston Toronto London: Little Brown and Company, 1990).

Lash, Joseph P., *Eleanor and Franklin*, (New York: W.W. Norton & Company, Inc., 1971).

Lash, Joseph P., *Eleanor: The Years Alone*, (New York: W.W. Norton & Company, Inc., 1972).

Lewis, Sinclair, *Main Street*, (New York: Grosset & Dunlap, Copyright 1920 by Harcourt, Brace and Company, 31st printing, November 1922).

McCoy, Donald R., *Landon of Kansas*, (Lincoln: University of Nebraska Press, 1966).

McCullough, David, *Truman*, (New York: Simon & Schuster, 1992).

Mencken, H.L., *In Defense of Women*, (New York: Time Incorporated, 1963, first published by Alfred A. Knopf, 1922).

Mills, Kay, *A Place In The News*, (New York: Dodd, Mead & Company, 1988).

Murdock, Victor, *It May Chance of Wheat*, (Kansas City, Missouri: The Lowell Press, 1965).

Neal, Steve, *Dark Horse*, (Garden City, New York: Doubleday & Company, Inc., 1984).

Notable American Women: The Modern Period, (Cambridge, Mass.: The Belnap Press of Harvard University, 1980).

O'Donnell, Kenneth P. and Powers, David F., *Johnny, We Hardly Knew Ye*, (Boston: Little Brown and Company, 1970).

Rand, Ayn, *The Fountainhead*, (Indianapolis New York: The Bobbs-Merrill Company, Inc., 1943).

Roosevelt, Eleanor, *The Autobiography of Eleanor Roosevelt*, (New York: Da Capo Press, 1992; originally published: New York: Harper & Brothers, 1961).

Roosevelt, Elliott and Brough, James, *A Rendezvous With Destiny*, (New York: G.P. Putnam's Sons, 1975).

Ross, Ishbel, *Ladies of the Press*, (New York and London: Harper & Brothers, 1936).

Schlesinger, Arthur M., Jr., *A Thousand Days*, (Boston: Houghton Mifflin Company, 1965).

Sevareid, Eric, *Not So Wild A Dream*, (New York: Atheneum, 1976).

Sidey, Hugh, *John F. Kennedy, President*, (New York: Atheneum, 1964).

Sorel, Nancy Caldwell, *The Women Who Wrote the War*, (New York: Arcade Publishing, 1999).

Smith, Wilda and Bogart, Eleanor A., *The Wars of Peggy Hull*, (El Paso: Texas Western Press, 1991).

Taylor, Robert Lewis, *Vessel of Wrath*, (New York: The New American Library, 1966).

Tebbel, John William, *An American Dynasty*, (New York: Doubleday & Company, Inc., 1947).

The Diary of H.L. Mencken, edited by Charles E. Fecher, (New York: Vintage Books, 1989).

This Fabulous Century (1920–1930), (New York: Time-Life Books, 1969).

200 Years, (Washington, D.C.: Books by *U.S. News & World Report*, 1973).

Ward, Geoffrey C., *A First Class Temperament*, (New York: Harper & Row, Publishers, 1989).

Winfield, Betty Houchin, *FDR and the News Media*, (Urbana and Chicago: University of Illinois Press, 1990).

INDEX

CPSIA information can be obtained at www.ICGtesting.com
Printed in the USA
LVOW040951150911

246410LV00002B/20/P